THE NEW IMAGE
OF THE COMMON MAN

BOOKS BY CARL J. FRIEDRICH

RESPONSIBLE BUREAUCRACY:
A Study of the Swiss Civil Service
(WITH TAYLOR COLE)

FOREIGN POLICY IN THE MAKING:
The Search for a New Balance of Power

CONSTITUTIONAL GOVERNMENT
AND DEMOCRACY:
*Theory and Practice in Europe
and America*

INEVITABLE PEACE

THE PHILOSOPHY OF KANT (*Editor*)

THE NEW IMAGE OF THE COMMON MAN

CARL J. FRIEDRICH

THE NEW
IMAGE
OF
THE
COMMON
MAN

Boston · THE BEACON PRESS · 1950

To my Mother

Foreword

to the 1950 edition

THIS BOOK is an expanded edition of my *The New Belief in the Common Man*, which appeared in 1942. In order to be able to use the existing plates, it was decided to embody my additions in a Prologue and an Epilogue. The Prologue, "Image and Reality," undertakes to relate the book's main theme to some major viewpoints with which it has been contrasted, as well as setting forth the reasons for calling this *The New* IMAGE *of the Common Man*. This, if the truth be told, was my favorite title from the beginning. The central discussion is about a new *image*, or concept, of the common man — without which, I believe, the old *belief* in the common man can no longer be held securely and confidently. The Epilogue, "Looking Backward and Forward," seeks to sketch in broadest outline, and at the same time assess, the basic events of the ten years which have elapsed since the original was published, in the light of a prediction made at the time the book first appeared. It also casts a hesitant glance into the future.

Neither Prologue nor Epilogue pretends to be definitive or dogmatic. They are as tentative and suggestive as the best common man's street-corner conversation where "one man's guess is as good as another's." Indeed, they owe their existence to the friendly and encouraging enthusiasm of the Beacon Press. For this I owe thanks, as indeed I do to the many friends the book has made over the years.

Preface

to the 1942 edition

THIS BOOK has been in the making for almost ten years. It is therefore impossible to thank all those who at one time or another have helped in clarifying the issues. Wherever possible, acknowledgment has been made to printed works, but such references are obviously inadequate.

My thoughts on the role of the public in a democracy crystallized finally as a result of an invitation to offer a course of lectures at the Lowell Institute in Boston. This forced me to formulate my conclusions. I am grateful to President A. Lawrence Lowell and Mr. Ralph Lowell for their invitation, and to Mr. William H. Lawrence, the Curator, for his unfailing kindness. May I add that the growing audience in their enthusiasm encouraged me greatly? The last of these lectures was delivered on the Tuesday after Pearl Harbor, when Boston had its first air-raid alarm, yet we forgathered to discuss the unity of mankind.

But that is not all. For some time past I have found myself working closely with a number of men from all walks of life. They had banded together to do their utmost to develop a broader grasp of the underlying issues of our times. They worked together democratically — disagreeing often, but yet co-operating in the task in hand. I owe a great deal to these friends, espe-

Preface

cially to Ernest Angell, Stephen Vincent Benét, Percy S. Brown, Lyman Bryson, Cass Canfield, C. D. Jackson, Walter Millis, Marshall Shulman, Raymond Gram Swing, and Ordway Tead.

Another source of continuous stimulation and encouragement has been certain of my students. Though I should like to mention all, I cannot. Hence I'll single out Edgar J. Kemler, Harold Winkler, and Fred A. Ossanna, Jr.

Dean Holmes of the Graduate School of Education was good enough to read the entire manuscript, and made helpful comments. Mr. Edward Weeks of the *Atlantic Monthly* particularly interested himself in the last chapter, and helped greatly in sharpening its conclusions. Mr. C. Raymond Everitt also read the entire manuscript and, like a real old-time publisher, acted as a most effective Dutch uncle. Finally, Mrs. Frances Burns, research writer for the Council for Democracy, Mrs. Talcott Parsons, and more especially Miss Miriam Berry gave me invaluable help in putting the manuscript into shape for publication.

As I look back upon all those friendly critics, I am reminded of Goethe's *"Man glaubt zu schieben und man wird geschoben."* Truly, in outlining the basis for a new belief in the common man, one seeks to state things common to those who believe in the future of freedom.

C. J. FRIEDRICH

Concord, Massachusetts

Contents

[xi]

Contents

[xii]

Contents

[xiii]

Contents

Contents

Image and Reality

THERE IS no symbol comparable to that of the *common man* in French, Italian, or German. Even in England the thought patterns of the country's aristocratic past have kept the image of the common man indistinct, though democratic movements have gained ground and eventually triumphed, after the war. Curiously enough, even in the United States the intelligentsia, whether benevolent or malevolent, continue to think of "the masses" or at any rate of "the other fellow" when they speak of the common man. Henry Wallace's *The Century of the Common Man* which appeared in the same month as my book is full of this condescension:

> Everywhere the common people are on the march. Thousands of them are learning to read and write. . . . These people are learning to think and work together in labor movements, some of which may be extreme or impractical at first, but will eventually settle down to serve effectively the interests of the common man.[1]

Time and again I have had to point out that "the common man is you and me" — that the common man

The New Image of the Common Man

is "everyman" when not concerned with his specialty. The matter is quite fully stated in Chapter I (pages 32 ff.); but in spite of this, reviewers and readers have lapsed into the false image of the common man as the uninformed, the impecunious, the illiterate. At the same time, there has been a persistent unwillingness to seize upon the other side of this analysis: the common man as presented in these pages cannot develop, cannot to any extent even survive under tyrannical conditions. His image as we see it presupposes a social reality in which discussion is not hampered, information can be gathered without governmental interference, character can be shaped and personality developed by each man in accordance with his likes. "I wear my hat as I please, inside and out" — this puckish remark of Walt Whitman's cannot be made and will not be made by those human beings who have to live under any form of autocracy, except for the few who will brave the terror to build an oasis of resistance. For resistance under these conditions is a matter of the spirit rather than one of effective organization, nowadays almost impossible.

The critics of democracy throughout the last century and a half have always dwelt upon the incompetence of the masses. In a famous book, Ortega y Gasset dwelt on the revolt of the masses, and while he himself was a high-minded intellectual, his thought fed anti-democratic mills. His description of the mass-man is inspired by a real sense of despair. Contrasting the "noble life" and the "common life" as effort and inertia, he deduced his image of a mass-man as the multitudinous or average man, creature of material ease, when the worker is "assured" of his existence, when the average man finds no social barriers raised against him, and when, *horribile dictu*, "the ordinary man learns that all men are equal before the law." Ortega thought that three things had made possible this new and unprecedented world: liberal democracy, scientific experiment, and industrialism. He concludes his "psychological chart" of the mass man of today by two fundamental traits: "the free expansion of his vital desires" and "his radical ingratitude towards all that has made possible the ease of his existence." In short, his is "the psychology of the spoilt child." One is forcefully reminded of Nietzsche's outcry in *Thus Spake Zarathustra:*

Alas! There comes the time of the most despicable man, who can no longer despise himself. A little poison now and then: it makes pleasant dreams. And much poison finally for a pleasant death. One still works, for work is a pastime. But one takes care lest the pastime fatigue. No shepherd and one flock! Each wants the same, each is the same: he who feels differently enters the insane asylum of his own accord.[2]

This mass-man troubles Ortega and many others of similar views today because "the masses intervene in everything"; this "absurd type" of human being may be called the "rebel mass." The anti-democratic implications of such a view can, however, not be laughed off; the totalitarian societies of our generation give ample support to the negative aspect of this analysis. Totalitarian tendencies in existing democratic societies confirm it. When Ortega cries out against the mass-man's dislike for all discussion, for all consideration of other viewpoints, one is forcefully reminded of the witch-hunts which are sweeping contemporary America. "The mass-man would feel himself lost, if he accepted discussion," he observes, and then exclaims: "Restrictions, standards, courtesy, indirect methods, justice, reason! Why were all these invented, why all these complications created? . . . By means of all these there is an attempt to make possible the city, the community, common life. . . . Civilization is, before all, the will to live in common." In short, to the image of the mass-man, the Spanish philosopher juxtaposes the image of the citizen. But he is so disturbed by the ordinary man's shortcomings, as he sees them from his intellectualist standpoint, that he pleads for an elite of superior men, a guardian class. Like Nietzsche's idea of the superman, as an alternative to the mass-man, this idea of a noble elite of superior men strikes at the roots of a free society. But we cannot cope with it by merely reiterating the old slogans.

There is enough of substance in the challenge of these

critics of contemporary society to call for a radical re-construction of the view of man. The new image of the common man which we sketched in terms of some of the basic issues of contemporary politics seeks to pro-vide that view.

Mass-man and superman belong together as the joint products of despair over the imperfections of demo-cratic society. Regardless of Nietzsche's more subtle and qualified concept, the "superman" has come to mean the man who can do what other men cannot. He is the type who by strength, whether of body or of mind, can accomplish "wonders," and who is consequently "be-yond good and evil." Mass-man admires him, because the feats of superman are those which he himself would like to achieve. It thus happens that the societies in which the mass-man has become the supporter of totali-tarian "managers" are at the same time those in which the idea of a self-appointed elite or superman (*Führer*, *duce*) has been widely accepted. I am convinced that it is of decisive importance to rescue the citizen of the free world from being identified with this mass-man, by carefully analyzing the limitations within which he operates.

A new belief in the common man, as I envisaged it in 1941, depends upon a new view of man, a new image of the common man.[3] It was disquieting to me that so many took this analysis to suggest a return to a view of man which is no longer tenable. The image of the common man, on the contrary, seeks to elicit a realization of what men have in common and what enables them to form communities. All men have it in varying degrees, and what is more, this complex of qualities is capable of growth and development. Many writers, like Henry Wallace, overlook the fact that in a very real and disturbing sense the common man withers away under dictatorship and totalitarianism. The communal side of man requires for its unfolding the setting of a free community. Fortunately, some human beings have such strong inclination toward the development of these traits that they will maintain small groups of resistance even under the most formidable terror. There are, even after a generation of totalitarianism, enclaves of genuine community left. The policy of democratization would have little chance of success under the quasi-dictatorship of military occupation if it could not count upon these surviving common men to grasp the torch and carry it.[4]

The elitist escape from the full meaning of a free society is so tempting in face of the present totalitarian perversions of democracy that leading thinkers recurrently revert to it. Karl Mannheim, in his *Man and Society in an Age of Reconstruction*,[5] high-lighted the role of elites, as the "culture-creating" groups.[6] Like Pareto earlier,[7] Mannheim identifies without explicit justification the political with other cultural activities, and thereby misses the distinctively *common* core of civilization which the free community provides for its citizens

[xxii]

in organizing their cooperation for common tasks. He writes:

We may distinguish the following types of elites: the political, the organizing, the intellectual, the artistic, the moral and the religious.

Though he then proceeds to contrast the political and organizing elites as integrating, this vital distinction falls by the wayside in his further analysis of the development of elites, so that, instead of clarification, a confusion arises. By linking the development of elites to class aspects of society (reflecting Mannheim's earlier Marxist views), he prevents a distinct appreciation of the *vitally different* basis of different kinds of elites. Hence he arrives at a dead alley:

We have no clear idea how the selection of elites would work in an open mass society in which only the principle of achievement mattered. It is possible that in such a society the succession of elites would take place much too rapidly, and social continuity . . . would be lacking in it.

As a result, Mannheim dropped the emphasis on elites in his *Diagnosis of Our Time* (1943) and instead demanded a militant democracy. Turning back to traditional values and virtues, such as brotherly love, mutual help, decency, social justice, freedom, respect for persons, etc., Mannheim then urged that defense of these and of the right procedure of social change was the core of militant democracy. It is clear that this complete turn-about fails to fill the vacuum left by the disappearance of the elites from the social pattern. Mannheim's attempt at substituting democratic planning is unsuccessful, because it lacks the basis of a new view of man.

Mannheim's approach has more recently been put by T. S. Eliot into the center of his own cultural analysis. This noted conservative, strongly antagonistic to the common man in America, deserves the most careful consideration. The tendency of certain writers to brush aside the cultural criticism of men like Eliot is unfortunate, and not in keeping with a professed concern with freedom. For Eliot, no less than Mannheim and Ortega, is deeply disturbed by the rising trend toward the oppressive mobocracy which destroyed Athenian freedom in the name of democracy. Eliot, in *Notes Toward a Definition of Culture* (1949), voices the Platonic belief that no society without a governing elite can hope to transmit the culture it has inherited. What is this governing elite?

The governing elite, of the nation as whole, would consist of those whose responsibility was inherited with their affluence and position, and whose forces were constantly increased, and often led, by rising individuals of exceptional talents.

This notion of a governing elite is deeply embedded in the English tradition. In the very early days of Massachusetts Bay Colony, this issue came to the fore as John Winthrop and his assistants attempted to maintain a governing oligarchy. It was vigorously defended by John Milton, when he sensed in 1660 that the majority of Englishmen were turning away from the good old cause of the commonwealthmen. In his *Ready and Easy Way* he wrote: ". . . if there be a king, which the inconsiderate multitude are now so mad upon, mark how far short we are like to come of all those happinesses which in a free state we shall be possessed of." To him, the only remedy was a "grand council firmly constituted to perpetuity . . ." He, too, stressed the moral virtues and values.

It is, however, one thing for Milton or Marx to plead for an elite that is qualified to govern because they have embraced the definite views which are held by them to be essential to well-being, and quite another to plead for such an elite without any clear idea as to what exactly it is that provides the standard for selection. Is it not precisely the purpose of a constitutional democracy to make it possible for everyone to participate to the extent of his intrinsic ability in the process by which such standards are determined and remolded, as different common men make appeal to the rest for their views upon the general public interest?

In short, the bitter critics of the reality of democratic politics and of the common men have, often with the best intentions, been prone to "empty the baby with the bath." They have undermined the belief in man as a communal being — the belief in the common man — by distorting his image. Misled by superman and mass-man, the corruptions of the common man in contemporary society, they have urged a return to an acquiescence in the rule of the uncommon man, the self-appointed governing elite. It is against these "prophets of the past" that the image of the common man as he marches into an uncertain future is set. Without a belief in man there can be no future.

THE NEW IMAGE
OF THE COMMON MAN

CHAPTER I

The Common Man in American Poetry and Politics

---

*We have changed our prepos-
sessions, and our ambitions must
therefore change.*

— J. H. ROBINSON

T HE BELIEF in the common man is the core of the democratic creed. The idea of a free people is inconceivable without it. How can a people be free if its members cannot think and act for themselves? And why should they be free if their thoughts and their emotions are unworthy of respect?

And yet it is a rather extraordinary belief. Few and far between are the occasions in the history of mankind when that belief has been held by many men. For long ages before the modern democratic era the common man was looked upon by political philosophers and men of practical experience alike as a ward to be taken care of or exploited for the greater glory of God, or of Empire, or of the rulers themselves. Throughout the seventeenth century, and well into the eighteenth, the mass of the people were at best an object of solicitude for benevolent rulers. Even so "enlightened" a mind as Voltaire appealed to the good will of kings in his efforts to help the common people. If the common people themselves showed signs of thinking, speaking, or acting by themselves, they and their leaders were denounced. This was equally true in aristocratic England and in monarchical France or Prussia. The common man was held incompetent to judge what was in his own interest, let alone what was in the general or public interest.

THE PROBLEM

Throughout the nineteenth century, critics continued to assail the belief in the common man as contrary to experience and even absurd.[1] It is often assumed that the belief in reason and the belief in the common man went hand in hand. This assumption is contrary to the facts. Eighteenth-century rationalists frequently took exactly the opposite view, and this tendency continued through the nineteenth century. Reason, they felt, was the possession of an intellectual elite. The "philosopher" was seen as the high priest of this esoteric group of intellectual men. Even powerful rulers, such as Frederick the

Great of Prussia and Joseph I of Austria, were keenly interested in being members of the charmed circle of "philosophers."

The belief in the common man crystallized and was proclaimed in the French and American Revolutions. "We hold these truths to be self-evident . . . that all men are created free and equal." So far are these truths from being self-evident that they had never been accepted before the Declaration of Independence. What is more, they have again and again been challenged since. Their constant repetition in Fourth-of-July oratory has given them a ritualistic significance, but it has not heightened their standing as realistic conceptions appealing to practical men. Somehow, they have been put away with the Sermon on the Mount as to-be-remembered-on-Sunday.

The ringing phrases of the American credo are echoed in Thomas Paine's conclusion to his *Age of Reason* (1794–1795): "Certain I am that when opinions are free, either in matters of government or religion, truth will finally and powerfully prevail." Here we have the new secular gospel in a nutshell: Give the simple mind of the ordinary man the facts, and he will see the rational, the reasonable way to act; and having seen his way, he will follow it.

The belief in the common man consists of three equally important parts. Let us state these assumptions more fully. First, ordinary men, when confronted with a problem, finding themselves in a "jam," will think hard and get all the facts they can. Second, they will reach sensible conclusions as to the right way to get out of the jam — right technically and morally. Common men will reach such conclusions without the help of "experts," and it is part of their "common sense" to recognize an expert when they see one. That is what the belief in the common man implies as to the mind. But it is equally important that, third, the common man is believed to possess the character to go through with the solution, to follow the right road as seen, to act rationally as well as to think rationally.

HOW THE IDEA UNFOLDED

Now it will be seen upon reflection that the first two assumptions are assumptions concerning the mind of man, while the third is an assumption concerning man's character. And the sad fact is that if you ask people whether in fact they think that human beings, ordinary men and women, are like that — do seek facts, do draw sound conclusions, and do stick to these conclusions — it will be found that many would answer in the negative. Since that is so, we are confronted with a series of questions. Are these assumptions sound, in spite of very widespread doubt? If not, can other assumptions be substituted so as to give us a sounder basis for a new belief in the common man, or do we have to abandon the belief in the common man altogether, and maybe a belief in democracy with it? Perhaps a brief examination of how this belief arose will help us in answering these questions.

Three stages seem to me clearly marked in the evolution of the attitude toward the common man. In the first, or rationalist, stage the belief in the common man rested upon contrasting him with decrepit princes and aristocrats. In this period the common man is essentially a *petit bourgeois*. In the second, or emotional, stage the belief flowed from the boundless enthusiasm and optimism of pioneering America; the common man has become a farmer or a worker. In the third stage, the realist stage, the belief rests upon an unquestioning acceptance of the democratic society. The common man is everyman.

FIRST STAGE: PAINE AND BENTHAM

The rise of the modern view of human nature implied in the belief in the common man has a long history. In the age of its flowering it found in the English-speaking world two radical exponents, Tom Paine and Jeremy Bentham.[2] They exerted a broad popular influence. They may be taken as representative. However, Bentham did not, in his earlier writings, show any faith in the common man. Along with Hume and other utilitarians, he rather believed in a benevolent tutelage for the common man, furnished by the better class. This English version of the continental doctrine of benevolent despotism Bentham grounded in the belief that ordinary men were unlikely to take a rational view of their self-interest, or to follow it if they saw it. While there might be an identity of interests in the strictly economic realm, an artificial identification of interests, he argued, had to be achieved in other spheres. The principle of utility, according to which a man's interest is to increase his pleasure and to decrease his pain as much as possible, was true for all men. Yet this principle was perceived by only a minority. At the time of the French Revolution Bentham was, strictly speaking, a Tory rather than a democrat.[3] He believed in the uncommon man, the aristocracy.

Not so Thomas Paine. In his *Rights of Man* (1791–1792) as well as in his earlier *Common Sense* (1776), he stoutly insisted upon the capacity of the common man to take care of himself. "As Nature created man for social life, she fitted him for the station she intended. . . . She has not only forced men into society, by a diversity of wants, which the reciprocal aid of each other can supply, but she has implanted in him a system of social affections, which, though not necessary for his existence, are essential to his happiness." Paine believed in the spontaneous capacity of every man for social life and in the almost complete capacity of men "for reciprocally accommodating the wants of each

other." Hence he insisted that "the instant formal government is abolished, society begins to act. A general
association takes place, and common interest produces
common security." What is more, "the more perfect
civilization is, the less occasion has it for government."
This faith in man's ability to work together borders
on the anarchist doctrines of men like Godwin. "All
the great laws of society are laws of nature." Referring
time and again to the experience of the American Revolution, Paine felt proudly confident of the rational and
sociable nature of all men.[4]

However ardent Tom Paine's belief in the common
man was, it lacked a convincing foundation, either in
history or in psychology. The sparse references to the
American Revolution carried little weight. But Bentham
undertook to provide this foundation. Abandoning his
antidemocratic bias, he and his school labored to provide a rational basis for such a belief. Their final conclusions are most effectively stated in Bentham's *Constitutional Code* (1827). Without quoting Bentham's
abstract and involved language, it can be stated un-
equivocally that by that time he considered the majority of men the best judge of what is good for the
community; they know what will provide the greatest
happiness of the greatest number. A careful reading of
his exposition will reveal, however, that Bentham had
arrived, not so much at a belief in the common man,
as at a disbelief in the uncommon man. His continuous

disappointments as a reformer had undoubtedly contributed to his conclusion that no monarchy or aristocracy was likely to interest itself in realizing the principle of utility, that is to say, the greatest happiness
of the greatest number. Disillusioned, he had concluded that most men act in accordance with the principle of "self-preference." This principle he defined
as "that propensity in human nature by which every
human being is led to pursue that line of conduct which,
according to his view of the case, taken by him at the
moment, will be in the highest degree contributory
to his own greatest happiness, whatsoever be the effect
of it in relation to the happiness of other similar beings." [5]

As a natural corollary of such a radical disbelief in
any uncommon man, Bentham proceeded to formulate
the proposition that a man's aptitude to make wise use
of political power is inverse to the altitude of his position in the scale of political influence. Wealth, power,
and prestige (or as Bentham calls them, opulence,
power, and factitious dignity) all reduce a man's moral
aptitude to judge of the *public* good. The simple reason
is that prominent men are remote from the needs of
the masses, are unsympathetic to their suffering, and
hence unlikely to think of the greatest happiness of
the greatest number. That the opposite opinion could
have prevailed for so long Bentham believes was be-

cause of the undeniable fact that wealth and power are surrounded by adulation. The "delusion" that the wealthy and powerful possess special aptitude is caused by the flattery expressed in the spoken and written discourses of their intellectual retainers. With a sideward glance at Burke and other patronized "leaders of thought," Bentham, the independent radical, exclaims: "As long as wealth and government have had existence, the powers of poetry and oratory have been employed in singing the praises of the powerful, the dignified, and the wealthy."

All the delusions created by the adorers of wealth and power are "instruments of misrule: a means of exercising it: and thereby an encouragement and incitement to exercise it." The only method for checking this unbridled propensity of any man of power or wealth to increase his own happiness (i.e. to serve his own interest) at the expense of others is to make his power wholly dependent upon others. In other words, only elective office (and regulated wealth, an implication which Bentham neglects) will be compatible with the principle of utility for the people at large.

The principle of utility has led Bentham to a radically democratic position, simply because this principle takes the skeptical view that every man is out for himself. The common man is rational, but hardly reasonable.

The New Image of the Common Man

THE AMERICAN REVOLUTION AND AFTER

Although English gentry provided the leadership in the revolutionary fight for independence, the bulk of the "rebels" were common men of all stocks. Harry Emerson Wildes has recently painted a graphic panorama of the encampment at Valley Forge. He rightly insists that this encampment marked the turning point of the Revolution. The men who came to Valley Forge "were battered, hungry, sick and in distress. . . . A disciplined, resourceful, and heartened army marched away from Valley Forge." He describes how through that terrible winter the men carried on, clung to their ideals. "The lesson of Valley Forge must not be lost. The Continental troops, who came as unrelated, virtually independent groups from separate states, went forth a welded national army. Their Spartan endurance of distress and disaster had taught them the need for a federated union of free men, enlightened and politically equal, if their ideals of liberty, democracy, and the pursuit in peace of happiness were to be realized." The same story is told in dramatic simplicity in Walter Edmonds' *Drums Along the Mohawk* (1936). The unquenchable spirit of simple farmers, their willingness to fight against overwhelming odds for their right to be independent, is here portrayed with a convincing realism. Along with Washington and the Adamses, the common men fought and won the Revolution against the British Empire, which was then an aristocracy. In America, rationalism and Puritanism, the frontier life and the melting pot, a rural economy of small farmers — they all had their share and played their part in the molding of the belief in the common man.[6]

But the leaders were afraid of the common man. The writings of Hamilton and other Federalists are full of animadversions against the common people, whom they called "the mob." Like its European counterpart, the wealthy upper class of America had no liking for democracy. It quickly recoiled from the forces it had led to victory.

The terrible distress into which the common people were plunged after the war led to the widespread uprisings of debtors in what is known as Shays' Rebellion. The Federalists saw in it the portent of an impending revolutionary upheaval — the anarchy which results from democracy. On the other hand, Jefferson sympathized with the exasperated debtors. They were the little men who had given their all in the fight for freedom only to find themselves driven from their homesteads by those who knew how to take advantage of the depreciation of the currency. Edward Bellamy, in *The Duke of Stockbridge*,[7] has vividly portrayed the chasm that had opened up between the commons and the "gentry" — between the men who through their participation in the war had become imbued with the democratic spirit and the squirearchy which remained attached to the oligarchical system of colonial society.

A number of the great revolutionary leaders became leaders of the common man. Sam Adams and Thomas Jefferson, James Madison and Benjamin Franklin, started the procession, which includes Andrew Jackson and Abraham Lincoln, Theodore Roosevelt and Woodrow Wilson. In wave after wave has been carried forward the revolution which started with the men at Valley Forge and Bunker Hill: the march of common men.

Down the years, however, a distinction has remained, which early divided Jefferson and Sam Adams. Sam Adams' faith in the common man was fully as strong as Jefferson's, but there was this significant difference between these two staunch republicans: whereas Jefferson put his trust in the American farmer, Sam Adams' common man was a townsman.[8] No clear line can, of course, be drawn between the countryman and the townsman, but the believer in the farmer is a believer in property, even though it be the small property of the man who tills his own soil.[9] On the other hand, those who believe in the townsman have gradually shifted the emphasis from the small shopkeeper and craftsman in Sam Adams' day to the class-conscious proletariat of the industrial age. Thus Veblen, in *The Vested Interests and the State of the Industrial Arts* (1919), speaks of the habits of thought engendered by the machine system in industry and by the mechanically standardized organization of daily life under this new order — a familiar theme throughout his work. Only in Veblen's eyes the countryman had been assimilated to the industrial worker. This countryman, though seemingly remote from "the habits of thought engendered by the machine system," was in fact part of Veblen's inspiration. In spite of such views (concretely expressed in the Farmer-Labor movements of the Central Northwest), there has remained down to the present day a marked difference in general outlook between those who think primarily of farmers and those who think of workers when talking of the common man.

WHITMAN, EMERSON, THOREAU

The fact of the matter is that the rather general belief in the common man which has been traditional in America since the Revolution was not effectively implemented by the intelligentsia until the mid-nineteenth century. The common man took possession in fact before he became generally accepted in theory. Though the common man became the mainstay of American democracy in the aftermath of the Jeffersonian "revolution," the intellectuals were slow to respond to the idea. The intellectual is predisposed toward the uncommon man; he strives to be uncommon. But the triumph of the common man was so complete in America that eventually even the intelligentsia became infected with his spirit. Walt Whitman knew the issue and put it very simply: —

One's-self I sing, a simple separate person,
Yet utter the word Democratic, the word En-Masse . . .

Though the voices that sang of this new spirit are many, let us listen to three: Whitman, Emerson, and Thoreau. All three were born at the turn of the century, all were children of the new age. Whitman was literally drunk with enthusiasm for the common man. The son of a Long Island farmer and carpenter, he was to belong completely to the life of the common man.[10] Time and again he returns to this theme. In the "Carol of Occupations," first published in 1855 and later re-published under the titles "Chants Democratic" (1860) and "To Workingmen" (1867), he concludes: —

Will you seek afar off? you surely come back at last,
In things best known to you finding the best, or as good
    as the best,
In folks nearest to you . . .
The popular tastes and employments taking precedence
    in poems or anywhere,
You workwomen and workmen of these States having
    your own divine and strong life,
And all else giving place to men and women like you.

Or in "With Antecedents" (1860): —

I know that the past was great, and the future will be great,
(For the sake of him I typify — for the common average
    man's sake — your sake if you are he;)

And that where I am, or you are, this present day, there
  is the centre of all days, all races,
And there is the meaning to us of all that has ever come
  of races and days, or ever will come.

For him, the belief in the common man and democracy is all rooted in strong erotic impulse; the brother-
hood of men is no idle phrase: —

For you these, from me, O Democracy, to serve you, ma
  femme!
For you! for you I am trilling these songs,
  In the love of comrades,
    In the high-towering love of comrades.

In these and many other similar lines Walt Whitman
displays his enthusiasm for *Man* as such. He truly could
have said, with the Roman poet, "Nothing human I
consider alien."

Emerson was very explicit in his determination to
make the belief in the common man the mainstay of his
conception of a democratic society, even of all society.
The very title, *Representative Men*, was chosen in
studied opposition to Carlyle's hero worship. "Great
Men!" said Emerson, "the word is injurious!"; what
makes an individual is his capacity to represent the
general.[11] But from this sound view, Emerson goes on
to state more extravagant views. The belief in the common man becomes, as in Whitman, a limitless Utopia
Emerson made this view most explicit in a lecture entitled "New England Reformers," the last of his *Essays*

The New Image of the Common Man

After proclaiming that a man is equal to the church and equal to the state, he flatly pronounces that "he is equal to every other man." "The net amount of man and man does not much vary," he tells us. "Each is incomparably superior to his companion in some faculty. His want of skill in other directions has added to his fitness for his own work." Nowhere to our knowledge has the belief in the common man been stated with more uncompromising exaggeration. To labor an obvious point: take the millions of good, competent housewives or farmers — in what faculty is one of them "incomparably superior" to any of the others? Indeed, these assertions are so palpably contrary to fact that one is puzzled to know how anyone ever could have set them down on paper.

Having stated Emerson's extreme belief and pointed out its weakness, the question remains: what was he trying to get at?

What was the sound kernel of his argument? It seems that Emerson's key point was that most men (and women) possess some aptitude which assures them of their place in society. It is a protest against the conceit of the uncommon man who, because he can write poetry or command an army, assumes a superiority that is absolute over the farmer, forgetting that the farmer can do other things well. When seen in that perspective Emerson's position is sound enough, so far as it goes. But it fails to deal with the crux of the elite doctrines:

that the work of the farmer does not compare in *importance* with that of the uncommon men; in short, that the farmer's skill is a common skill, whereas the statesman's is an uncommon skill. The reason for this failure comes from Emerson's individualism, from his making the comparison one between individual men, rather than the collective judgment of the many.

His younger friend, Thoreau, was more clearly aware of the collective problem. Indeed, there is a definitely collective strand running through Thoreau's thinking, which is, of course, particularly apparent in his political essays, *Civil Disobedience, Slavery in Massachusetts*, and *A Plea for Captain Brown*. Although his view appears at first blush to be an extreme of individualism, further reflection reveals a powerful collective impulse in the insistence upon the individual's responsibility for collective wrongs. In *Civil Disobedience* he proclaims this view in its sharpest form: "Under a government which imprisons any unjustly, the true place for a just man is also in prison . . . the only house in a slave state in which a free man can abide with honor." "I cannot for an instant recognize that political organization as *my* government which is the slave's government also." The "oaken strength" of his sense of communal responsibility is further emphasized and well expressed in the opening sentence of *Slavery in Massachusetts:* "I lately attended a meeting of the citizens of Concord, expecting, as one among many, to speak on the subject of slavery in Massachusetts; but I was surprised and disappointed to find that what had called my townsmen together was the destiny of Nebraska, and not of Massachusetts." This insistence upon the moral issue leads him to challenge sharply the authority of the majority: "What is wanted is men, not of policy, but of probity — who recognize a higher law than the constitution, or the decision of the majority. . . . What should concern Massachusetts is not the Nebraska Bill, nor the Fugitive Slave Bill, but her own slave-holding and servility."

Was Thoreau, then, a believer in an intellectual elite, a Platonist? Was he a believer in the uncommon man? Far from it. His appeal is addressed to all men of good will, but more especially to the common men around him. It was to the villagers of Concord that he addressed his *Plea for Captain Brown*. But his view finds clearest expression in the chapter on "Reading" in *Walden*. "It is time that villages were universities. . . . Shall the world be confined to one Paris or Oxford forever? . . . In this country, the village should in some respects take the place of the nobleman of Europe. . . . *To act collectively is according to the spirit of our institutions.* . . . Instead of noblemen, let us have noble villages of men." Thoreau's passion for craftsmanship is clearly associated with an ardent belief in the common man, animated by what Veblen was later to call the "instinct of workmanship." [12] For workmanship is closely related to character. Here is the bridge from Henry Thoreau and his *Walden* to Veblen. This emphasis begets a curious blend of radicalism and conservatism.

It is a striking fact that all three men, Thoreau, Emerson, and Whitman, responded enthusiastically to two representative common men of their time: John Brown and Abraham Lincoln. Each of them at once seems to have sensed the symbolic significance of the fanatic preacher who expressed the deep-seated urge to act regardless of consequences. He reminds one of the American youth who, when asked why he joined the Lincoln Brigade to help republican Spain, answered simply, "Somebody had to do something." That each of them should likewise have perceived the depth of Lincoln's representative quality confirms their kinship in being close to the common man.

John Brown and Abraham Lincoln were curiously linked in the struggle against slavery. The epic of that struggle has found its poet in our own day in Stephen Vincent Benét. His *John Brown's Body* is so extraordinary because it succeeds in a hitherto unprecedented fashion in bringing the common man onto the stage of history. Farmers and workers, craftsmen and merchants, English and Scotch, Poles and Germans, but Americans all — the "Invocation" conjures up the colorful pageant that is America. No matter where they come from, they join the procession of the common man.

The New Image of the Common Man

Stepchild of every exile from content
And all the disavouched, hard-bitten pack
Shipped overseas to steal a continent
With neither shirts nor honor to their back.

MODERN POETRY

In turning to Benét, we have arrived at the third stage in the evolution of the belief in the common man. Benét is not unique in his portrayal. Sinclair Lewis and Carl Sandburg, Robert Frost and many others, have each in his own way expressed belief in and affection for ordinary people. But the belief now has new overtones. Babbitt, while depicted with a sympathetic regard for the type of go-getter businessman which he represents, has nevertheless clownish traits. The smart and the intelligentsia overlooked Lewis' sympathy so completely that many of them found their feelings of superiority confirmed by his work. Both here and in Europe Babbitt became a byword of condescending disdain. The voices were few which, like the reviewer of *Babbitt* in the *Frankfurter Zeitung*, reminded people that "it was consoling to find that people in America and in Germany are so much alike." Most people overlooked the implied belief in the common man which took Babbitt simply for granted. At the same time, the common man as portrayed by Sinclair Lewis has lost the glamour which he had for Tom Paine or for Walt Whitman. Looked at by himself and realis-

[22]

tically, the common man possesses features which he lacked when he was being contrasted with moronic kings and depraved and corrupt courtiers. But what the common man may have lost in appeal as an ideal, he has gained in distinctness and vitality.

Is it not the essence of all realism to look at things "as they are" and to pay little attention to what they are supposed to be? The realist fails to bring into adequate perspective those differences between individuals which reflect their efforts to attain a norm or standard. But the realist compensates for this failure by the more vivid portrayal of the actual world. As no man is great in the eyes of his butler, so to the realist all men are common men.

The villagers and countrymen of Robert Frost live, not in noble villages, but in a vivid world of stone walls that need mending and of cows that eat fallen apples and get sick. Where Thoreau had vacillated between the romantic's dislike for ordinary men who "live a life of quiet desperation" and an idealist's appeal to these same men to become something far beyond their natural aptitude and inclination, Frost and the poets of our time comprehend the human kind around them with admiration or affection tempered by amusement, mockery, or occasional straight derision. In Frost the democratic atmosphere is completely part of the felt reality. His mocking disbelief in any kind of outward success frees him from all those delusions which obscure

The New Image of the Common Man

the vision of the panderers to the elites of wealth and power. But there is something more here: a quest for the native, rooted strength of the established ways of common folk. It is the poetic search for the visible, touchable, sensuous reality which leads him and other poets of our time toward the common man.

Clearly, then, the view of the common man has greatly changed. The *esthetic* impulse of contemporary poetry is a far cry from the *ethical* bravado of revolutionary days, when the European intellectual, Thomas Paine, and the Virginian Grand Seigneur, Thomas Jefferson, joined in befriending the common man. Most intellectuals despised Tom Paine for doing this. Struggling hard to develop a belief in culture and refinement, which was sadly lacking in rough, newly settled America, these intellectuals found the belief in the common man unpalatable. John Adams' epithet, "filthy Tom Paine," well epitomizes the abomination of the more genteel.

Today we see an alignment of brain and brawn. The thinkers and poets of America have turned to the common man with a new enthusiasm, born of their search for "the peculiar, the American thing." The cataclysm of the first World War finally gave America her full sense of self. No longer self-assertive and subservient in turn, American thought turned inward. The American spirit became conscious of its own form. And as American thought turned inward, sought to dis-

cover America as she is unfolding the human experiences of the people, the common man was rediscovered
as a *fact*, in shop and factory, farm and field. Rol-
vaag's *Giants in the Earth*, Willa Cather's *My Antonia*,
or Steinbeck's *The Grapes of Wrath*, revealed the
new vision of the common man as the quintessentially
American thing. They certainly did so as much as the
philosophizing of so representative a thinker as John
Dewey. But the explicit philosophy permits logical
analysis. To that task we now turn.

THE BROAD ISSUE: JOHN DEWEY

In *The Public and Its Problems* (1927) John Dewey,
after exploring the decline of democracy and the eclipse
of the public, turned to the local community as the
place where both might be reborn. The democratic
public, "still largely inchoate and unorganized," cannot "adequately resolve its most urgent problem: to
find and identify itself." "Democracy must begin at
home, and its home is the neighborly community." It
is here, in the intimate contact of the neighborhood,
that the public, that is, the mass of common men and
women, can become articulate. From Dewey's point
of view, the dislocation and unsettlement of local communities is probably more responsible for the crisis
than industrialism. "There is no substitute for the vitality and depth of close and direct intercourse and attach-

ment." This insistence upon the importance of direct intercourse is based upon the conviction that "the essential need is the improvement of the methods and conditions of debate, discussion, and persuasion." Dewey's view of this need rests upon an unqualified belief in the *rational* common man. He feels that it is easy to exaggerate the amount of intelligence and ability which may be required to judge the bearing upon common concerns of the knowledge supplied by experts. All he thinks we need is greater publicity. His appeal to do away with secrecy, prejudice, bias, misrepresentation, and propaganda has a quaintly familiar ring. It clearly rests upon simple rationalist assumptions. These assumptions no longer seem acceptable, as we saw earlier. A clearer, more fully differentiated view of the common man as he actually is will give body to Dewey's propositions, and thereby bring them closer to practical reality.

THE ANTIRATIONALIST CHALLENGE

The unrealistic assumptions concerning the common man have now collapsed under the cross-fire of a number of antirationalist challenges. More especially Marx, Pareto, and Freud may be said to typify the sociological and psychological contradictions in our outlook. Their viewpoints are characteristic of our dilemma. It is not intended to suggest that they have been dominant influences, but rather that they are representative types.

Karl Marx, far from believing in the common man, expounded two related views of man. On the one hand, there was the bourgeois businessman and enterpriser, a helpless automaton acting in accordance with economic law. In him Marx embodied what he had learned from that dismal science, deterministic economics. On the other, there was the Communist elite, the intellectual leaders of the class-conscious proletariat — more especially himself. In them Marx embodied what came to him as the tradition of the feudal and bureaucratic Prussia in which he grew up. Between the bourgeois and the Communist, the common man cut a sad figure, and still does in the thinking of all good Communists.

Pareto, like other sociologists of the end of the nineteenth century, made the idea of the elite the very center of his general theory of society. Like others before him, he held that government is always government of the few who are smart enough to know how to run things and have the will to do so. Without going into the esoteric jargon that Pareto developed to express his rather simple ideas, it is possible to summarize his notion of society thus: Most men are motivated by self-interest, by emotions or sentiments, and by ideas as to what is right. But the first two are much more important than the last. In order to know how society works, let's look at the past. Let's be "realistic" and consider the facts. Since the past has been largely undemocratic, Pareto comes away with a radically undemocratic doctrine.

Freud was, of course, a doctor. He found a lot of psychopathic persons leading repressed sex lives. He undertook to explore the relationship between sex and all the rest of men's psychic behavior and rediscovered the enormous importance of sex. Humans, he found, are the helpless creatures of their traditional environment, prescribing modes of behavior without regard to their sexual needs. Like Pareto and Marx, he was basically a determinist with a savior complex. Humans, he taught, were at the mercy of fate, unless saved by Saint Sigmund.

Between them, Marx, Freud, and Pareto left the common man stranded. The rational creature whom Bentham believed ready to act according to a sensible calculation of pleasure or pain these modern witch doctors described as the hapless victim of inexorable forces. They (and most of us with them) saw the average human as tossed about on the seas of class struggles, emotions, and drives, without the faintest chance of making head or tail of what is going on — except for those who happened to agree with the particular revelation. I shall explore these elite doctrines more at length in a later chapter.

BELIEF IN THE COMMON MAN RESTATED

Enough has been said now to show that a radical restatement of the belief in the common man is required, if he and democracy with him are to have a "new birth of freedom." To this task we must now address ourselves.

We are back where we started. Let us recall what was said above concerning the belief in the common man. "Give the simple mind of the ordinary man the facts and he will see the rational, the reasonable way to act, and having perceived this way, he will follow it." There are assumptions here, we saw, concerning the mind as well as concerning character. Neither of them is compatible with the "findings" of Marx, Pareto, and Freud which we have just sketched. Must we then abandon the belief in the common man and the belief in democracy with it? This has been the conclusion of Communists and Fascists alike. It is the most deep-seated issue of our crisis.

In their discussion of public-opinion polls and how they work, George Gallup and Saul Forbes Rae [13] start with the phrases: "What is the common man thinking? The life history of democracy can be traced as an unceasing search for an answer to this vital question." Public-opinion polls "provide a modern answer on the basis, not of guesswork, but of facts." There can be little doubt that "the public" has re-emerged into view as a result of these polls. But is it a public we can respect? Are its opinions worth polling? The answer to this question (which Gallup and Rae take for granted) depends upon whether we can restate the belief in the common man in such a fashion that the antirationalist challenges are met. For who could care about the opinions of a public which is believed to be the victim of social forces, subconscious drives, and the lures of mass propaganda?

It is my contention that we can restate the belief in the common man in such a way as to allow for what is sound in these antirationalist doctrines and yet retain what is essential for democracy. This restatement has four facets. To anticipate what I hope to show at greater length in the chapters to follow, let us review these four features.

THE COMMON MAN FALLIBLE

First of all, the belief in the common man should be stripped of those elements of excessive optimism which, in their extreme form, lead almost to a claim that the common man is infallible. Some of the earlier enthusiasts seemed to think that the common man could not be wrong. This absurd distortion of a tempered confidence in the common sense of ordinary men resulted in part from the fact that in the pre-democratic age groups of the elite often had advanced such claims for their own infallibility. For not only the Pope and his ecclesiastical hierarchy, but princes and noblemen, went a long way in demanding obedience by claiming that they possessed a highly esoteric knowledge. In the sixteenth and seventeenth centuries a substantial literature grew up which referred mysteriously to "the secrets of rule," the *arcana imperii*. Rulers such as James I were exceedingly fond of this idea.

The democratic movement had to combat these claims, and it did it by implying, if not actually saying, that the common man, too, is infallible, or at least almost always right. If only you give the common man the facts, truth will prevail, Tom Paine proclaimed. Similarly, the Bentham of the *Constitutional Code* felt positive that the majority knew what was good for the greatest happiness of the greatest number. John Dewey, as we saw, provided an echo of this confidence.

Now, there is no real need for advancing such claims. It is very possible that the truth may not prevail. All we do need is the much more tempered belief in the comparatively greater wisdom of the many. What we need is the belief that the mass of common men are, in the long run, less likely to be wrong than the individual judgment of any superman, or the limited judgment of any self-appointed elite.

THE COMMON MAN COLLECTIVE

In speaking of the mass of common men, we have already touched upon the second feature of a new belief in the common man. Historically, the rise of the common man is associated with the rise of individualism.

The New Image of the Common Man

As a result, the belief in the common man became linked with a belief in the individual common man. In that form it is impossible to maintain. But why need we assert that Garbage Collector John Doe is, as an individual, better able to judge an issue confronting the country than Professor Bill Roe? We do not. But the collective judgment of all the John Does is quite a different matter. John Dewey tries to get at this angle by talking about the common man as "the public." If we leave aside for the moment the distortions of judgment resulting from special interest, using judgment becomes essentially a matter of gauging probabilities. On any matter involving common values, it stands to reason that three people consulting with one another are less likely to make an error in judgment than one, no matter who they are. There will be exceptions, of course, but by and large, that is the probable outcome. And the larger the collective group, the less frequent become the instances in which one person is apt to be right as against the collective judgment of all.

COMMON JUDGMENTS

In speaking of "ordinary human values," we have brought in the third feature of the new belief we are seeking to outline. For it is necessary to eliminate from this belief all matters of exceptional or rare value, more especially all matters of taste. A good deal of argument in favor of the elite and against the common man grows out of the well-founded feeling of sensitive intellectuals that common men often do not recognize the difference between a Rembrandt and a contemporary magazine cover. Likewise, the common man cannot distinguish between the intellectual level of a popularizer, such as Will Durant, and of A. N. Whitehead; to him they are both obscure, and he is likely to think that Durant, being a bit more understandable, must be better. Such objections, in terms of culture and refinement of judgment, have, as we saw earlier, been popular with the educated classes right along.[14] While sound enough, so far as they go, the facts which give rise to such objections do not oblige us to abandon the belief in the common man. They do suggest that we omit such matters from the field to which the belief in the common man applies. Such judgments of perfection are not properly the concern of the common man.

CHARACTER AND JUDGMENT

There is a fourth feature of the belief in the common man which requires restating, and that is this: In the forming of political judgments, character is more important than intellect. What does that mean? Character, the dictionary tells us, is "moral vigor or firmness, especially as acquired through self-discipline." A man of character is a man who knows his values, or at least senses his values, and sticks by them. He is a man who seems consistent in his actions, who seems to follow certain principles. We need not necessarily agree with his principles. Here is a Chinese, practising polygamy, and here is an American, practising — divorce. Yet both are men of character. They show high consistency in their conduct.

This consistency is what matters in the judgments involved in most political decisions. The British people are so successful in their operation of a popular government because on the whole standards of conduct are stable among them. So when a new situation confronts them, they tend to consider the alternative courses of action in relation to fixed standards. There may be a good deal of discussion, but generally there is an even keel. Sometimes this consistency may be very irrational. The way in which the British public reacted to Nazism affords a good illustration. In confronting the Nazis, the British hesitated to believe them criminals until they had so proven themselves. Different Englishmen were, of course, inclined to accept different actions as proof, some the persecution of the Jews, some the invasion of the Rhineland, some the invasion of Austria, still others Munich. But finally, when the Nazis seized Prague contrary to their agreement in the Munich pact, the British were through. Now they knew, and nothing could stop them. (The failure to understand this adherence to a standard is said to have led Hitler to believe that the British would not march.)

COMMON NEEDS AND COMMON JUDGMENTS

This importance of character, of consistency in judgment, brings out a very interesting point. It shows that intellect interferes with character. The more clever you are, the less likely you are to stick by your convictions regardless. The more clever and smart you are, the more likely it is that you will see a way of escaping the consequences of a "jam." The common man is likely to stick it out. His standards are set. From this vantage point, the antirationalism of our time actually reinforces the belief in the common man. More apt to follow sentiment, the common man is more apt to be consistent.

This is, in fact, true of the other three features of our more realistic view of the common man as well. They all are in line with the requirements of a democracy.

We do not need to concern ourselves with his refinement, because matters of public interest do not generally involve the exceptional, but rather only the usual, situation. Public policies deal with the needs of ordinary men most of the time.

Again, it is not necessary to call upon the common man individually; through voting and other democratic procedures, his participation is a collective one.

Finally, to admit that common men are not infallible, even when voting in overwhelming majorities, provides a most welcome foundation for the protection of minorities through civil liberties.

These four elements in the proposed restatement of a firm belief in the common man are further strengthened by an equally firm disbelief in the uncommon man. We saw that Bentham had already formulated this corollary with great succinctness, so far as the man of wealth, power, and prestige is concerned. This disbelief holds true, of course, only where matters of *communal concern* are under consideration. But in this realm such disbelief should be sharp and unqualified.

Politics is concerned with policies. Policies often call for changes of *existing practice*. We do not start from scratch in communal affairs. The community is already a going concern. The judgment which is required of the common man, collectively, is of the kind which says, "This change of policy is bad because it runs counter to our cherished values and beliefs, customs and habits of life," or conversely, that it is a change which is acceptable because it does not do so. For as far as the technical issues are concerned, the public will be ready enough to follow the experts. In this matter of consistency, as we have called it, the majority of average men is much more likely to score, because the view of these men is not obscured by the technical enthusiasm of the specialist. Theirs are very different kinds of judgment from those which proclaim: "This is a profound truth," or "This is a superb work of art," or even "This is a saintly act." Such superlative evaluations do not enter into public policy, because *policies deal with average acts of average persons*. It is with reference to these that the judgment of the uncommon man is untrustworthy, just because he is an uncommon man.

THE PLAN OF THE BOOK

With these propositions set down as working hypotheses for a new theory of democratic government, we are now prepared to survey the major problems which the belief in the common man touches. In the chapters that follow, we shall seek a reconstruction of our belief which will at the same time afford us much opportunity to test these hypotheses.

First we shall examine the confusion which has reigned as a consequence of the continued use of the ideas of state and sovereignty. These two ideas are intimately linked to the belief in the uncommon man. They are incompatible with the idea of democracy. The state as God has been the Golden Calf around which modern pagans have been dancing, from Rousseau to Hitler. The world chaos with which we are confronted calls for a complete destruction of these neo-pagan gods.

The development of modern propaganda presents a second and insoluble dilemma for the older belief in the common man. A realistic survey of propagandist activities will reveal that that dilemma disappears when we take the view of the common man here delineated. It incidentally provides us with a practical yardstick as to what is what, in regard to propaganda, and how to distinguish propaganda clearly from education.

In the light of these insights we shall then be able to take a new and more sensible view of majority rule. Instead of the timeworn antithesis of majority rule and minority rights, we shall show how majority rule works out its own practical limitations, in terms of the common man as he really is.

The old controversy over majority rule and minority rights hinged upon the insistence on "agreement upon fundamentals," which has plagued political thought from Burke to the present day. A rapid survey in one of the chapters will show this agreement upon fundamentals as the happy hunting ground of antidemocratic theorists throughout the period of democratic advance. From the "gusts of popular passion" upon which Federalists loved to dwell, to the "class struggle" which Communists and Fascists alike denounce and propose to resolve into the higher "unity" of their party tyrannies, the enemies of democracy have been aided by our inability to make realistically clear democracy's need for dissent and her capacity for stomaching such dissent. The new belief in the common man makes a clear realization of this need and this capacity possible.

Even more formidable an obstacle to the future of democracy has appeared to many to be the insoluble conflict between democracy and bureaucracy. This dilemma hinges upon the problem of responsibility. Unless citizens can "think things out for themselves," how can they stay on top of the experts? They simply can't, cry some, and turn against democracy. They simply must, cry others, and turn against the expert and become demagogues. There is possible, however, a new concept of responsibility which rests upon the sense of workmanship in the common man, which makes him naturally turn to the expert. Thus bureaucracy and democracy are merged in a responsible government service composed of mutual servants.

From this vantage point, a solution of the further dilemma of expanding government control and free institutions becomes possible. Constitutionalism appears merely as the starting point of planning.

After the new belief in the common man has been tested by these six crucial problems, we return to the problem of the common man versus the elite. All elite theories have a common origin and a common error.

The New Image of the Common Man

It is a prerequisite for a democratic future that we should radically eliminate them from our thinking. Such theories are being rapidly discredited, but as one passes, another makes its appearance. The present crisis threatens to produce another such in the form of an American superiority complex. It is no sounder than any of the others. The belief in the common man comprises a belief in the common man of all mankind. But this posits a fundamental issue.

The new view of the common man is heralded in a new conception of education. The older conflict between classics and civics gives way to a modern version of education of free men for democracy. Such a conception, to be lasting, must transcend any nationalist limits. Here the capacity of democracy to absorb dissent provides possibilities for a world-wide humanism which would merge classics and civics in a pan-human idea of free men which is unhampered by dogmatic fetters.

Here, then, is the central contention of these pages: In spite of modern psychology and industrial technology, the belief in the common man is not only vital to the democratic creed but quite tenable. But it is tenable only if we state it in terms quite different from those which have come down to us from the visionary prophets of the democratic age. Naught but ill results from the thoughtless repetition of outworn formulas. The almost incredible faith in the omnicompetence and rationality of the common man, of you and me, must be replaced by a tempered yet firm conviction of the common man's *political* capacity. We need to insist, first of all, upon this *limited* competence, indeed upon the fallibility of every man, be he ever so uncommon. Whether there be an ultimate right or wrong, good or bad, no man knows what it is. In the absence of such absolute standards, communal policies depend upon calculations of probability. The common man, even in the aggregate, is not infallible; far from it. But he perceives more readily than the expert the general impact of proposed policies. The judgment of the common man in which we believe is a collective, not an individual, judgment. Therefore, judgments involving discriminating evaluation of exceptional achievement are altogether outside the sphere of these judgments of the common man in which we can trust. The common man is trustworthy because he is, in the aggregate, a man of character rather than of intellect — consistent, and averse to highfalutin deviations. He is "safer" than the uncommon man.

While a tempered belief in the common man is basic for democracy, a limitless belief in him results in the "revolt of the masses" and is part and parcel of totalitarian dictatorship.[15] Here a popularly acclaimed "leader" is the final judge of everything. Hitler is the common man run amuck. He poses as the incarnation of Rousseau's "general will," the builder of a "real" democracy. It is belief turned into superstition. Limitless and without real content, the belief in the common man destroys rather than maintains constitutionalism and democracy.

But if, as a result of such superstitions, we allow ourselves to be frightened into abandoning the belief in the common man altogether, if we become despondent and lose faith in ourselves, our plight is worse. What we need is a balanced confidence in our power to operate a community of common men by common judgments upon matters of common concern. Exceptional men, if truly exceptional, will devote themselves to the exceptional tasks. The mass of common men will gratefully acknowledge the achievements of such uncommon men by the time they have become common property — part of the life of common man.

CHAPTER II

The State as God: Modern Man's Golden Calf

*So spake the Fiend, and with
necessitie,
The Tyrants plea, excus'd his
devilish deeds.*

— MILTON

MUCH of the exaltation of the common man in nineteenth-century Europe and America was a reaction against the absolutism of the preceding age. Is it strange that the reaction to the democratic faith should in turn have exalted the absolute value of the state? The expounders of the faith in the common man, Emerson, Thoreau, Whitman, were all hostile to organized religion, though Whitman literally reverberates with the type of emotionalism which William James has so well described in his *Varieties of Religious Experience*. Indeed, Whitman himself was quite conscious of the religious impulse which animated him; but the religion of the self of which he sang remained barren to many whose religious impulses drove them to seek a higher entity in which to merge their selves. Whitman succeeded in merging his self in the future of America and of mankind. It is the glory of America that such comprehensive social idealism has been associated with the nation's aspirations. But in Europe men groping for a spiritual anchor turned toward the state or the nation.

Invented in the sixteenth century, the concept of the state has gradually come to overshadow all other political terms. Its importance is reflected in endless theorizing and in literally dozens of definitions. And yet, curiously enough, the word "state" has never entered American folk speech. Or is it curious? The growth of language is a mirror of the thoughts of the people who speak it. Up to the present, Americans have not needed that word to say what they desired to say. They talk of "country," "government," "people," "nation," and of just plain "America," but they do not speak of "*the* state," except in academic circles. Why? Is the common man king? What use is the word in European tongues? How did it arise? To what does it refer?

THE MONARCHICAL STATE

In a slow process that lasted several generations, the modern concept of the state was developed. It was forged by political theorists as a tool of propaganda for absolute monarchy. They wished to give the king's government a corporate halo roughly equivalent to that of the church. The State was the "estate" of the king; in France, where the idea was most effectively developed, the word *État* still covers both "estate" and "state." This is no place to trace the tortuous history of these dialectics. Suffice it to add here the second key concept, sovereignty, without which the state concept would be indistinctive.

Although many "definitions" have been offered since the ideas were first expounded by Jean Bodin, it is still valuable to look at them in their original form. Every state, said Bodin, in order to be well ordered, requires one single sovereign, that is to say, a person or group of persons to possess supreme power over all other persons. A sovereign, therefore, can change any existing law.[1] No state without such a sovereign, no sovereign without a state. In spite of many variations in detail, these have remained the main features of the ideas of state and sovereignty.

As an ideology for monarchical absolutism, this doctrine was perfect. Hobbes and Spinoza radicalized the doctrine by constructing a more extreme "philosophical" basis in natural law. But in spite of their almost universal sweep on the continent, the ideas of state and of sovereignty were slow in finding a home in England. At last Bentham and Austin in the nineteenth century proclaimed the sovereignty of Parliament, Austin largely under the influence of German jurisprudence. It was a curious sequel to the Reform Act, this proposition that Parliament is sovereign.

POPULAR SOVEREIGNTY

The concepts of state and sovereignty were already losing their utility. Numerous writers, amongst whom the most important was Jean-Jacques Rousseau, had undertaken to undermine the monarchical mythology. They claimed "sovereignty" for the people. That's what the ablest opponents of monarchical pretensions, the monarchomachs in sixteenth-century Europe, had insisted upon two hundred years earlier.[2] Few noticed that "sovereignty," when applied to a vague aggregation such as the people, lost its distinguishing characteristic: to identify the final law-making authority. For obviously the people cannot change the law, any law. Had this difficulty been clearly perceived, both "state" and "sovereignty" might well have paled into insignificance and died that natural death which comes to words that have lost their utility.

On the contrary, popular sovereignty became the battle cry of all good democrats. Even the concept of "state" was kept alive by popular sovereignty. There then ensued a comic-opera battle of words, a tilting at windmills by learned knights the equal of which had

[46]

not been seen since the days of decadent scholasticism. All would have been well if France, unified and centralized by the Revolution and Napoleon, had been the only country to consider. But unluckily there were federal states to torment the expounders of the antiquated doctrines. The Americans, and later the Swiss, did not seem to fit into the pattern of state and sovereignty at all. Hence, both in America and in Switzerland, voices arose which insisted that the only genuine "state" was the component unit of the federal setup. Calhoun especially set forth ingenuous ideas along such lines. In both countries the claim, tied as it was to grave political issues, eventually was settled by a civil war, but the problem of "state" and "sovereignty" remained. While it elicited some interest in academic circles, it lost its practical importance. The people forgot about "sovereignty."

STATE SOVEREIGNTY

In Germany, where the federal system was compounded of principalities, each ruled by a prince jealous of his position as sovereign, the situation was different. A veritable galaxy of learned men at once set out to find both the state and the sovereign under this federalism. Unfortunately, all the ingenuity of their metaphysically trained minds could not find what was not there, namely, a sovereign. It was not the people; oh my, no: the component parts were monarchies, even if constitutional. The princes individually were not sovereign, because if they were there would be no Reich. But neither were all of them together sovereign, because there was the King of Prussia, and the Reichstag.

Slowly the earnest searchers thought they saw the light: since the idea of sovereignty was essential to the idea of the state, and since no sovereign could be found, why, the state must be sovereign. This ingenious "solution" is one of the most startling instances of word magic. It would take many a day to follow all the tergiversations and mental acrobatics through which these learned jurists went to prove that the idea of state sovereignty was the last word of wisdom. Fortunately, it has been done for us brilliantly in a volume published some years ago.[3] From this maze one emerges with a feeling of utter futility, for to say that the state is the sovereign is either completely tautological or merely refers to its independence from other states. Such independence, while often in fact claimed or desired, is exposed to challenge at any time. With a sigh, one might lay aside all this latter-day scholasticism, were it not for the new life which the totalitarian movements have given to state and sovereignty. In them, the state once more presents itself as the *ultima ratio*, the final and absolute value, the earthly God to which all common men must be subordinated, yes, even sacrificed.

Modern Man's Golden Calf

In these movements we confront, of course, a rough parallel to the absolute monarchies of yore. But whereas the monarchs acknowledged themselves to be subject to a moral law or to right reason, our contemporary "leaders" quite flatly reject any such hocus-pocus. From this standpoint, a Hitler fits the original conception of a sovereign completely: he can change any law. Whether his state is well-ordered is another matter; but then, states have all along seemed more recognizably well-ordered to their immediate beneficiaries, whether French noblemen, Prussian officers, or Fascist party members, than to some of the common men whose well-being was presumably the state's objective. From the viewpoint of nineteenth-century jurisprudence this is, of course, all a great mistake.

The comfortable abstraction of the "state" when made concrete in such persons as Hitler or Stalin has a most distressing way of reaching for academic authorities and putting them into concentration camps. But let us not get too contemporary — just enough to remind us that all this is rather relevant to our broader problem. Americans have come to despise theory to such an extent that they have completely forgotten Ralph Waldo Emerson's "thoughts rule the world." To them, a theory is almost by definition "something wrong." It is the beauty and the terror of a revolutionary age such as ours that theories are probably the most important "facts" altogether.

PLURALISM

Some years ago misgivings concerning the adequacy of the conceptions of state and sovereignty, which had been brought to English and American academic halls from Germany, crystallized into what became known as "pluralism." Pluralism, though it meant to argue that there were a number of sovereigns, a plurality of them, actually amounted to denying the idea of sovereignty. For as we saw, sovereignty to be meaningful is indivisible. It is the sovereign who makes the ultimate decision. If there were several sovereigns, who would have the last word? Whoever it is, he is the real sovereign, then. But in spite of this obvious logical objection to pluralism, it served a useful purpose. As Francis Coker put it: "They [the pluralists] have been more explicit and concrete than earlier writers in demonstrating the activities . . . of the numerous occupational groups in the modern community, intermediate between the individual and the state." [4] Pluralism brought out how unrealistic the conventional concept of sovereignty is.

Practically all of the pluralists got themselves involved in obvious contradictions when they retained the concept of the "state." It was common for critics to point out that whatever functions the pluralists assigned to the state, in fact the idea of sovereignty was involved, since the state was left as the final arbiter. This criticism is weak in that the classical concept of sovereignty, as expounded by Bodin, Hobbes, Rousseau, Bentham, and Austin, is no mere bundle of limited functions. But it is true that the state concept leads back to sovereignty as its essential concomitant. The most striking illustration is afforded by the work of Harold Laski. When a pluralist, he was most radical in his rejection of monistic sovereignty.[5] But later he adopted the most comprehensive state concept, namely, that implied in all-inclusive state socialism.

LASKI'S PLURALISM

Laski, it will be recalled, actually made the individual "sovereign." The individual conscience is the only valid source of law. When the claims of various associations conflict, the individual conscience is the final arbiter of where the allegiance lies. In expounding such views, Laski offered a striking juristic application of the American folklore of anarchic democracy; his was a commentary upon Austin in terms of Thoreau, so to speak. Indeed, Laski's insistence upon the individual conscience as the court of last appeal in matters of political allegiance and obedience is a mere elaboration of the views so eloquently stated in Thoreau's essay on *Civil Disobedience*.

After his return to England, Laski found himself once more face to face with a highly organized government. Vested minority interests were strongly entrenched behind its established institutions. His views thereupon changed. There is little pluralism in *The State in Theory and Practice* (1935), which is a skillful exposition of the Marxist theory of the state. This theory is double-faced in that it sees the state at one time as the executive committee of the exploiting class and at another as an agency for the overthrow of capitalism. After that, the state withers away. Harold Laski bridges the difficulties involved by the belief that the common man's conscience demands a thorough collectivism. Thus the pluralist forces coalesce into trade unions; the unions achieve a majority; and the majority then proceeds to collectivize the means of production. It is very interesting that an outstanding theorist of "the state" thus finds himself thrown back upon a particular belief in the common man for resolving the paradox which the concept of the state posits for democracy.[7]

THE STATE AS SOVEREIGN ASSOCIATION

But there have been other than Marxist attempts. Under the impact of the pluralist attack, the state has been reinterpreted as an association. But while the state resembles other associations, it has a very particular function, and that is to act as a "unifying agent."[8] "Sovereignty," according to one of these views, is the will of this association. But the difficulty with such a concept is expressed in the question: how can the state unify if it is not *higher* than other associations and possessed of greater power? With that question we are back at the original issue.

One recent writer [9] has squarely faced this issue and has called the state the "sovereign association"; i.e., omnipotent within a territory. But that assertion of omnipotence is precisely what the pluralists had attacked.

It is our contention that the error of this and similar views consists in believing that *one* theory of the state can cover the governmental practice of absolutism as well as constitutionalism. Actually, the only thing that can be said about both types of government is that they are ways of organizing the exercise of power in the community. But they are antithetical in the patterns which they provide. Absolutism in its various forms provides for a concentration of power, while constitionalism in its various forms provides for a divided exercise of power.[10] This could be put another way by saying that such sovereign associations or "states" do exist at some times and in some places, but there are other times and places when there does not exist any association which can be said to be omnipotent. The United States and Switzerland are two countries where no such association can be shown to exist.

No definite meaning can be given to the statement: "The American people are omnipotent." For if power be conformity between the action of one person and the expressed wishes of another,[11] all we can say in the United States is that the actions of the American people conform to the expressed wishes of the American people. Hence, what is lacking is precisely the phenomenon of power which presupposes that the persons expressing the wishes and the persons taking the actions are different. But should we not distinguish between the people acting collectively and the people acting individually? [12] In a democracy the people acting collectively is compounded of the people acting individually and in groups. Over any length of time no one person, but all of them together, are acting, and they do it in accordance with their own wishes — another way of saying that there is no state or sovereign involved.

THE SOVEREIGN MAJORITY

There has been still another conventional way of trying to escape from this dilemma. According to this view, there is a "sovereign" majority. In other words, we are asked to distinguish between the majority of the people and the whole people. We shall return to this view later. Here it must suffice to remark that if the majority be the state, the state would be constantly changing. For who is associated in and constitutes the state, the whole people or the majority? We should have to maintain that we have one state when the Republicans are in power and another when the Democrats are in. Therefore it must be the whole people who constitute the state. This leads to the paradox that the whole people constituting the state are a sovereign association, and yet the majority are also sovereign.

In short, the state and sovereignty are historical phenomena which may or may not exist at any particular time or place. They very probably do exist in the totalitarian countries today; they did exist wherever absolutism held sway in seventeenth- and eighteenth-century Europe. States are indeed associations of men; like *il stato* of Lorenzo de' Medici, from which they derive their name, they are parties (gangs or brotherhoods) of men occupied with establishing or maintaining power over other men. The common man, by definition, cannot be part of a state in this sense, because if he were, he would become an uncommon man. The belief in the common man and the belief in the state are incompatible.

MONOPOLY OF FORCE

The foregoing provides a basis for a critical attack upon another aspect of the state concept. It has often been asserted that the state exercises a "monopoly of force." More refined theories recognize that you cannot depend on force alone, that, in a picturesque phrase, you cannot sit on bayonets for very long. But the emphasis usually remains on coercion. If persuasion or, more broadly speaking, consent is given the superior place which it in fact occupies in providing a basis for power,[13] the antithesis between the sovereign state and the self-governing community becomes clear.

A political community is governed in one of two ways. Either a constituent group has organized a pattern providing for the expression of consent by the common man (constitutional democracy), or a conquering group has set up a system of controls providing for effective constraint of the common man. The contrast is obscured, but not invalidated, by the fact that at times the exclusion of many common men gives the government an aristocratic flavor, as was the case in England in the earlier nineteenth century, or the conquering group has included so many men in its system of controls that its government possesses a plebeian flavor, as in Stalinist Russia and Nazi Germany. But the basic difference remains, and it was the government built on constraint that the concepts of state and sovereignty were constructed to idealize in the seventeenth century. Any close analysis reveals, however, that the central bureaucracies, supported by their armies, conquered the medieval constitutional systems from within, destroyed their pattern, which provided for the expression of consent by the common men, and established the monarch as the final arbiter of what should be done.

It has since been assumed by all but the pluralists

that such a final arbiter must be there and is to be found in every well-governed territorial segment of the earth's surface. In fact, a continuous, ever-present final arbiter is not only not essential for a democracy, but does not come into play except at intervals, and even then only imperfectly.[14]

OUR BASIC DILEMMA

The decisive point here is this: a basic dilemma has developed between the traditional belief in the common man and the continuous extension of the state concept. Why? Because under constitutionalism the common man is supposed to consent freely, rationally, deliberately, while the state concept posits sovereignty as the omnipotence or near-omnipotence of somebody within certain territorial limits. The crisis of democracy consists precisely in this: that many men upon becoming aware of this conflict and paradox throw overboard the common man and the belief in him; their dependence upon Father State has become so great that they are seized with fear and trembling at the thought of losing him. It does not, at this point, matter whether the omnipotence is that of a majority or that of a minority.

Omnipotence raises the question: Who is or can be omnipotent so long as the common man's consent is believed to be essential to legitimate government? Totalitarians, whether Communist, Fascist, Racist, or Nativist, "solve" this problem by limiting the concept of the common man to whoever fits their ideology. Thus the Communist common man is the class-conscious proletarian, the Fascist common man the "true" Italian or Spaniard who is conscious of his nation's mission, the Nazi common man (with only a slight variation upon the theme) the "pure" folk member who is conscious of his race's mission, while the Nativist American common man is the "100 per cent American." The last named species may be described as an American whose ancestors came here so long ago that he has entirely forgotten what they came for. Each of the totalitarian views of the common man carries with it the degradation of those whom it excludes. Thus capitalists, kulaks, Jews, Marxists, or just aliens are readily looked upon as subhuman.

All this is only too well known, and to the candid observer is such an obvious *petitio principii* as to amount to a fraud. Unfortunately, such insight may blind us to the equally apparent fact that we who consider ourselves believers in democracy have not yet discovered any solution to the dilemma either. For a common man who is broadly conceived, who here in America comprises all the nationalities and viewpoints, including our pet aversions, is incompatible with any state concept conceived in terms of sovereignty as just discussed. Such a common man will even, in some situations, engage in mob action, i.e., seek to use coercion and constraint for bringing into line fellow men whom he cannot persuade. If we insist upon maintaining our belief in this common man, we must abandon the concepts of state and sovereignty, or rather, accepting them, we must learn to restrict them to those political communities where they correspond approximately to ascertainable realities.

ORDER, YES – BUT

We are face to face with the recognition that Bodin and all those who followed in his path since have, in one form or another, overstressed *order*. That was their unexplained major premise; that order is more important than anything else or, to put it in more modern terms, that security was more important than anything else. There was an assumption here that complete security or order can be attained. This assumption has rarely been faced. Does it rest upon any foundation of fact? Obviously not. And yet by assuming it one becomes predisposed to consider order and/or security threatened. From such fears arose the clamor for effective action to maintain, restore, establish order and/or security. This kind of perfectionist demand represents a great danger to democracy. Crankish fads of one kind and another pervade a democratic electorate year after year; the Technocrats and the Townsendites are two of the more recent examples. It will not suffice to denounce these movements as demagoguery; they are usually led by sincere fanatics, perfectionists who honestly believe in their cure-all. Invariably these schemes are built upon the idea that complete order and/or security can be achieved if . . .

The difficulty for democracy consists not in its actual inability to provide complete order, for no government does that. It lies in its inability to silence the prophets of the millennium. In this respect, Hitler and Stalin have a great advantage; the common man is not permitted to voice or hear voiced the opinions of those who feel insecure or who dislike the lack of order. Concretely speaking, the Nazis were able to go on governing Germany in spite of a vast amount of corruption, previously practically unknown there. We say "advantage" — but is it really an advantage? Or is it actually a disastrous disadvantage? We shall have occasion to develop this problem more fully in the next chapter. Right now, let us sum up thus: By exaggerating the value of order and security we promote the idea that the government can do more than is possible, that it is all-powerful. This idea of omnipotence is traditionally associated with the deity. By just another step, we envisage the government as state to be God, and those administering the communal tasks as high priests, if not demigods.

Leaving aside for the moment the question of whether or not the common man is inclined toward such views, we can clearly see that a belief in the common man is incompatible with them. Order and security by themselves are not so important as *what* is ordered and *what* is made secure. The famous cry, "Give me liberty or give me death," has now been stated in terms of the four freedoms; the freedom of speech, the freedom of religion, the freedom from fear, and the freedom from want.[15] These are beacons on the road into the future. Unlike "order," they possess a meaningful content for the common man.

It is highly significant that the prophets of the belief in the common man have been indifferent to order. It was not a primary value to Walt Whitman. His great ode to the pioneers is hardly inspired by any desire for order and security: —

> For we cannot tarry here,
> We must march, my darlings, we must bear the brunt of danger,
> We the youthful sinewy races, all the rest on us depend,
> Pioneers! O Pioneers!

> Have the elder races halted?
> Do they droop and end their lesson, wearied over there beyond the seas?
> We take up the task eternal, and the burden and the lesson,
> Pioneers! O Pioneers!

The New Image of the Common Man

All the past we leave behind,
We debouch upon a newer mightier world, varied world,
Fresh and strong the world we seize, world of labor and
the march,
Pioneers! O Pioneers!

Whitman's entire body of poetry breathes this air of expansive adventurousness; his voice gave a superb expression to the spirit of the common man in America. In fact, so far is all this from the deification of Father State that, as we have seen, Emerson, Whitman, and especially Thoreau contain anarchist elements. This has been a persistent strain in American thought and feeling. Throughout the nineteenth century, and not only in America, anarchism accompanies the rampant individualism which inclines to neglect the group and class structure of society.

These historical associations of the belief in the common man are not likely to continue. Indeed, if the belief in the common man cannot be freed from its connection with some of them, it is probably doomed. But there is no reason why the only alternative to robust individualism should be the deification of the state. If the common man is seen as participating in such groups and as a member of such classes, *order through consent* is readily achieved. Indeed, far from being a mirage, it is the most common, the most natural occurrence in communal life. The common man is religious in the primordial sense, that is, as necessarily a participant in rituals which he shares with large numbers of others. A pattern of rituals, arising from a balance of many groups, will provide a measure of order which is sufficient for most practical purposes. Any realistic study of America, or Switzerland, or any other constitutional system, will show this clearly.[16]

THE REALISTIC VIEW OF POWER

A realistic view of politics and political institutions thus is indispensable to a sustained belief in the common man. It shows under what conditions of group and class composition and balance communal life can persist without coercive integration. It also points toward a thorough analysis of the institutional safeguards which are indispensable for such a democratic community. It promotes a realization of the fact that neglect of these safeguards may at any time offer the opportunity for a concentration of political power, and the establishment of a state and, hence, of sovereignty.

There is a peculiarly powerful impulse toward this sort of analysis in our own civilization, for it has been at once the progenitor of the modern state and of its most bitter critics. General disapproval of political power and secular government is deeply linked to our Christian heritage. At an early date, Saint Augustine coined a very effective slogan when he described the state as a "robber band," or a bunch of gangsters — to use contemporary American. Mind you, Saint Augustine was talking of a pattern of politics quite definitely in line with our view of "the state."

The piratical view of the state is coming more and more into favor amongst those who study the political reality of contemporary dictatorships. G. A. Borgese, in a moving indictment of Mussolini's *Goliath* (1937), pictured Il Duce as the Evil One who, an anarchist at large, seeks to destroy contemporary civilization with satanic glee. A comparable interpretation of Hitler has been given by Rauschning in his *Revolution of Nihilism* and *The Voice of Destruction*. Both Borgese and Rauschning are eloquent and persuasive in pointing out the kinship of these totalitarian doctrines to anarchism, nihilism, and absolutism. They show that these doctrines are preoccupied with power as the final arbiter of all things, and therefore leading to state idolatry. Is there, then, any kind of standard by which to judge this earthly god, the monster state?

Suppose the state is essentially a gang, does it follow that those composing the gang are "gangsters" in the American common man's sense of that term? Gangsters are bad men, yet the gang of guardians to whom Plato would entrust the state are supposed to be supermen. How are we to judge? The answer is: We cannot judge; that is precisely why we don't want *any* gang. Nor do we want to be cajoled into accepting such a gang by being told that the people are some kind of mystical

[64]

whole which can make ultimate decisions. The people contain both those governing and those governed, divided into changing groups which are fighting for temporary ascendancy and predominance. That is the view of those who have expounded the belief in the common man. Bosses come and go, machines are built and destroyed, gangs form and dissolve, but they are not an elite which is either stationary or circulating, but common men wielding temporary power as a result of their skill in securing support from other common men.[17]

ORIGIN OF THE STATE AS GOD

It is contrary, then, to the democratic way to look upon the "state" as some kind of neutral god charged with looking after the national interest. It is also alien to Christian dogma. Where, then, did it come from? Political ideas do not grow in a vacuum. They provide the basis for institutions which develop in response to an urgent need. The state builders of the sixteenth and seventeenth centuries met such a need. But where did they get the ideology with which to surround the naked reality? And why should they have sought to clothe this reality in such a garb? It was because Christian tradition was suspicious of political power that a justification for power was needed; the pagan doctrines of classical antiquity provided a similar pattern of ideas.

[65]

The New Image of the Common Man

The state as an institutional device for achieving the "highest" good traces clearly to the political doctrines of Plato and Aristotle. Both thinkers, pagan in their religious background, are of course merely the culmination of a long line of efforts to express in abstract and general language what constituted the essence of Greek, as contrasted with barbaric, politics. When Aristotle talks about the *polis* as the highest community and hence organized for the highest good, he has in mind a political community built upon the principle of group solidarity, in matters not only of politics but of religion and social life as well. Each of these *polei* had its own local gods or goddesses, and the struggles between the *polei* were mythologically symbolized in quarrels between their "gods." In the Homeric legends these epic struggles found beautiful expression. Ideas of this kind were part and parcel of the tradition of each *polis;* religion and politics were cut from the same cloth.

Polis designates, properly speaking, both state and church rolled into one. Only by thinking of government and church as one can we get a full conception of the Greek *polis.* Mixed in with this pagan idea of the state-church and constituting an essential aspect of it is the concept of the blood clan. No reader of Aristotle's description of the development of the constitution of Athens can fail to see how the whole *polis* rests upon the idea that in the last analysis all the members of the *polis,* all the citizens, are and ought to be relatives; indeed, their most distinguished families usually traced their descent from the local deities.

It is only in these terms that the Greek acceptance of slavery can be understood. No matter what aliens might be at home, they could have no moral standing in the community to which they had no blood relationship. The Roman law likewise did not treat them as persons, but as things. The modern concept of the common man, therefore, could have no meaning for a Roman or for a Spartan or an Athenian in the fifth century B.C. The idea of equality was inconceivable, because the idea of individual personality was remote. A man was what he was through the community and the clan to which he belonged. Once taken from that context he sank to a subhuman level.

The emphasis then in the Greek state-church is upon blood kinship and was decisive in bringing about the politico-religious community. Of course, we must remember that these people had the excuse of complete ignorance concerning even the elementary data of genetics, which their present-day emulators cannot offer. But though race theory be pure nonsense, there can be no doubt that the Aristotelian *polis* is in part built upon this foundation. The failure to keep this basis of Greek political thought in mind has occasioned much confusion; the Aristotelian concept of popular government and what *we* mean by democracy are not the same. Characteristically, Southern apologists for slavery before the

Civil War used to dwell upon the Aristotelian ideas as representing "true" democracy, much as advocates of race discrimination might today.

CHURCH VERSUS STATE

Now it is precisely this linking of religion with the clan, the common blood descent, which Christ most uncompromisingly rejected. Some Jewish prophets had done it before him. Other great prophetic religions, like Mohammedanism and Buddhism and Confucianism, also are opposed to it.[18] But Christian ethic was as explicit as any ethic could be in this respect. One reason was that the common Jewish tradition was not very different from that of the rest of the Mediterranean world. Hence we can say that the Greek *polis* conception as expounded by Plato and Aristotle is incompatible indeed with the Christian idea of men as fundamentally alike and equal in the face of their Creator. From the Christian standpoint, the *polis* is not at all the highest and the most comprehensive community, nor is it instituted to realize the highest good. To put the same thought more succinctly, the Christian view denies the religious functions of the *polis*, thereby splits the state-church into a church and a secular counterpart, the government. "Render therefore unto Caesar the things which are Caesar's . . ." Once this Christian view gained the ascendancy, there could not be any *polis* in the Aristotelian sense.

There is a breadth to the classic *polis* conception which the modern idea of the state as primarily a system of government could not properly claim. And yet to use it was very tempting for those who, from Bodin and Hobbes to Hegel and Marx, wished to surround the government with the halo of a supernatural sanction. It is an attempt to assign to the state a spiritual significance which it does not in fact possess within a Christian culture. All the expounders of the more extreme state conceptions have, characteristically, been antichurch, if not antireligious. Hobbes, in the too infrequently read last book of the *Leviathan*, thunders against the church as the most iniquitous institution.[19] Precisely because religious life has become the concern of churches, explicitly separated from the government in the United States, the government lacks spiritual significance. Here, too, democracy explicitly rejected what the monarchies of Europe had tried to finagle by linking church and state together.

Throughout their history, the concepts of church and state developed together. Of the two, the church was the first offspring of the *polis*, the Roman *civitas*. But whereas the *civitas* had been a clan, and even the Roman Empire had never succeeded in shaking off the fetters of this conception, the church was built on faith and dogma. As such it was profoundly different from the *polis*, and could truly claim for its faithful that it was the highest and most comprehensive community, and that it was instituted for the highest good, namely, the salvation of man's immortal soul. Thus the pagan *polis* became the bride of Christ. The church challenged and eventually superseded the Roman emperors who had persecuted it with such ferocity. Incidentally, the fierceness of the persecutions was motivated by the correct realization that the Christian faith, with its emphasis on the equality and equal dignity of all men, meant death to the pagan *polis*. Was not the emperor the divine head of the Roman *civitas?*

The disappearance of the empire and the emergence of the church did not eliminate the need for secular government. But since the church was charged with the religious tasks, the governments stood in need of its blessing in order to acquire authority. The Christian faith, teaching the value of the individual and the crucial significance of personal salvation, demanded that all such government be conducted according to law, more especially divine law.

A first attempt at realizing this conception culminated in medieval constitutionalism. It rested upon the faith in a higher law, fixed and immutable; the clergy was supposed to interpret doubtful issues. Governmental authority was divided between the king and the "estates"; together they expounded the law through the high court of parliament. All this is familiar enough, as is the fact that no "state" concept arose in medieval times.

THE MEDIEVAL VIEW: SAINT THOMAS

Yet in the Middle Ages there was a germinal beginning of a state concept. Unhappily Saint Thomas Aquinas, in undertaking to work out the relationship between Aristotle and the Christian faith, failed to reject Aristotle's politics as basically incompatible with the Christian view. He suggested this danger more by implication. In his commentaries upon the *Ethics* and *Politics* of Aristotle he imperceptibly shifted the emphasis. He did not openly protest the suggestion that the *polis* is organized to achieve the highest good.

Accepting the Aristotelian teleology, Aquinas reiterates Aristotle's argument that each community is organized for some good, that every *civitas* is a community, and that therefore every *civitas* is constituted for some good. So far so good. But then the premise of the all-inclusiveness of the *civitas*, which forms so essential a part of Aristotle's and other Greek political thought, is reiterated by Saint Thomas. This is startling, because such a premise is manifestly out of keeping with the reality of the church in medieval society, even if the *civitas* be considered coextensive with the Holy Roman Empire (which does violence to other parts of

Aristotle's premises). Saint Augustine's doctrine of the invisible church quite apart, the church was certainly not considered as comprehended within the *civitas*. Still, Saint Thomas claimed that it is manifest that the *civitas* is the *communitas principalissima*. Now how can that be maintained in view of the Christian ideas concerning the overwhelming importance of the human personality and its immortal soul? Saint Thomas, in paraphrasing Aristotle's assertion about the highest good, had slipped in a more decisive qualification: Saint Thomas speaks of it as the highest amongst human goods, i.e., goods to be realized in this world! But the distinction here implied between *human* and *divine* values is quite alien to Aristotle's whole way of thinking. Once accepted, this distinction dissolves all of Aristotle's political philosophy, inasmuch as there may then be a community like the church, serving higher values and hence entitled to the primary allegiance of men. As this community, too, is composed of human beings, it transcends the *civitas*.

Here the conflict is hidden between Aristotle and Saint Thomas, between paganism and Christianity.[20] The decisive passage in which Aristotle states that men, in order to become moral, must live under laws which are backed by force, is accepted by Aquinas. He adds that a father's teaching or any other persuasion will not do it, but only a law which is promulgated by a king. Only such a law is a *sermo procedens ab aliqua prudentia*

[72]

et intellectu diligente ad bonum (a lesson proceeding from prudence and a mind seeking the good). This view fails to perceive the problem around which all modern constitutionalism revolves, namely: how to discover what is good, what is the right thing to do, and how to find ways and means of realizing it. So by accepting the hidden premises of Aristotle's pagan conception of the *civitas* as the all-inclusive and highest community, Saint Thomas and the scholastics allowed Western political philosophy to become encumbered with the idea which stood at the center of the Greek tyrannies and the deification of the Roman emperors, the political idea against which the Christian faith had most explicitly revolted.

THE RENAISSANCE: REVIVAL OF THE PAGAN STATE

Saint Thomas, of course, had no thought of deifying the state. But as the Christian faith declined, men proceeded to stress exclusively those *bona humana* which Saint Thomas had admitted were realized by the *civitas*. The Renaissance culminated very naturally in the political doctrine of Machiavelli. The great Florentine, far from being a faithless cynic, asserted that the state, the *civitas*, was the highest of all values. In doing so, he went far beyond Aristotle's ideas. Aristotle, with the life of the Greek city before him, had seen the *polis*, or state-church, as the framework within which the fulfillment of man's destiny had to be achieved, and had described the *polis* as nature's most admirable product. Machiavelli, looking at the *condottiere*, the gangster leader of the Italian city-state, and knowing that the cultural life was quite independent of whatever these governments did, asserted that the state was the highest, the most remarkable work of art. The state, like other works of art, had to be created by man. Only the most skillful use of all the known techniques of warfare, military as well as civilian, could bring results. Machiavelli's, therefore, is a clear, unqualified belief in the *un*common man. He is an elite theorist, pure and simple. Here, then, was the creation of supermen, more awe-inspiring than the greatest work of art. But in the godless Machiavelli there was as yet no "deification" in the more comprehensive sense of the age of absolutism. Enough has been said, though, to show that the views of Machiavelli, while derived from Aristotle, are totally different in their emphasis.

If Machiavelli's new paganism was a challenge in its radicalism, it was nevertheless merely the culmination of a general trend. The climate of opinion in Renaissance Europe, devoid of awe for the Christian religion, but thrilled by the discovery of classical antiquity, was favorable to the erection of a golden calf, a symbol of the awe-inspiring forces of nature. Two English thinkers, steeped in the spirit of Tudor absolutism and of humanism, finally fashioned the new idol: Francis Bacon and Thomas Hobbes. They combined Machiavelli's un-christian doctrine of the "reason of state" with the state-church doctrine of the reformers. Besides, they were both ardent believers in the intellectual elite. It was a peculiar amalgam. "Reason of state," or the rational calculation of political advantage, embodies, of course, a principle of action that is indifferent to all moral codes. Even if stated descriptively, it tends to glory in <u>success</u> as the standard of evaluation.

THE REFORMATION: LUTHER AND ANGLICANISM

The early reformers had little use for that outlook. Indeed, Luther's revolt had drawn quite a bit of its immediate inspiration from its indignation over just such practices within the church. The brazen methods used by some churchmen for collecting funds for worldly purposes had provided much fuel for popular oratory against the "whore of Rome." Resuscitating the other-worldly purpose of the *ecclesia*, Luther and his followers objected to the universal church and its claim to be the guardian of the higher law, but they neverthe-less took over the Aristotelian tradition of scholasticism in regard to moral and political fundamentals. Fatally, they even extended it by linking church government and secular government. Though Luther presumably was inspired by Saint Augustine, he failed to follow

The New Image of the Common Man

Saint Augustine in the realm of politics. Instead of maintaining that the government is a "bunch of gangsters," he attributed to the prince the function of heading the church. Such mixing of secular and ecclesiastical functions meant moving toward the Greek idea of the church-state. By doing this, Luther prepared the ground for the secular papalism of a James I (and the point was further elaborated by Aristotelians like Melanchthon). Hence Luther, and with him the entire Lutheran and Anglican tradition in political philosophy from Hooker on, was bound to lead to a "deification of the state."

The recognition of the ambivalence of Luther's thought on the state must not blind us to the fact that he and his followers gave the greatest impetus to the belief in the common man that it has ever received. This was, of course, due to the Protestant doctrine of "salvation through faith," of the inner light, which made the individual's conscience the final arbiter in matters of faith. The radical democratic implications of that idea became apparent almost immediately in the tragic Peasants' War. Luther, terrified by the violence of this popular uprising, turned sharply against all such political inferences. Predominantly religious in his interest, he evidently felt that the religious reforms must not be jeopardized by such secular applications. But the inner logic of his outlook could not permanently be prevented from coming to light. People, shaped in their viewpoints by the Protestant doctrine, were when they became secularized bound to put the individual conscience to secular account. The next great upheaval conditioned by this inner logic was, of course, the English Revolution, and more especially the Levelers' radical democracy.

Against such tendencies, as we said, this deification was achieved in England in the philosophy of Bacon and Hobbes, in Germany in that of Friedrich Wilhelm Hegel. The neo-Hegelian revival at Oxford toward the end of the last century was a natural confluence of persistent streams of thought. All that was required for this modern idolatry was a gradual weakening of the ecclesiastical and moral moorings of Lutheranism and Anglicanism.[21] After they were gone, the "state" remained as the only focal point of human allegiance. Was it not headed by the head of the church, anyway?

While the deification of the kings and of their monarchical governments went forward apace, medieval conceptions fought a rear-guard action in the doctrines of Protestant and Catholic writers who expounded and defended the murder of tyrants. But theirs was a lost cause; they became known as the *monarchomachs*, the killers of kings. A little-known Scotsman, Barclay, called them that in 1600, and they have been called it ever since. Yet these expounders of the ideas of medieval constitutionalism became the forerunners of modern constitutionalist doctrine.[22] They fought the concepts of state and sovereignty which were then gaining ascendancy, showed that the concepts were incompatible with constitutionalism. The present situation presents us with a very similar issue. Stalinism, Hitlerism, and Fascism are different variants of a pagan approach. They, like Aristotle, maintain that some secular community, either the proletariat, the nation, or the race, are the highest community.

Thus from the sixteenth century onward, state idolatry slowly expanded. The growing exaltation and adoration of the "state" naturally meant a continuing emphasis upon "sovereignty." And the most radical expounder of the limitless claims of this sovereignty remained Thomas Hobbes, ex-secretary of Francis Bacon — cold intellectual *par excellence*, precursor of Bentham, Rousseau, and Hegel, Austin and Marx, Stalin and Hitler. Underlying all the many arguments and disagreements between these modern thinkers, we find a common core of worship for the secular political community and its organization — a deification of the state.

Is there any escape from this pseudo-theological claptrap? Can we hope to get away from the specter which haunts our thinking on man and society, the mirage of the Aristotelian heritage — this heritage which is not only beyond our deepest convictions but also contrary to our most obvious experience? For not only is it inherently contrary to the Christian view but it obstructs creative innovation both at home and abroad. At home it prevents our progressing beyond the present impasse between labor and its employers; abroad it keeps us from looking at the world in terms of a common humanity and its emerging common ends. There is no answer to these questions except in terms of a radical change of mind. We need to assert that in a democracy *the state does not exist*. There are governments, peoples, countries; there are kings, parliaments, dictators, parties, and concentration camps; but there is no evidence in support of the idea that some sort of holy unity, some mystical transcendence, need be attributed to them, that they indeed should be seen as an ordered whole.

Humanity is a whole, but not government, of whatever kind. If the Nazis should conquer, or the Stalinists, mankind would, no doubt, be treated to some idol of a world-state; governing gangs wish to see themselves identified with the oppressed human beings over whom they hold sway. Against this infernal threat, the brighter vision of a mankind freely united in a democratic union has been set forth by many.

We hope to have shown that both "state" and "sovereignty" are symbols of totalitarian government, that they are indeed fraught with implications that are incompatible not only with democracy but with the essence of Christianity. Great spiritual forces in other cultures, fortunately, are likewise opposed to the state idolatry of totalitarianism. The belief in the common man of all races and all religions is a necessary prerequisite of world government. Nations will take their place along with churches and professions and other free groupings of men within the broader organization of a liberated mankind.

CHAPTER III

Independence of Thought
and Propaganda

---

*Remember, Dick, to keep close
to the people — they are always
right and will mislead no one.*

— LINCOLN

THERE can be little question that the war "to make
the world safe for democracy" caused the collapse of
the belief in the common man in America. Men felt
themselves terribly, tragically duped, sold down the
river by J. P. Morgan and Company. George Creel's
brazen title, *How We Advertised America*, was the
knock-out blow; similar revelations by British propaganda agents completed the havoc. The "lost generation" turned away with bitterness and mockery from
politics and democracy. The common man became
Babbitt — a clown.

The New Image of the Common Man

THE SPECTER OF PROPAGANDA

A new belief in the common man must face the issue raised by propaganda. Unless that is done, the new belief remains untenable. This is no academic issue; it is a decisive hurdle we shall have to take. If it cannot be taken, democracy is finished. The evolution of Walter Lippmann's writings is very revealing in this respect. As editor of the *New Republic* and author of *Stakes of Diplomacy* (1917), he was animated by the traditional belief in the common man. He appealed to the rational mind of independent citizens.

But the response was discouraging. Again and again he found himself confronted with irrational responses, prejudices which no appeal to the mind seemed capable of dislodging. So Lippmann turned against the rational common man. To account for the average person's resistance to rational argument, he coined the imaginative word "stereotype." The formula has made history. Every literate person today knows that a stereotype is a pattern of perception conditioned by an individual's background, training, and experience.[1] But even though the public reacted according to stereotypes, Lippmann still assumed that there was a public opinion.

Three years later, in 1925, Lippmann had lost that hope, too. In *The Phantom Public* he set forth the view which the title suggests, namely, that there is no public at all; that the belief in the common man was so far wrong that you could not even expect the mass of men to pursue an irrational course with any consistency. It may be well to remind the reader at this point that the diametrically opposite view has been suggested in this book — namely, that the conduct of the common man shows ordinarily a very high consistency.[2]

Lippmann's skeptical opinion can be traced to his being a New York newspaper writer. As such, he was inclined to picture the public as the heterogeneous mass of metropolitan newspaper readers. Actually, this "mass man" is not in any sense representative of the common man in America (or elsewhere). This "mass man," uprooted and without standards or traditions, is, in fact, the very opposite of the common man upon whom the functioning of democracy depends. His reaction to propaganda is very different. John Dewey realized this fully when he urged a return to the communal level for a revival of democracy.[3] But he did not go far enough in combating the phantomizing tendency of Lippmann.

Much of the pro-democracy oratory with which the market place is filled at the present time is little more than escapism. Freedom may still be a cause, but it is unlikely to be served by offering up incense at the altar of bygone views — views begotten in a day when no methods of mass communication, controlled by huge corporate enterprises, had undermined the moral and intellectual independence of the common man. The Northcliffes and Beaverbrooks, the Hugenbergs and

Cotys, the Hearsts and Howards, the Sarnoffs and Paleys and Luces, are different champions of liberty from Benjamin Franklin. And since George Creel and Sir John Reith and Goebbels and Gayda are surely not the democratic answer, what is? Shall we call in another Don Quixote-Thurman Arnold to ride against the windmills of corporate monopoly in the field of mass communication?

Before such a question can be answered, broader issues must be considered. To repeat, public opinion is the mainstay of popular government, seeing that no meaning can be attached to the phrase "the will of the people" unless there is a politically active group which can be called "the public." A phantom cannot guide us into the future. It's got to be a real, living public. If it is nothing but a collection of marionettes manipulated by the unseen hand of the propagandist behind the scenes, if it is made to cheer, howl, sulk, and cry as the lords of press and radio (and, in times of crisis, the government) decide, then the belief in the common man is ridiculous, as obsolete as the belief in ghosts and witches.

PROPAGANDA: HOW DEFINE IT?

What, then, is propaganda? What is this fiendish thing that has arisen from the bowels of a free society to destroy it from within? Attempts to define propaganda are already legion. Psychologists have been particularly fecund in such definitions, each variation bearing testimony to a different psychological slant. Pychoanalysts and Gestaltists, as well as every other school, have each given birth to a "definition" spiced with its favorite technical terms. It would be wearisome to survey all of them here. What is the use of a definition, anyway? A definition draws a line, a limit, a boundary. When we deal with living reality, a definition serves primarily to mark off, to distinguish, and to classify. Hence in defining propaganda much will depend upon what we desire to distinguish propaganda from. For the theory and analysis of the democratic process, it is of primary importance to distinguish propaganda from two related functions: information and education. Most psychological definitions fail to do this.[4]

It is common knowledge that the popular view of propaganda is simply: lies. But while lying may at times be a method of propagandists, it often is not. When Lord Haw-Haw reminded the British of their evil deeds in India, he was not lying. When we say that democracy has been the peculiar American creed, we are not lying. Yet who would deny that these statements may be part of a propaganda campaign? That they can be propaganda? That, at any rate, such statements have a propagandistic effect?

Moralizing never gets you far in social analysis. Obviously, propaganda depends upon communication. So do information and education, so that is not a distinguishing characteristic. What kind of communication is propaganda, then, as contrasted with information and education? In answering that question, analysts have concentrated upon (1) the content of the communicated message; (2) the effect of the message upon the recipient; (3) the originator of the message, and more especially his purposes.

Content analysis has not led to the discovery of satisfactory general distinguishing characteristics of propaganda. The reason is simple: Any message may have a propagandistic effect; none need have it. It all depends upon the context. This context is composed of the propagandist who originates the message and the audience for the message, the recipient, who has been jocularly dubbed the "propagoose."

Psychologists have been preoccupied with defining propaganda in relation to the propageese; i.e., in terms of what happens to those to whom the propaganda message is addressed. The student of politics is more interested in the originator of the propaganda. Both approaches are needed for a full understanding of the propaganda process.

It may be well to leave aside for the moment the psychological approach, because it is clear that all writers on the subject have tended to minimize the distinction between education and propaganda. Psychological definitions of propaganda include, rather than exclude, education and information.

THE ROLE OF THE PROPAGANDIST

But an inspection of the propagandist and his purposes yields a definite distinction between these communication processes. All propaganda presupposes a propagandist. A propagandist is a person who hands out information, generally in order to gain ideal or material advantages for himself or the group he is acting for. More specifically, he seeks to get people to take or not to take particular actions which ideally or materially benefit the group for which he is carrying on the propaganda campaign. Ordinarily, the group will pay for this service. Therefore, usually, if we want to ascertain its purpose, we can look for the person or group who pays for a propaganda campaign. The particular actions which are sought may be of a great variety, moral, amoral, immoral: Join the Red Cross; Vote Republican; Praise Hitler.

Actually, a great deal of propaganda turns out, upon closer inspection, to be directed toward two objectives: to get people to join an organization, or financially to support an organization. This, you might say, is the hard core of the work of a propagandist, while around it cluster the more general activities which bring about in people a disposition to do these things. In these borderline regions, however, the propagandist's activity overlaps extensively with that of the educator.

Before we explore this insight further, let it be remarked that any rational effort at propaganda, any successful propaganda campaign, involves a calculation of cost. No propagandist worth his salt will spend a thousand dollars to gain financial contributions of five hundred. That is, only if

$$\frac{a}{e} \geqq 1$$

where a stands for advantage, e for cost, will a propaganda campaign be undertaken.

I might illustrate this by the activities of Goebbels in the United States. Before 1939 his ministry might have taken the position that the pro-Nazi propaganda should be calculated in terms of possible trade gains. German imports to the United States were worth $64,-550,000 a year. Suppose that the profit on them was 10 per cent, or $6,455,000. Up to that sum, expense would be justified. The Nazis might have doubled that sum to take account of the exchange advantages and argued that an outlay twice as large might be justified, if it offered reasonable prospects of forestalling trade discrimination. After the war commenced in 1939 (but before our entry), the situation was, of course, radically altered. While trade was off, the Berlin propagandists might have maintained that the advantage of keeping the United States out of the war and preventing aid to Britain was so great as to justify almost any expenditure. The only limit then would be their available resources. At this point the rational calculation of effort or expenditure (cost) in relation to gain breaks down.

The case of Nazi propaganda, fictitious though it be, reveals that even these more general efforts to gain advantages are related to a specific action, such as "Americans' not going to war." If propagandists and propaganda campaigns are paid for by someone, realistic inquiry will seek to determine the sources of the funds. Such knowledge can then be related to the activities of the propagandist and the nature of the advantages, whether material or ideal, can be ascertained. The evidence is not likely to be conclusive, however, and superficial cynicism on this score has been rife in various quarters. Frequently, ideal and material advantages and motivations are mixed; nor are human beings necessarily aware of their motives. But the fact remains that we have become increasingly alert and skeptical, so that the shaping of public opinion does appear, not so much as the result of spontaneous response and genuine thought, but rather as the directed impact of manipulative forces which permeate all corners of contemporary society.

PROPAGANDA OF THE ACT

In watching and understanding modern propaganda campaigns, it is quite important to get away from the common error of considering only propaganda of the word. Although vast quantities of verbiage are poured forth by propaganda organizations today, every propagandist knows that one act is worth many thousand words. Even when the art of propaganda was not so highly developed as it is now, the promoters of causes realized the attention-arresting quality of the active challenge. The woman-suffrage movement is a striking illustration. The fact that women were willing to undergo such trials as they did had a cumulative effect upon the general male public. The almost helpless opposition of true Christians to the Nazi terror and race persecution has derived more genuine support from Pastor Niemöller's courageous stand than from all the words of all the refugees taken together. For Niemöller's martyrdom dramatized and hence aroused sympathy for their plight.

Skillful propagandists will make every effort to stage acts if they do not occur, and to publicize them in any case. Sometimes, from the viewpoint of outsiders, such staged affairs may be extremely clumsy. The Nazis' Reichstag fire impressed none but their own party followers for any length of time, but it probably served a useful purpose at the time in confusing the public. The Zinoviev letter incident, dramatizing as it did the British Labour Party's unpopular policy of collaboration with the Soviet Union, was a similar, though far less vicious, hoax. Our own Republican Party's social-security stunt in the election of 1936 was an unsuccessful attempt at that sort of thing. Here it will be recalled that about two weeks before Election Day, some industrial plants distributed pay-roll envelopes furnished them by the Republican organization and bearing this legend: —

PAY DEDUCTION — EFFECTIVE IN JANUARY 1937

We are compelled by a Roosevelt "New Deal" law to make a 1 per cent deduction from your wages and turn it over to the government. Finally this may go as high as 4 per cent. You might get this money back in future years — but only if Congress decides to make the appropriation for this purpose. There is NO guarantee. Decide before November 3 — Election Day — whether or not you wish to take these chances.

Nothing was said in this about the fact that the employer was to match the wage deduction, nor about the benefits to the employees.[5]

But much propaganda of the act is a natural part of any great movement, whether governmental or otherwise. The meeting of Roosevelt and Churchill in mid-Atlantic is a good example here.

The New Image of the Common Man

THE VICTIMS OF PROPAGANDA

As was said at the outset, more interesting psychologically are the people to whom the propaganda is addressed. Just what are the psychic effects of various kinds of propaganda upon the people to whom it is addressed? Unfortunately, the answer to such a question is still very much in doubt. Different psychological approaches have brought a number of things to light; without question the gander does something to the geese. Politically speaking, the pragmatic test — that the propageese are acting in accordance with what the propaganda intended them to do — might seem sufficient. But how to explain these effects is the psychological problem.

The 1941 USO campaign, for example, did succeed in making tens of thousands of Americans contribute money to a cause which only a few months earlier they would have considered "militarism." This campaign was skillfully built upon symbols acceptable to the community. National defense, morale, inter-faith co-operation, and service were the four central symbols which the campaign handbook featured in describing the campaign objectives. This is what they said: —

To make our citizens realize that their help is needed in a key problem of national defense — maintaining the morale of our fighting forces and defense workers.

To show that the danger spots to morale are the places

where local resources are inadequate to provide decent, attractive, and worth-while places and activities for the off-duty soldiers, sailors, and men and women defense workers.

To convince everyone that the United Service Organizations have the qualifications and the right program for effectively meeting this problem.

To arouse a desire to work for and give to the USO as part of a great inter-faith demonstration of united patriotic action.

Whatever the particular campaign, under the competitive conditions of democracy there are always opposing groups on hand to point out the fact that propaganda is being made. War, antiwar, isolationist, interventionist, socialist, capitalist — these and dozens of other issues are being dramatized by skillful propagators of the opposing viewpoints and action programs. An impression is thereby created of the citizen's being completely at the mercy of the propagandists.

Actually, a good deal of the propaganda is neutralized in the clash of competing claims. This is owing to the fact that much propaganda is directed toward getting the propageese to act in a manner contrary to the interest of someone else. Propagandist X, acting for A, urges people to join an organization which adversely affects the interests of B. B thereupon starts a counter-campaign. If the advantage of A is roughly equivalent to the disadvantage of B, then both A and B will be inclined to spend the same amount of money and get the same amount of propaganda, and the situation is likely to remain unchanged. It was interesting to learn that the Committee to Defend America and the America First Committee had spent roughly the same amount of money, operated organizations of about the same size, and probably kept each other from having any substantial effect, except in so far as they intensified feeling and thus contributed to a rising tension level.[6] Yet it would be unrealistic to try to dissuade either group from carrying forward its campaign — as unrealistic as trying to persuade cigarette companies to abandon advertising.[7]

Such an equilibrium of interests need not necessarily be the situation, however, and often does not exist. If no serious disadvantage corresponds to the advantage sought by the original propaganda campaign, no opposing campaign will develop. This might, for example, be the case in government propaganda campaigns. Such campaigns are often directed toward securing the public's adherence to an action program which is part of an adopted and generally approved public policy, such as the Social Security Act or the Alien Registration Act. Efforts to interfere with such a propaganda campaign will occur only if there is strong opposition to the policy.

Counterpropaganda may fail to develop or may be weak where the persons adversely affected by a propaganda campaign are widely dispersed, so that each person's disadvantage is small as compared with the advantage sought by the propagandist. Much of the success of the Nazis has been built upon this circumstance; attempts to organize campaigns to counteract Nazi propaganda in this country have until very recently been fatally handicapped by lack of financial support. A folder of a large national organization realistically opened the statement of its case thus: "In the eight years since 1933, the Nazi Ministry of Propaganda and Public Enlightenment has spent $2,000,000,000 trying to undermine the democratic system and destroy the democratic idea. This Council exists to work and spend in the defense of that system and the aggressive promotion of that idea." [8] This case, incidentally, brings out another facet: The extent of the financial support is not necessarily a gauge of the "pull" of a propaganda campaign; for if the psychic resistance is very great, a countercampaign may be able to counteract it effectively even though it has to work with much more limited funds. In sum, even with the vast outpourings of propaganda of all kinds which our mass-communication media feed to the public today, there still stands at the receiving end Mr. Common Man seeking to determine what course of action to follow, whether to give to the Red Cross, the Bundles for Britain, the USO, or to the beggar in the street, whether to read the *Saturday Evening Post*, the pamphlets of the Council for Democracy, or Dorothy Thompson's column, whether to join the League for this or the Committee for that.

PROPAGANDA ANALYSIS

Those who would curb this torrent forget that restrictions would have to be administered by common men, and that these would be human, having their own prejudices, preferences, and convictions. There can be only one conclusion, and that is the conclusion that under democratic, that is to say, free competitive conditions, the only cure for propaganda is more propaganda. What this means is that the only cure for propaganda you or I don't like is to make more propaganda for what we do like, to speak up for whatever we believe in and get others to do likewise. As compared to this need for affirming one's own view, the "detection" of propaganda is rather unimportant. A great deal has been made of it in recent years; there isn't really any great mystery about it. And even if you do detect it, you have not necessarily destroyed its effectiveness in influencing yourself, let alone others. The propaganda of terror, for example, which the totalitarians have used so extensively, is meant to be "detected."

Quite apart from the important propaganda of the act, even word propaganda cannot be detected by merely looking at the words. The familiar pattern of the Institute for Propaganda Analysis distinguishes seven devices: Name Calling, Glittering Generalities, Transfer, Testimonial, Plain Folks, Card Stacking, The Band Wagon. It is valuable to know these devices, but too much reliance should not be placed upon them. For one thing, they rest upon too broad a conception of propaganda. You can convince yourself of this by going over any piece of writing, a poem of Shakespeare's or the Bible, for that matter; you will readily find examples of one or more of these devices. Any writing that touches upon values, upon what someone believes in as true and good, will contain "glittering generalities" and so on.

What is more, the Institute's whole approach is based upon that eighteenth-century rationalism, and the conception of the common man which we have inherited from this rationalism. For while the Institute recognizes the fact that propagandists appeal to "feelings," its own appeal is almost entirely built on the assumption that its readers are highly rational beings. This implies, of course, a holier-than-thou attitude which assumes that the Institute's presentations can be free from propaganda. Actually, every one of their intrinsically valuable studies is itself a skillful piece of propaganda. The very act of calling others "propagandists" is employing the "name-calling" device. The Institute's own studies rely most upon the Card Stacking device, but Testimonial and Glittering Generalities are common, while Name

The New Image of the Common Man

Calling and Transfer are also found. Once again, the very word "device" is an instance of Name Calling — as are their several names, such as Card Stacking.

Characteristically, the Institute claims in one of its publications that "the effect of propaganda on an uncritical audience jeopardizes democracy in that it opens the way to a fascist demagogue." [9] The emphasis upon the "critical" quality of the audience which that audience presumably would derive from familiarity with the Institute's publications shows clearly the lack of confidence in the judgment of common men. It is our contention that an audience, when confronted with the claims of rival propagandists as it is under democratic conditions, usually is able to judge for itself between these rivals as to what and who is "right."

The real issue in propaganda analysis arises from the fact that there are endless differences as to what are ends deserving of approval. In short, if we are candid, we have to admit that the propaganda we are worried about is the propaganda of our enemies. Not so much for ourselves. *We* readily recognize such propaganda; hate makes us clairvoyant. But we fear its effects upon others. If the propaganda is open, if it is carried on in broad daylight, our actions must be directed toward combating it. No problem of detection is involved. But if the propaganda is veiled, we must detect its source.

That is the real problem. No mere reading of the stuff we suspect is going to help much. Most of us find no difficulty in recognizing the outpourings of Father Coughlin as propaganda. But whose propaganda is it? Some of his misstatements read exactly like the outpourings of Goebbels' machine. Is Father Coughlin directly or indirectly in their hire? Such charges have been made, and some evidence has been brought forward in support of them. How could the source of Father Coughlin's questionable items be learned? You can see from this question how exceedingly difficult it is to "detect propaganda" in a realistic sense; that is to say, how difficult it is to detect the hidden propagandist and destroy him.

EDUCATION VERSUS PROPAGANDA

Nor is the detection of propaganda nearly as important as independent thought and action. But how can thought be independent? How can people be got to think for themselves? Most of us would answer: through education. But how shall we distinguish education from propaganda? At the outset of this discussion of propaganda it was said that propaganda should be so defined that it could be clearly distinguished from education. By this we did not mean to suggest that a hard and fast line could be drawn between the two; that is rarely possible between related social phenomena. Let us recognize at the outset that the two overlap. Nevertheless, there is a real difference. In other words, there are activities that are so clearly either one or the other that no misunderstanding can arise.

There are three primary conceptions of education prevalent in the United States today. Hence, if one is merely a man who teaches, one approaches the subject with some trepidation. Each exponent sees his as the right idea, of course, and each one feels that democracy would be best served by people educated according to its principles. Indeed, some of the more ardent exponents of each philosophy feel that democracy is incompatible with any other but their own philosophy.

What are the three strands of educational outlook? Discarding the more conventional labels, they might be called the pragmatic, the humanist, and the authoritative views of education. The pragmatic or realist view stresses the informational and the training side of education — learning how to think, how to solve problems, and so forth. The humanist view emphasizes the importance of a cultural heritage, a broad appreciation of basic values, both moral and esthetic, but assumes that these values can be taught by the free teacher who has been himself trained in that heritage. The authoritative view, while also emphasizing the importance of moral values as the central goal of educational effort, would make the Catholic Church, as the dispenser of divine revelation, the fountain of doctrine and truth concerning them. Other churches incline toward this view also, and many denominational colleges bear the earmarks of that conception, but they have not developed so comprehensive and consistent an educational philosophy as the Catholic Church. Such, then, roughly are the three educational views: the pragmatic, the humanist, and the authoritarian. These labels are, of course, rather general, and there are many intermediary positions and viewpoints. But it is clear that educational effort in the United States should be viewed in the light of their joint operation.

All three philosophies have something in common, however. They all seek to mold and develop a human being. All education is inspired by an ideal of what a human being should be like to be perfect. Education is perfectionist. Not the doing of some particular thing, such as joining a church or giving it money, is the purpose of the educator. Education in its efforts to mold and develop a human being, to make him a more perfect person, employs standards. If you endeavor to make a young person as fine a person as you know how, you will do it, of course, in terms of what seems perfection to you. You may be a Christian, or a Communist, or a Nazi, a Buddhist, or a Mohammedan, or a Confucian. Each of these "creeds" claims to possess a vision of human perfection. This claim, this faith, is a vital part of any creed. Perhaps they are all wrong, and the cynical sensualist is right who would let humans be what they will.

As long as we claim that human beings require forming, that they ought to be shaped in accordance with our ideal, we will, if we are at all fair, admit that there are other ideals and that the educational efforts of rival viewpoints are externally, functionally similar to our own. If we believe in one of these creeds with all our heart, we shall find it harder to admit this similarity of an opposing pedagogical effort, but it is there. Believing strongly in the humanist ideal, I find it very hard to "understand" Communist or Fascist education; I tend to view it as propaganda. But with some effort I can see how they understand it. Any effort to mold human beings according to some ideal, according to some standard of what is good, beautiful, and just, constitutes genuine education.

It should be clear now what distinguishes the educator from the propagandist in a functional sense. Whereas the educator seeks to mold and develop a human being, the propagandist is essentially an organization man. He takes a manipulative view of all matters touching the creed. For him, it is always a question of what an issue will do to the organization to which he is attached, be it the Soviet Union, the Democratic Party, or the Catholic Church. When dealing with spiritual and intellectual matters, the propagandist will usually ask: "What is their material value to us today? Do these proposals strengthen or weaken us?" The creed itself may entail disadvantages from a propagandist viewpoint. In such cases, the propagandist tries to soft-pedal the issue. Not so the educator. He cannot allow such opportunism. All politically active creeds have had to face this problem; all have at times been rent by the clash between the educator's and the propagandist's views, none more so than the Christian churches.

A DRAMATIC SCENE:
THE GREAT INQUISITOR

In its extreme form, this difference between the propagandist and the educator and the bitter melancholy of the struggle between them has been dramatically depicted by Dostoevski. In "The Great Inquisitor," part of *The Brothers Karamazov*, Dostoevski has Jesus reappear in sixteenth-century Spain. The Inquisition takes him into custody, and in the ensuing examination the Great Inquisitor tries to convince Jesus that it is impossible for them to allow him to go about preaching the Word. It would bring their organization tumbling to the ground. "All has been given by Thee to the Pope," the Great Inquisitor exclaims to the Son of Man, "and all, therefore, is still in the Pope's hands, and there is no need for Thee to come now at all. Thou must not meddle for the time, at least. . . . Thou didst Thyself lay the foundation for the destruction of Thy kingdom, and no one is more to blame for it. . . . I swear man is weaker and baser by nature than Thou hast believed him. Can he, can he do what Thou didst? . . . We have corrected Thy work and have founded it upon *miracle, mystery,* and *authority.* . . . We have taken the sword of Caesar and in taking it, of course, have rejected Thee and followed *him.* Oh, ages are yet to come of the confusion of free thought, of their science and cannibalism. . . . (But in the end) all will be happy, all the millions of creatures, except the hundred thousand who rule over them. For only we who guard the mystery shall be unhappy. . . . What I say to Thee shall come to pass, and our dominion will be built up. I repeat, tomorrow Thou shalt see that obedient flock who at a sign from me will hasten to heap up the hot cinders upon the pile on which I shall burn Thee for coming to hinder us. For if anyone has ever deserved our fires, it is Thou. Tomorrow I shall burn Thee. *Dixi.*" Whereupon Jesus walks up to him, without a word, and kisses him.

Here we have the conflict between the educator as true believer and the organization man, the propagandist, in its extreme form. Georges Bernanos has beautifully depicted it in his *Diary of a Country Priest,* as has Ignazio Silone in his *Bread and Wine,* a moving indictment of the political compromises of the church under Fascism. The old priest who is the hero of Silone's novel says: "The Church has made religion a drug for the poor people. What belongs to God is given to Caesar, and what ought to be left to Caesar is given to

God. The spirit of the Lord has abandoned the Church, which has become a formal, conventional, materialistic institution, obsessed with worldly and caste worries."

THE INTERDEPENDENCE OF EDUCATION AND PROPAGANDA

It is part of the conflict that neither educator nor propagandist can do without the other. That is what often gives the situation the inescapable quality of a Greek tragedy. The educator needs the support of the organization which the propagandist creates and maintains; the propagandist is helped greatly in the long run by the efforts of the educator to mold human beings in accordance with whatever ideals inspire the organization. Indeed, any such organization is dependent upon the efforts of the educator, because it is he who creates and perpetuates lasting predispositions for the support of the organization. But in creating such dispositions, the educator also produces the propagandists' most severe critics. By instilling an ideal into youth, the educator creates a dogmatic fervor which is liable to be bitterly disappointed when confronted with reality. Many American parents have recently had to face this kind of clash, and it has been deeply disturbing to them to find themselves confronted by decidedly pacifist views among young people who have admittedly been brought up with that ideal.[10]

[105]

The New Image of the Common Man

In short, the clashes between group ideals, as taught by the educator, and the realities of group life, as utilized by the propagandist, are inherent in the distinctive functions of the two. The tragedy of the conflict will be intensified when the propagandist strives to make extensive use of established ideals, as he is apt to. The experience with the Creel Committee is most instructive here. At the root of the questionable aftereffects of this ably conducted experiment lies the problem of the common man's place in democracy.

To repeat it once again, the democratic ideal has as its core the belief in the capacity of the common man to think and act for himself. The neglect of this aspect of the American ideal turned the propaganda success of 1917 into a major disaster. James Mock and Cedric Larsen have recently analyzed the Creel Committee experience under the title *Words That Won the War*. It would have been more appropriate to call the book "Words That Lost the War." For although our arms prevailed, the outcome of the war turned into a gigantic defeat for democracy, due to our own failure to guard our ideal against abuse by the propagandist. Everyone knows that the wave of disappointment which followed the war to make the world safe for democracy was sharpest amongst young men who had been brought up in an unquestioning acceptance of the democratic ideal.

THE POSTWAR CONFUSION

In short, the sudden awareness of the fact of mass propaganda challenged the traditional belief in the common man. No one expressed the shock more vividly than Henry L. Mencken. "He had to deal," to use the brilliant characterization of Ludwig Lewisohn, "with a society putrescent with gross and ugly and tyrannous delusions, with the tragic hypocrisy of the 'war for democracy,' with the rebirth of a nativism that sought to make helots of all Americans not of one special blood, with the apparent triumph of moral and intellectual repressions that degraded every man to a potential spy upon his neighbour and covered the land with a spawn of informers and defamers and lynchers of the body and of the mind." Against this America Mencken protested: "Wilson: the self-bamboozled Presbyterian, the right thinker, the great moral statesman, the perfect model of the Christian cad." Mencken's cynicism was pure nihilism, a confused striking out in all directions, condemning the good with the bad, and the indifferent into the bargain. But it was none the less a challenge.[11]

The challenge of postwar disillusionment has not been met. Nor could it be met in terms of a return to earlier views. Though the reactionary escape has an everlasting appeal to the timid, a radical challenge demands a deeper search to uncover the maladjustments which produced it. Though we have stewed for twenty years in the broth of Menckenian cynicism, we do not believe in the common man today any more than we did in 1920. The New Deal was largely manipulated by benevolent despots, intellectuals with a realistic grasp of patronage and ward politics, even though they often used the rationalist slogans of a bygone day.

If the new war had not come along and changed the issues, beyond the shred of a doubt another wave of reaction, another cry of "back to normalcy," would have engulfed the land. Such a reaction would have re-assured the masters of our economy concerning the workings of democracy; but would it have revived a belief in the common man? The ill-concealed spectacle of a gigantic struggle between the propaganda of the ward bosses, the Kellys and the Hagues, on one side, and the masters of wealth and mass communication on the other, was apparent even in the summer of 1940. While French democracy was collapsing under the battering of the Hitler legions, American democracy was under attack from right and left by the forces that despise the common man, even while they protest their love for him.

Here, then, is the true paradox: Organized propaganda and mass communication, though begotten by the belief in the common man, have caused its eclipse. Only within a democratic setting could the vast extension of propaganda take place which has occurred in the last two or three generations; yet having taken place, it put into jeopardy the very belief upon which democracy rests. How shall we explain this development, and having explained it, how shall we remedy it? In order to answer that question we need *to change our conception of the common man*. Mass propaganda brought to light the fact that man, the common man, was quite different from what eighteenth-century rationalism and individualism assumed him to be. It brought to light the irrational in him. This was inevitable; for the propagandists, competing for the support of the common man, rapidly developed ever more subtle techniques, ever more elaborate skills for ensnaring him, capturing his attention, and goading him into action. That's why we have to state our belief in terms more limited and more precise, more sensible and realistic than were formerly used.

THE UNCOMMON MAN

Modern propaganda, if it has knocked out the underpinnings of our old belief in the common man, has dealt even more mortal blows to all beliefs in uncommon men — so-called "elite theories." This is often overlooked, yet it is just as potent when you consider the facts. Not only is the uncommon man the helpless victim of the governmental propaganda machine under a totalitarian system. Of that we have distressing evidence in the behavior of men of outstanding ability who have fallen under the spell of a Goebbels. The uncommon man also appears to be more vulnerable to the everyday appeals of propaganda in a democracy. Quite a few studies have shown that intellectuals of all kinds are more volatile than the common man. The common man is slow in his intellectual reactions, and that serves to protect him against the propaganda of the word, while his rough-and-tumble existence after graduating from the school of hard knocks makes him less likely to be thrown off balance by a skillful piece of propaganda of the act.

In recent decades, the uncommon man has assumed a new role; he is the voice or symbol of the collective aspirations. He, too, has seemed the victim of propaganda and the playball of forces and trends, uncommon only in his greater susceptibility to propaganda. Did not the most learned of German scholars step forward to defend the aggressive policy of the Kaiser's *Reich* as if they were a bunch of children? Did not American and English poets sing of democracy, as if their talent were for hire to the committees of propaganda? Such occasions have shown that the uncommon man is exceptional only in his particular field of work; in the common concerns of the community he is as apt to be as much of a propagoose as any ordinary citizen, if not more so. His proper field is some creative realm of activity which in no wise proves his ability to govern the community. Indeed, the very fact that their talents are exceptional in art, literature, or science leaves the uncommon men preoccupied with other matters than the affairs of common men. Nietzsche, who cried out so passionately for men of uncommon traits, was not able to manage even the simplest of human relationships, nor would the superman he projected in his own image have been much more successful. In his comments upon the Franco–Prussian War he shows himself the naïve victim of official propaganda.[12]

The nearest to an uncommon man recognized by modern America is Abe Lincoln — common man incarnate and self-consciously cognizant of that fact. Lincoln most sharply disbelieved in the uncommon man: "Remember, Dick, to keep close to the people — they are always right and will mislead no one."[13] This was said in private and to a friend, not in a public speech to flatter the multitude. Lincoln, then, was uncommon only in the extent to which he embodied the traits which the belief in the common man called for: "One of the very few Christians in the bloody history of Christendom."

WHO IS A COMMON MAN?

Taking Lincoln as the archetype of the common man illustrates well the five basic aspects of the nature of the common man.[14] Lincoln also may serve as a reminder that we are speaking of ourselves. The common man includes that not inconsiderable group of common citizens in all walks of life who try to figure out why they do what they are doing. What is more, they are known to do so by their neighbors, with the result that their views are accepted by the people around them as the "best bet." Such people may be just plain, ordinary men and women, or they may occupy one of the many positions of intimate "leadership" in which the person counts heavily — positions which are held because the holder excels in his particular work, whether as worker, as farmer, as teacher, or as anything else. They are not a "class," although much of the writing on the middle class is in part inspired by unconscious images of this group. They are recruited from all classes, occupations, and skills.

Because such persons excel in whatever they are doing, because they possess what Veblen called "the instinct of workmanship," they are usually ready to recognize the special skills and aptitudes of others. Their own judgment is needed where it is a question of determining that a certain policy is bad because its runs counter to our cherished values and beliefs, customs and habits of life, or conversely, that it is good because it does not so conflict.

Independence of Thought and Propaganda

THE RANGE OF COMMON JUDGMENT

How the judgment of the common man dovetails with that of the expert can be illustrated rather well by the following: —

The people at large do not determine whether a given statute is constitutional or not. Nobody has ever proposed or argued such an arrangement, to my knowledge. A decision as to constitutionality involves complex legal considerations entirely beyond you and me, entirely beyond the comman man. The "best judge" is a man learned in the law. But what *ought* to be constitutional is indeed a matter of judgment for the common man; hence we provide for constitutional amendments. In the long run, the common man collectively is a better judge as to what is good for him than any self-appointed elite. The various specialists, groups of uncommon men with particular knowledge or interest or skill, compete in appealing to that collective judgment; but unless they can make their points convincing, they do not prevail.

There are many other illustrations. Take for example the budgeting practices of the federal government in recent years. Many experts have thought that we were spending too much, that we ought to balance the budget. Others took the diametrically opposite view. If these learned men had to settle the argument without recourse to the judgment of their common fellow-men, they probably would end by using force. One or another of the groups would have to seize the government and then impose its view upon the other experts and the rest of us. But appeal to the collective judgment of the people means that both arguments will have their day in court. The one major difficulty arises from the fact that more money may be expended on one side of the propaganda fence than on the other. But there is no pretense here, anyway, that the collective common judgment is necessarily right. It is merely maintained that in matters of this kind the judgment of many men is better than the judgment of the specialist. There is a social-psychological reason for that: Such decisions are related in manifold ways to the prevailing folkways of the community. For effective functioning and execution, such decisions require integration with these folkways.

THE NEW BELIEF EXEMPLIFIED IN THE METHODS OF THE UNITED STATES DEPARTMENT OF AGRICULTURE

Very interesting pioneer work, based upon these assumptions, has been done by the United States Department of Agriculture. This department has developed a number of valuable techniques for tapping the farmers' response to important issues of policy. A system of committees and discussion groups has been worked out under the AAA and under the Soil Conservation Service, and lately in connection with defense work. In these committees a continuous effort is being made to stimulate farmers to consider the government's policies and activities in relation to what we might, theoretically, call the folkways of the community. For instance, soil-conservation practices are considered in relation to the existing pattern of soil treatment. Many of these problems are very concrete and practical. Thus contour plowing, the method recommended to check sheet erosion, is so contrary to prevailing community practices that little progress has been made in New England, though other parts of the country have responded more readily. Folkways are not so firmly established in some; the erosion problem is more serious in others. Likewise, the treatment of pastures has been extensively discussed and after discussion altered by the adoption of practices which the government pushes through "benefit payments." It has been a folkway, throughout Northern New England, to permit cattle to graze over large tracts which are partly wooded. This practice is unsound from a technical viewpoint and should be supplanted by separate handling of woodland and pasture. Farmers have been clarifying the issues, and by a series of steps the program is being realized. The latest development is concerned with forest practices; here, too, existing folkways need to be altered in the light of changed technological conditions.

The New Image of the Common Man

The Department has also fostered broader discussion and acceptance of its work through the method of farmers' referenda. These referenda have helped to give a broader democratic base to the regulatory activities of the government. They have been inspired by the conviction that if the common man, in this case the common farmer, is given a chance to figure out not only the rational benefit but the irrational, felt associations of a given policy, he will be helpful in shaping such policy and in putting it into effect. However, there are still significant shortcomings in this program of farmer consultation. These shortcomings are rooted in an insufficient confidence in the common man's judgment. Some of the referenda have, for example, contained half a dozen or more questions without an opportunity to answer them separately. At times it has been difficult to know just what was being asked. Lengthy documents worded in the abstract language of the law have accompanied the ballot without any clear indication of what would be the practical consequences of the changes suggested. When such questions are coupled with so definite an appeal to special interest as "whether to raise the price of milk," it is easy for people to get the impression that something is being put over on them that they do not understand and that they are being goaded into accepting by the higher milk price dangled in front of them. But in spite of such shortcomings, the methods developed by the Department of Agriculture are of the greatest importance, because they seek to find a new and significant place for the common man in a complex technological society.[15]

Lately the Department of Agriculture has commenced to utilize the testing techniques of the public-opinion polls for ascertaining the opinions of the common farmer. Monthly tests are carried on in all states of the Union, providing detailed information based on interviews with individual farmers. These interviews cover highly technical matters connected with soil conservation, production increases, and similar matters. It is obvious that such polls, if carried out fairly and effectively, greatly increase the awareness of officials and thus enhance their responsiveness to commonly felt needs and complaints in connection with agricultural policies.

FOREIGN AFFAIRS — AN EXCEPTION?

There is, however, one extremely important field of governmental activity in which most of what we have said concerning the judgment of the common man does not necessarily hold. That is the field of foreign affairs. The decisions in this field are of a nature that removes them from the average man's grasp. Nor do they bear any striking relationship to his folkways, traditions, and beliefs. Occasionally, to be sure, a great issue such as the defeat of Hitlerism presents itself and arouses a genuine popular response. It is quite revealing that in this case the common man in America has right along been more nearly sound than more vocal experts. The polls of public opinion have shown that. But then this was a simple, basic issue. When foreign policy calls for judgment of a complex situation, the common man recoils from it because of his lack of knowledge.

A democracy should, strictly speaking, have no foreign policy. The author has dealt with these problems at some length in a volume entitled *Foreign Policy in the Making.*[16] Here the difficulties of democratic foreign policy are fully explored, and it is shown how these difficulties drive democracy on toward world organization. Democracy is universal in its reach; by its mere logic, it is propelled toward including *all* common men, all mankind. Since the common man — that is, democracy — shuns foreign policy, such policy in democratic national government oscillates, as American democracy has oscillated, between isolationism and internationalism.

Only after a world government has been brought into existence, and the functions of world-wide scope have been assigned to that organization, will the common man as world citizen be able to function effectively.[17] Then, instead of national governments maneuvering against each other in secrecy, a world government charged with our common concerns will be subject to the participation of all. Toward the achievement of that goal, every extension of democratic organization, such as is envisaged, for example, in plans for "Federal Union," is a step forward.

Foreign affairs, then, are excluded from the basis for the new belief only because the idea of rival states contending for their interests by the use of force is in conflict with the democratic principle.

CONCLUSION

In short, the collective judgment of common men is valuable for communal work, not because it is based on independent thought, but because it is based on interdependent thought. It is valuable, not because it is purely rational, but because it is traditional, grounded on a vivid sense of traditional values as they relate to the issue in hand.

This fact, to be sure, offers the propagandist an opportunity to distort issues by manipulating the stereotypes. But "you can't fool all of the people all the time," and as the public becomes more sophisticated about propaganda and its uses, its collective judgment improves. The polls have shown that, time and time again, the people as a mass has had a sound view of basic issues. Anyway, have we not already recaptured a good deal of ground from the cynicism engendered by the shock of propaganda? Is it not already clear that most propaganda, precisely because it seeks to win support by meta-rational appeals, reinforces the judgment of the common man, which is built upon a perception of common values?

Torn by conflicting appeals, assailed by propagandists on all sides, participating in propaganda campaigns ourselves from time to time, we, common men and women all, can still remain ourselves and as a symbolic gesture display what headgear we fancy, exclaiming with Walt Whitman: "I wear my hat as I please, indoors or out."

CHAPTER IV

Majority Rule[1]

The common man is constantly and increasingly exposed to the risk of becoming an undesirable citizen in the eyes of the votaries of law and order.

— THORSTEIN VEBLEN

LANGUAGE, in the opinion of Thoreau, provides a clue to the hidden mainsprings of tradition. "Let us know what words they had and how they used them, and we can infer almost all the rest." How many people going to town meetings in New England have accepted as a matter of course the "moderator" who presides over the annual get-together, without being conscious of the tradition which this word "moderator" reflects? And yet this moderation, which the moderator is there to maintain, is a quality of utmost importance if democracy is to function. The lack of it was the fatal defect of democracy on the Continent, except in Switzerland.

THE MODERATOR

It is the job of the moderator to prevent differences of opinion from becoming too violent, and to seek a majority consonant with the weight of the decisions made. In very decisive matters, it is his task to bring about as near unanimity as possible, or to delay a decision until a sufficient measure of agreement is reached. No one can speak unless the moderator recognizes him, and thus the moderator exercises a dominant influence over the conduct of business. When controversy runs high, and he is known to be on one side of the argument, he will have to be a man of strongly judicial temperament to avoid partiality, and of course moderators often fail in such situations. But as one of them remarked when asked whether he ever took sides: "Yes, indeed. But they have elected me for thirty years, just the same."

MAJORITY VERSUS MINORITY

It is unrealistic and contrary to fact to assert that a bare majority has unlimited power in a democracy. It is worse to define democracy in such terms, because such a view neglects the actual workings of democratic institutions and, if adopted, would jeopardize their successful maintenance. The tendency to define democracy thus is usually most pronounced in quarters where the interest in democracy is a matter of expediency rather than a basic conviction. Such writers usually profess great concern for the common man. Yet the public, in America and elsewhere, has rarely accepted the rigid majoritarian position. Going by common sense rather than theory, the public vividly feels the confusion of the abstract *either-or* which contrasts majority rule with minority rule. The public is for majority rule, to be sure, but it perceives the need for flexibility in determining what shall constitute a majority. The common man is, on the whole, less oblivious than the political partisan to the fact that a working scheme of cooperation among men of different views and interests calls for a sense of mutual obligation.

But, of course, the view of the common men of this or any other land does not settle the matter. The vital issue as to whose views shall prevail in a democracy, whose views *do* prevail in a democracy, has never been too clearly analyzed, either by the public spokesmen or by the political theorists. In recent years the issue has been much beclouded by the bitter controversy over the role of the courts in the American past and future.[2] Majority rule is in this context usually identified with congressional majorities or presidential programs, and contrasted with minority rule, epitomized by the "nine old men."[3] Who, being a believer in popular government, can be in doubt when the issue is thus clearly one between majority and minority?

The other side of this political controversy is just as smart in obscuring the issue by a verbal antithesis;

the rule of law versus the rule of politicians is the battle cry in this quarter. Who, being a believer in constitutionalism, can be in doubt if the issue is raised in such terms? [4] And yet Edwin Mims, Jr., though sticking squarely to majority rule, has insisted that there is a limitation on the power of the existing majority: the principle of majority rule itself. For this principle "guarantees the eternal right of the individual and the minority to work openly at all times toward the formation of a new majority." [5] That is the reason why any attempt to identify majority rule with totalitarian dictatorship is absurd. Such attempts have been very popular in anti-New Deal quarters, where Roosevelt's policies were freely denounced as "dictatorship" by men who were in the very process of building a majority to defeat him. You cannot, of course, expect scientific consistency from political partisans, but the issue reveals the confusion that has arisen over the problem of what is the democratic balance between majority and minority. This balance may be stated in terms of rights, or of powers, or of rule; whichever the frame of reference, it is a question of balance rather than a clear-cut alternative between majority and minority.

WHAT CONSTITUTES A MAJORITY?

The extreme majoritarian view has recently been stated with trenchant emphasis as follows: "In any decision-making group one half of the members, plus one, have a *right* to commit one half of the members, minus one, to any policy they see fit to support." [6] This principle the author of the statement claims as the essence of democratic government. The advantage of this flat statement of the majoritarian position is that it avoids all subterfuges. It is ostensibly advanced by the author out of a concern for the common man as against the "scientific elite"; it is set forth as the acme of radical progressivism.

In my opinion, the flat majoritarian position represents a common error made by many progressives, and it is in the interest of a progressive majority that it should be opposed. Modern democracy urgently requires our abandoning this abstract, mathematical view of the problem of majority rule. There are three crucial unexplained major premises involved: (1) that there is no difference in importance between several "policies," though such a difference is implied in the American tradition of constitutional versus ordinary legislation; (2) that a majority will necessarily respect the minority's right to work openly toward the formation of a new majority; (3) that policies are merely matters of willful "decision," that is to say, that there is no difference between policies which can, and policies which cannot, be enforced.

All three of these assumptions are untenable. To begin with the last, statute books are littered with enactments which are dead letters because they are unenforceable. The fact that a majority in the state of North Carolina, indeed, in many states of the Union, holds fornication to be illegal does not commit the considerable minority opposed to such a policy to quitting their fornicating. Unless you are prepared to put a policeman behind every man and woman, you cannot enforce such a statute. Nor can you enforce a statute "to maintain competition" when the economic factors make for monopoly. The minority opposed to such a statute is going to prevail, not because its "will" is superior, but because its insight is; for nature's laws are always enforced. One of the most common failings of majorities, particularly when they are compounded of diverse groups, is to enact statutes with mutually exclusive objectives. Such statutes can never be enforced intact, and the majority's will is to that extent nullified. Even a minority of one, if grounded upon a sound recognition of nature's laws, will prevail against an overwhelming majority.

Second, there is, unfortunately, plenty of evidence to show that on many occasions the majority will not respect the minority's right to build a majority. Indeed, this right has to be hedged about by numerous constitutional safeguards protecting the freedom of expression. Freedom of speech, of the press, and of peaceful assembly are continuously imperiled by the majority's inclination to deny the minority's right to build a majority. Even the most casual examination of the records of the Civil Liberties Union during the last twenty-five years will destroy any illusions on that score. Many of these rights, even though constitutionally guaranteed, are continually being curtailed by the majority's pressure and violence. The endless procession of labor organizers being browbeaten by vigilante groups, "Reds" being ridden out of town, Negroes being lynched without trial and being kept from voting in Southern states, all testify to the ever-present readiness of the majority (even in America) to oppress the minority. The mere fact that the minority is supposed to be protected by constitutional safeguards constitutes no actual protection.

Would any man, then, seriously question that there is considerable difference in the importance of popular decisions? That it is one thing to decide to increase the income tax, and quite another to abolish freedom of speech? Since the radical majoritarians are always citing Rousseau as their great authority, they may be reminded that Rousseau sharply differentiated between the majorities required for different kinds of decisions. This is important, because Rousseau was certainly an ardent believer in democracy. He left no doubt about democracy's being his ideal. He stood ready to accept the judgment of the common man without equivocation or recourse to a "higher law." Yet how did Rousseau feel on the subject of majorities? "The vote of the majority always binds the rest." Does Rousseau mean by a majority a majority of one? Far from it.

There are two general rules [that may serve to regulate the relation between voting and the general will]. First, the more grave and important the questions discussed, the nearer should the opinion that is to prevail approach to unanimity. Second, the more the matter in hand calls for speed, the smaller the prescribed difference in the number of votes may be allowed to become: where an instant decision has to be reached, a majority of one should be enough. The first of these two rules seems more in harmony with the laws, and the second with practical affairs. In any case, it is the combination of them that gives the best proportions for determining the majority necessary.[7]

According to Rousseau, a majority of one is restricted to instant decisions! It is restricted to outright emergencies. Here we have, in clear form, the tradition of grass-root democracy in Switzerland and America, the tradition embodied in the word "moderator." Democratic practice has become less cautious; simple pluralities are accepted for many "grave and important questions," general laws of far-reaching consequence. But let no one cite Rousseau as authority for the majority-of-one doctrine. On the contrary, it should be clear from this that Rousseau would strongly have approved of the provisions for a specific amending power in the American constitution. Indeed, he was always cited to similar effect in the course of the French Revolution.

Sieyès's celebrated proposal for a constitutional jury was specifically built upon the notion of a higher constitutional "will of the people," the *pouvoir constituant*.[8]

THE CONSTITUENT POWER

The constituent power — that is to say, the residuary power of the people "to reform, alter, or abolish" the government — stems from the great constitutional struggle which rent England during the seventeenth century. The idea has medieval roots, and it was persuasively stated by John Locke after the Glorious Revolution. It was repeatedly and flatly set forth by the makers of the American constitution, more especially James Wilson, Sam Adams, and George Mason. The term "constituent power" was central in the political thought of John Quincy Adams. All this is very well known. But it is equally true that throughout this body of thinking there is a lack of precision when it comes to explaining just what this constituent power consists of. When these writers speak of "the people," whom do they mean? A majority of one? Since the decision concerning the form of government is certainly a grave and important one, we may suspect that they do not. We cannot escape from this issue by constitutional provisions for an amending power. No matter how elaborate the provisions for an amending power may be, they must never, from a political viewpoint, be assumed to have superseded the constituent power, for the constituent power is the power that made the constitution. It remains forever in the people, who cannot be bound by their ancestors to any existing governmental pattern. It is the power to make a revolution. We say "power" deliberately, rather than "right." For it is a purely factual, norm-creating thing, this power to establish a constitution or a pattern of government. What more can be said about it?

The constituent power is exercised by the constituent group. The constituent group can come into operation only when the government fails to function constitutionally, i.e., becomes arbitrary and tyrannical. Its function results from the residuary and unorganized power of resistance in the community. The constituent group is neither a class nor any other established sector of the community; it forms spontaneously in response to the need of the revolutionary situation. The more intelligent and vital members of the community are apt to take things into their own hands when the situation becomes unbearable, for these men have a natural desire for freedom. Arbitrary power will not long be endured by them. But the traditional doctrine of the seventeenth and eighteenth centuries, the doctrine as we find it in Locke as well as in revolutionary America, has two important defects — defects which have tended to discredit it in its entirety. These two defects are (1) that the doctrine failed to make it explicit that the constituent group as defined can come into play *only* against arbitrary power, but not against a functioning constitutionalism [9] and (2) that the doctrine fails to emphasize the specific function of the constituent group, namely, to build a constitution.

The two defects are clearly corollaries, for there is not likely to be any widespread demand for a new constitution so long as the existing constitution functions effectively. Under such conditions, the demand for a new constitution would not receive sufficient support, nor could the building of such a constitution count upon general approval. And yet there is a difficulty in that there may be widespread disagreement as to whether an existing constitutionalism is functioning satisfactorily. The millions of unemployed are likely to take a view of present-day constitutionalism in America different from that of more successful groups in the community. In the last analysis, the community itself is the judge, according to the doctrine of the constituent power.

Before the advent of the New Deal, disagreement became so sharp that a revolutionary situation threatened. But no constituent group did arise in America in the thirties, although the more conservative members of the Supreme Court did their level best to convince the community that the existing constitutionalism no longer functioned, but served merely as a screen for the arbitrary exercise of power. The policies of the Roosevelt administration convinced the people, however, that there were as yet vast resources within the existing framework of government, and the revolutionary impulse subsided. Far from being the dictator that his opponents accused him of being, Roosevelt was, in fact, the savior of constitutionalism. He proved that it still was a functioning system in this country. The common man's judgment was definitely that American constitutionalism was not tyrannical and arbitrary. This is most important, because democratic constitutionalism is forever directed against the establishment of such arbitrary power; conversely, only the general conviction that such arbitrary power has arisen calls forth a constituent group and revolutionary action.

REVOLUTIONARY ACTION – WHEN CONSTITUENT?

But if such a group forms and revolutionary action takes place, it is constituent only if the group undertakes to set up a new constitution.

The fact that the constituent group possesses its power for the purpose of setting up a new constitution makes it inadmissible to call this group the sovereign, unless it be clearly understood that the word "sovereignty" is ordinarily used in an entirely different connotation. We have seen what that connotation is. No useful purpose is served by smuggling the sovereign back through another door in this fashion. A constitu-

tional democracy has no sovereign, but it does recognize
a constituent power, a residuary power of the community behind and beyond all government capable of
destroying the existing constitution and establishing a
new one.

This recognition of the ultimate popular sanction of
the constitution itself depends once again upon the belief in the common man. This belief at the same time
clearly implies the recognition of the constituent power.
Those who have argued that the Websters and the
Cooleys [10] abandoned the central tenets of democracy
are entirely right. Their views are certainly incompatible with those of the makers of the constitution. The
Websters and Cooleys were misled by the spectacle of
dictatorial usurpations, such as the rise of Napoleon in
France. Andrew Jackson was frequently seen, by those
whose interests he attacked, as another "dictator," and
cartoons depicted him as an emperor with crown and
purple much in the fashion of our own day's abuse of
Roosevelt. The obvious and all-important distinction is,
of course, that Napoleon and his present-day imitators
not only *destroyed one* constitution, but *failed to build
another*. No constituent power was exercised by any
constituent group in Germany when Hitler became dictator. It was an anti-constitutional reaction. The same
holds true of the two Napoleons.

The frightened "liberals" who turned against the
common man because of these developments failed fully

to appreciate that these reactionary movements were financed and led by threatened privilege and special "elites." The way to counter these corruptions of democratic constitutionalism is not to abandon the belief in the common man, but to set forth more realistically the actual nature and functioning of the common man, and hence of the constituent power. More especially must we never lose sight of the fact that this power is the outcome of the common man's desire for freedom, that is to say, for having a functioning constitution, free from arbitrary violence and tyranny.

QUALIFIED MAJORITIES

Rousseau buttressed his idea of a qualified majority for grave and important questions by his famous doctrine of the "real constitution." This he considered the most important of all kinds of law. It "is not graven on tablets of marble or brass, but on the hearts of the citizens." What Rousseau is here referring to is morality, custom, and public opinion. In his day, Rousseau could claim, though not quite justly, that these factors were unknown to political thinkers. Since his time, their force has come very much to the fore, and modern inquiry has obliged us to abandon Rousseau's view of them as part of the natural environment. We know morality, custom, and particularly public opinion to be continuously molded; we have already explored the issues which the exercise of this power of propaganda has raised. There can be little question that these developments force us to abandon Rousseau's views concerning the "real constitution." It is just as well; for that doctrine has been a potent weapon in the armory of reaction from Burke to Pareto.

In surrendering the "real constitution," do we have to surrender the idea of qualified majorities with it? Far from it. The idea of a qualified majority is part and parcel of a non-Utopian belief in the common man. The argument for qualified majorities rests upon considerations of political prudence, rather than upon metaphysical views concerning the general will, or the "real constitution." In an environment shot through with propaganda of all kinds, the common man's ability to think a matter out for himself requires more time if the matter is of great weight. Our more precise concept of the common man sees him as neither infallible nor superhuman in virtue. It stresses the quality of judgment and character which results from a vivid sense of values. As a matter of fact, there is nothing startling in this counsel of prudence; for the common man follows it quite habitually in his own affairs. That fact is the basis for the qualified majority.

If very deep-seated feelings are involved in a decision, even though only the feelings of a substantial minority, democratic government will hesitate to go forward upon the basis of a bare majority preference. The whole point of having a constitution is to demark clearly what are these graver and more important decisions. Obviously the gravest issue is the making of the constitution as a whole; the next after that, any alterations in its specific provisions. In England, where there is no single constitutional document, serious issues are continuously dubbed constitutional, and there is no more effective argument against any policy than that it raises a "constitutional question." There is an implied suggestion that the issue at hand should be submitted to the voter in a general election. To be sure, a mere plurality would, in fact, decide the matter if an election were held. But a detailed study of English practice reveals a hesitancy to proceed unless the majority is "substantial." [11] In any event, a general election consumes much time and money, and thereby provides an opportunity for a threatened minority to organize effective resistance.

These arguments are reinforced by a very practical consideration: the marginal voters. The relatively few who pass from one side to the other, and thereby spell victory or defeat for the government, keep the government majority alert to any substantial minority view. The complete disregard of any such minority is rather improbable. This does not, of course, apply to the extremists on the opposite side; e.g., the Conservatives may safely disregard the Communists, and Labour the Die-hard Tories. But they must respect their own extremists, as well as all the marginal groups who may go over to the other camp. On the whole it can be said that a country so closely knit and so definitely held together by its common heritage and imperial interests, and so well disciplined politically, as England, may go farther than other lands in discarding the safeguard of qualified majorities; its example may not be a safe one for less fortunate communities to follow. The fact is that English political tradition has evolved restraints upon the majority which are not available elsewhere.

MINORITY RULE, THEN?

However, at this point there arises the specter of minority rule. Does not, so runs the query, the insistence upon more than a bare majority confer exorbitant power upon the minority? For example, why should considerably less than half the people be able to negate a constitutional amendment? This is a serious problem, no doubt of that. But to be more concrete and practical: does the recognition of the requirement of a qualified majority mean embalming the present vested interests of our economy and protecting them against the majority will? This has been cogently argued time and again. It is, however, in the light of experience a gross overstatement of a palpable fact. To say that a qualified majority delays changes is almost tautological; if it didn't, what would be the purpose of having it? To say that a qualified majority prevents changes is largely untrue; if it did, the United States would have neither an income tax nor woman suffrage. The Interstate Commerce Commission and all the other regulatory agencies would likewise be nonexistent.

The usual argument about minority rule amounts to a play with the word "rule." The mere fact that certain actions can be prevented by a determined minority does not make that minority the ruler, even though it gives it a strong share in the rule. Nobody has yet been able to say how minorities can be adequately protected under a constitution without granting them such constitutional safeguards as will enable them to participate in ruling through their power of resistance. When the arguments of those who are provoked by the minority's right to share in the ruling are more closely scrutinized, it is found that they are all concerned with property rights. It may well be that the constitutional protection of property has no longer the support of the common man in America; if that be so, a constitutional amendment is in order.

The spiderwebs of judicial logic which have been spun about "due process of law" defy the layman's comprehension anyway. Fortunately, they are being brushed away by the Supreme Court itself. What is more, the use of the formula "due process of law" often constituted an expansion of the meaning attached to those words at the time the constitution was written. Hence perhaps all we ought to do is to adopt an amendment saying in effect: "The words 'due process of law' shall be strictly construed in accordance with their original meaning, to wit, the process of legislation as provided for by the constitution." If that were done, attempts at nullifying by judicial fiat legislation which the majority has accepted would be effectively forestalled. However, it is doubtful whether the present Supreme Court, manned as it is by believers in a strict construction of judicial power of review, will be much inclined to nullify legislation, anyway. It does not seem too much to say that the minority supporting absolute property rights has now shrunk to the point where it can no longer prevent the progressive redefinition of property in social rather than in individual terms. The whole development is a striking illustration of the fact that even qualified majorities will come into being in support of urgent social reforms.

CONSTITUTIONAL MAJORITIES – WHAT?

Let us accept, then, the proposition that qualified majorities are in keeping with the basic principle of majority rule, indeed that such qualifications frequently are the direct outgrowth of the majority principle itself. The only question that remains is: How shall they be qualified? It seems to many that our own amending process is too cumbrous. I share this view. I believe that the greatest service a political party could render to political improvement in this country would be to amend the amending clause so as to provide for a cheaper and swifter process. Certainly Switzerland has prospered under a much simpler plan; the same is true of many of our state constitutions. The danger of such arrangements is that a good deal of ordinary legislation is in course of time written into the constitution. This is, however, much less likely to be the case in the federal sphere, where a constitutional amendment will always necessitate a large outlay of funds.

It is, by definition, impossible to lay down rules as to the majorities required for revolutionary alterations of a constitution. It is apparent from what has been said, however, that the majorities required would probably be sizable, at least in the initial stages. The problem is largely of an academic nature, since it is both the hope and the experience of working constitutional systems to obliterate the need for such upheavals by yielding to the demand for changes, no matter how basic. There is, for example, little question that the government of the United States has developed into what some like to refer to as a "service state," others as a "welfare state," still others as "socialism." What all these words seek to indicate is the undeniable growth of numerous regulatory and service functions which the American government did not exercise a hundred years ago. There is, furthermore, reason to believe that the American government will continue to develop in whatever directions seem desirable to the people at large. Insofar as these developments are successful adaptations to a changed economic environment, they vindicate our belief in the common man. All these constitutional changes have, in the last analysis, been his work.

What we so easily forget when we chafe under the restraints which hinder us in doing the to us obviously right thing is that in a democracy we are committed to carrying the rest of the community with us. Nothing, in other words, is intrinsically right unless and until it is approved by suitable majorities. As was pointed out before, this does not mean that what majorities approve is therefore right — far from it. Majorities of common men are not infallible, any more than are the common men who compose them. They themselves are the first to realize that safeguards are needed. If such safeguards bring it to pass that self-interested minorities can entrench themselves and thwart the realization of the majority's interest for any length of time, then steps can and will be taken to smoke out such self-interested minorities.

But the protection of minorities as such cannot be surrendered as a principle simply because of such possibilities. In my opinion, the workers have least reason to espouse the doctrine of the extreme majoritarians. This needs to be stated quite emphatically, since quite a few men who consider themselves the special friends of the workers have enunciated such extreme views.

The New Image of the Common Man

Karl Marx insisted that the workers were bound to become the majority and could then go forward to realize Socialism or Communism. The fact is, however, that even now, a hundred years after Marx's analysis, the workers do not command a majority in any country, nor do they show any sign of commanding one in the foreseeable future. This is the conclusive reason for their interest in constitutional protection of minority rights, for the chances are considerably greater that "big business" may bring together a bare majority for a short time with the aid of a demagogue, such as Hitler. The experience in various European countries, but more especially in Germany, should go a long way toward proving that no greater disaster can befall the workers than that rigidly majoritarian views should prevail at such a time. Even at the risk of considerably delaying what they consider necessary social gains, the workers are more vitally concerned than any other group in the maintenance of constitutional democracy.

HITLER A CREATURE OF A MAJORITY?

A brief glance at Hitler's assumption of power is instructive. There has been a good deal of argument in years past over whether Hitler was or was not brought into power by the majority of the German people. Men like Max Lerner, in their anxiety to vindicate the unqualified majoritarian premise, have insisted that no majority ever voted *for* Hitler. Lately the general tendency has been to take it for granted that Hitler was the German choice, particularly among all those who wish to identify Germans and Nazis. Now the fact of the matter is that the truth lies in between these two views. Hitler rose upon a huge wave of popular support. No other political leader had ever before achieved such a massive electoral following in Germany. True, that support never exceeded 41 per cent, but the Conservative Nationalists were so sympathetic that they were willing to join hands with the Nazis. They were the first "appeasers," later to be followed by the French, the British, the Dutch, the Belgians, and all the other social reactionaries and conservative appeasers, down to our own America First Committee. Since these Conservatives polled another 10 per cent of the votes, the Hitler cabinet secured a total of 51 per cent in the election of 1933, the last halfway democratic election that was held in Germany. It is at times argued that the Nazis interfered with that election. They staged the *Reichstag* fire and then, charging a Communist plot, arrested a number of Communist candidates. But whether this interference really helped them is an open question. And even if it did, it is probable that with a little more patience they could have secured a majority anyway. But what is more, it does not really affect the argument. Nobody can deny that Hitler was *already* Chancellor of the *Reich* at the time of the election as a result of the workings of the rigid majoritarian principle. The advantage which he took of this situation is part of the reason for objecting to the dogmatic majority-of-one view. For, as we saw, the majority principle, soundly conceived, itself guarantees "the eternal right of the individual and the minority to work openly at all times toward the formation of a new majority."

It was precisely this guarantee which the Weimar constitution had neglected adequately to protect. For how can the right to form a new majority be protected, except by removing certain essential minority rights from the usurpation of a temporarily aroused majority? Everyone who has ever considered this matter at all thoroughly is aware of the fact that without the several freedoms of expression, the freedom of speech, of the press, and of peaceful assembly, it is impossible to safeguard the minority's right to work openly and at all times toward the formation of a new majority. The totalitarian outlook is dogmatically opposed to that conception. The Communist, no less than the Fascist, is unprepared to grant any such freedoms, because he is unprepared to admit the minority's right to an opinion contrary to his. All totalitarians look upon themselves as the elite which knows what is right, so "what is the use of an opposition?" The Weimar constitution, rigidly majoritarian in the numerical sense, gave such an outlook its opportunity. The task was simply to achieve a majority of one once, and then to use that majority to do away with the entire constitutional system by destroying the opposition completely. Indeed, by eliminating the opposition you eliminate also any possible comeback on the part of those who constituted the majority in the first place.

For here is the other side of the medal: While Hitler rose upon the support of the German masses, this support was fraudulently secured by lies and misrepresentations more crass and unscrupulous than any ever set forth by a demagogue before. In other words, the German people supported Hitler on what he said that he proposed to do; but there is not the slightest shred of evidence to show that they would have supported him if he had made it clear what he actually was going to do. Even in the summer of 1933 a free election would have resulted in a repudiation of the Hitler government. This is important, for at that time the German common man had not as yet been destroyed by five years of terrorizing propaganda — a propaganda which did not so much make him think as the Nazis desired, as it atrophied his political judgment altogether. I say purposely: The common man was destroyed; for the common man upon whom democracy depends does not survive the establishment of totalitarian government. The reason is that only democracy provides the conditions necessary for the average man's acquiring and developing those qualities which our belief in the common man posits.

It is, in this connection, worth remembering that these

conditions had not existed very long in Germany when Hitler made his appeals, and hence the German middle classes and peasants did not display that quality of judgment which the common man in a democracy must possess for its successful functioning. John Stuart Mill argues this point persuasively in *Representative Government*. He there points out that free institutions advance civilization, because they provide a free testing ground for the active spirit. There is much to be said for this contention, if civilization's advance is seen primarily in moral terms. In terms of art and music, the record is not so clear. Some of the most astounding achievements of human creativeness have occurred in times and places which were rather markedly unfree. But whatever the truth in this respect, it does not affect our view that only democracy provides the setting in which the average human being can develop those qualities which enable him to play his role as a citizen. They are acquired traits which require shaping. From this standpoint it can be seen that the common man presupposes democracy, just as much as democracy presupposes the common man. Democracy can, therefore, never be decreed by the stroke of a pen.

MINORITY RIGHTS

A leading theorist of markedly progressive views has recently written: "No majority, unless it abrogates democracy, can decide to kill the members of the minority . . . to repeal the rights of national or religious groups, or to prohibit the free and dignified expression of independent and possibly non-conformist opinions. It is only within certain constitutional limits that a majority can act and that a change in the majority . . . may affect the course of policy." [12] Although this view is a bit extreme in that it borders on the "inalienable rights" fallacy, it nevertheless puts well the general point we have been trying to develop. Written as it was with reference to the abuse of majority power by totalitarian governments all over Europe, it focuses attention upon the fact that the process of protecting the minority in opposition to the majority is part of the concept of majority rule itself.

It is hoped that we have shown conclusively that qualified majorities are the only politically practical method of insuring protection for the opposition. To argue against such qualified majorities on the ground that they permit minority rule is unsound. It is inspired by opposition to the traditional concept of property and the traditional inclusion of private property among the rights of the minority which a majority must not destroy. Although the traditional view of corporate property rights is on the way out, it is probable that the common man will, for a long time yet, retain a desire to protect small property against confiscation. Such protection may have social utility. Arbitrary dispossession has been so potent a weapon in the hands of totalitarian dictators that the inviolability of small-scale property rights probably should be recognized as an important buttress of that measure of independence of thought which the belief in the common man presupposes.[13]

At any rate, the common man in America seems as yet firmly attached to the idea of private property, in spite of an increasing readiness to place regulatory restraints upon corporate property. It will probably be whittled away in slow bits, with small-scale property-for-use remaining longest. Even so radical a picture of the common man as is contained in Steinbeck's *The Grapes of Wrath* draws its deepest inspiration from this struggle of simple working folk to find their way back to what appears to them the rightful inheritance of every free man in America, a piece of land he can call his own. It is pitifully, but powerfully, symbolized in the figure of Muley. Desperately he refuses to leave the land which his forebears have settled upon and tilled, even after the banks have taken the title away from him. He defies all laws to stay on.

The fact that the passion to own something does not animate the subtle and the intellectual should not deceive us. A Thoreau might find property nothing but an encumbrance. He might prefer to be a squatter and to smile at the people who, thinking they own a farm, are in fact "owned by the farm." The common man's sense of selfhood is anchored in such dependency. And maybe he is once again more nearly right than the intellectual elite. Faust, after his endless wanderings in search of the moment when he could say out of the depth of his heart: "Oh, that it last! This is so fine" — Faust finally discovers that moment in the act of securing new land for free men to settle upon.[14] He then exclaims, and the words have become immortal: "This is the last conclusion of the wise: He only earns his freedom and his life, Who daily has to conquer them again. . . . Such an activity I want to see — to stand upon free ground with men who're free!"

CONCLUSION

Realistically considered, rule by the majority of common men operates in accordance with what such men consider the nature of man's decisions. Such decisions operate upon several levels. Democratic constitutionalism recognizes the common man, acting as a member of the constituent group, as the final source of constitutional authority. It recognizes the same common man, when participating in the amending process, as the final source of governmental authority within an existing constitutional procedure. It recognizes the same common man, when participating in the election of various representatives, as the source of authority for legislative and administrative rules and regulations. When we consider this pyramiding of processes, we are led to the conclusion that the people are not one, but several, entities, each with its own specific function. The crux of the several functions appears to be the nature and weight of the decision involved and the majority required for it.

With these thoughts in mind, we can say that anything within a society ruled by a majority can be changed as long as the proposed change does not violate nature's laws. The idea of inalienable rights has been abandoned in favor of the idea of civil freedoms — freedoms which common men grant one another, not only because they like to have them themselves, but also because they are valuable for the society as a whole. The underlying idea is that such freedoms bring out the creative impulses in men. A majority of common men may, in response to urgent needs, abandon one freedom for another. They may fail even to realize the full import of these freedoms. They are not apt to be satisfied for any length of time with the loss of all freedoms.

CHAPTER V

The Need for Dissent

*America always has welcomed
diversity, variety, differences.*
— LOUIS ADAMIC

THOUSANDS of citizens, many of them radicals,
were forgathered in Madison Square Garden on August 19, 1941, at the National Unity Rally called by
the Council for Democracy. The emotional high point
of the main speaker's address was reached when he
exclaimed: —

Be you an interventionist or a noninterventionist; be
you for peace or for war; be you of English descent or
German or Italian or French or Irish; be you a Republican
or Democrat; a Catholic or Jew or Protestant or non-
believer; a rich man or a poor man; whether you like
Roosevelt or whether you don't; whether you are a farmer,
laborer, or businessman; whether you are a white man or
a Negro — you are, if you still think freedom is better than
slavery, if you still believe in our way of life, an American
first.

The New Image of the Common Man

What does this mean? What is it that is supposed to unite all these people, that is neither religion, nor nationality, nor yet a common view of the economy? Conventionally, the answer given to such a query is: "Democracy!" In other words, it is assumed that all these Americans would share a common faith in the fundamentals of democratic government, or even "the democratic way of life." But suppose we held a poll amongst those present as to what they thought democracy meant. The answers would reveal a great variety of viewpoints and emphases. Are there then no Americans? Indeed there are. But they are united by common modes of behavior and concrete objectives, opinions as to what needs to be done here and now, rather than by any abstract opinions or agreements on fundamentals.

John Tunis, in a telling series of studies, *Democracy and Sport* (1941), unfolds the close relationship between democratic behavior and sportsmanship. His concluding essay is called: "Who's Next?" In it, he describes the everyday barbershop scene, where each takes his turn as he comes in line. "Who's next?" When you hear that phrase again, remember what stands back of it. A hundred and sixty-five years of the tradition of fair play stand behind it. Generations and generations of people who felt that the best man should win — and tried to practice that belief, too; who respected the rights of others, the rights of the man beside you, waiting to have his hair cut. Who's next? — It's nothing. Yet it's everything. It's all democracy in that barbershop. What John Tunis has done here is to bring out with the simplicity of genius the real basis of unity: common modes of acting toward one another.

AGREEMENT UPON FUNDAMENTALS

These common modes of acting toward one another bring out again the importance of what we called character when sketching the new view of the common man. The steadfast adherence to communally established and traditional modes of conduct and the simple, straightforward judgment as to what is in keeping with them — these are the elements of consent and order in a democratic community. They are something very different from fundamentals in a rational or philosophic sense. They are embodied in proverbs, not in dogmas.

But the civic dissensions of our generation have, by a curious paradox, called forth urgent demands for agreement upon fundamentals. Such agreement upon the fundamentals of social and political philosophy are said to be an essential condition of a working democracy. More than thirty years ago Lord Balfour wrote: "Our whole political machinery presupposes a people so fundamentally at one that they can safely afford to bicker." In saying this, he summed up in a felicitous formula the political philosophy of British conservatives from Burke to Bagehot. It is a philosophy likewise implicit in the "fundamental rights" philosophy of American constitutionalism. The traditionalism of these writers always dwelt upon the wisdom of past ages, as contrasted with the present, and upon the wisdom of the intelligent and educated classes as the high priests of this precious heritage.[1]

Agreement upon fundamentals has, however, been expounded with almost the same insistence by progressive critics of contemporary society. Harold Laski, in his *Parliamentary Government in England* (1938), cites Balfour repeatedly. In *Constitutional Government and Politics* (1937) the writer himself took this view. It is also found in G. D. H. Cole and Robert H. Jackson. The conservatives and the progressives do not, of course, agree on this basic issue for the same reason. Balfour and his ilk insisted upon this agreement upon fundamentals as an antidote against such doctrines as the class struggle. Laski on the other hand stresses it to support his contention that parliamentary government is doomed. The class struggle is a fact with which you have to reckon. Parliamentary government was such an exquisite thing while it lasted; but it can be no more, he laments.

A gradual shift of emphasis since Burke first popularized the view has broadened the frame of reference of the doctrine of fundamental agreement. As we move from Burke to contemporary American views, we find a series of steps by which the doctrine is gradually given broader scope. It starts with the claim that such agreement is essential for the English government of the eighteenth century — the matchless British constitution — and it ends with the proposition that it is essential for democracy at large. For when Burke urged his traditionalism, he was thinking of government "by a territorial aristocracy," to use John Morley's trenchant phrase. Walter Bagehot gave the doctrine a broader sweep by relating it to British parliamentarianism, as it worked after the Reform Act, a government by the middle class as he saw it. Balfour, no doubt, had late-nineteenth-century popular government in mind, when he used the Balfouresquely vague "we." Harold Laski, in turn, speaks of *representative* government, a still broader category, as he claims that such government is based upon the prerequisite that the body of citizens be fundamentally at one upon all major objects of governmental activity.[2] Not only is there a broadening here of the type of government for which agreement on fundamentals is essential, but there is also a broadening of the amount of agreement required, when it is demanded that such agreement should extend to all major objects of governmental policy. Is not this requirement a denial of the two-party system? Oh no, says Cole, who has set forth the further claim that even the two-party system presupposes agreement upon fundamentals.[3] But even this sweeping extension of the need for agreement on fundamentals was not enough. Robert

The New Image of the Common Man

H. Jackson and others in America [4] have claimed that democracy pure and simple presupposes agreement upon fundamentals. "Democracy is doomed when there is not, or is no longer, common agreement at least on the point that political decisions have to be based rather on consent than on force. There can be no doubt that such an agreement presupposes in itself common fundamental objectives."

Let us look back. From aristocratic constitutionalism we have gone through parliamentarism, representative government, the party system, to democracy as presupposing agreement upon fundamentals. Here is a steady progression from the more limited to the more general statement of a principle. By gradual extensions, Burke's well-founded view has been stretched to the point of a paradox: democracy, based on the toleration of the view we hate, is possible only when there are no views of that kind; democracy, based on the ability to agree to disagree, is possible only when there are no disagreements serious enough to be dubbed fundamental.

There is only one step further that you can go in broadening the doctrine, and that is to adopt the seventeenth-century view of writers like Hobbes and his natural-law school, who generally insisted upon the agreement on fundamentals as a necessary condition for *all* government. The extreme position reveals the general direction of this tendency: it is absolutist or totalitarian in its implication. May it not be that modern constitutionalism and especially constitutional democracy are seeking to organize government precisely so that agreement on fundamentals need no longer be required? We are inclined to think so.

THE IMPORTANCE OF DISSENT

In spite of its extensive acceptance, "agreement upon fundamentals" is not in fact a necessary condition of either representative government or "democracy" or "constitutional government." It is not even clear that it is a desirable condition for free institutions. Eduard Lindeman has written that democracy cannot mean the same thing to everyone. "There should never be a time when every citizen means the same thing when he utters the word 'democracy.'" [5] The truth of the matter is that there has always been dissent in matters of basic significance. Totalitarian regimes are known to have made frantic efforts to secure uniformity of opinion and belief, but all they have succeeded in getting is outward conformity. Is not this insistence upon agreement on fundamentals, of unity in matters of belief, antidemocratic in its conception? Is it not the first step in the direction of totalitarianism? This question is particularly poignant at this time, when the country is reverberating with the demands for "national unity." National unity behind a specific objective, such as the defeat of Hitlerism or the winning of the war, is one

thing; national unity behind a social and economic philosophy (usually that of the man insisting upon it) is
quite another thing.

In the previous chapter we had occasion to allude
to Rousseau's doctrine of the *real* constitution. He saw
it as a set of general views, a unity of general outlook,
as morality, custom, and public opinion. We saw then
why such a conception should be discarded. Since Rousseau is generally considered the philosopher of democracy *par excellence*, his error in this matter has had
far-reaching consequences, since it seemed to buttress
the doctrine of the agreement on fundamentals. In the
light of modern propaganda, it is untenable to think
of morality and public opinion as part of a "natural
environment." To be sure, it is still true that "it (the
real constitution) takes on every day new powers, when
other laws decay or die out, restores or takes their place,
keeps a whole people in the ways in which it was meant
to go, and insensibly replaces authority by the force of
habit." But these changes are to a considerable extent
the result of conscious human effort, they do not just
happen, and a people's opinion and morality are not
one, but a mosaic of many different stones. If there is
unity, it is unity through diversity. As Louis Adamic
put it: —

This is not a nation but a teeming nation of nations,
a country in process of becoming a nation; it always has
been that, and, to my mind, it will be no tragedy should

it remain that for some time to come, even forever. It always has been a heterogeneous country, a mixture of strains and religions; which has been, and is, the basis of much of its uniqueness in the world and the source of its power. It may be no accident that many of the most dynamic cities and regions in this country have been and are those which include the greatest variety of national and cultural backgrounds. On its sound, positive side, America always has welcomed diversity, variety, differences.[6]

W. Y. Elliott - mythos

WHAT ARE FUNDAMENTALS?

It is a strange fact that none of those who have insisted upon the importance of agreement on fundamentals have given a clear indication of what are "fundamentals." Fundamentals are generally taken to be basic beliefs, starting points for all discussion or action, propositions that cannot be further analyzed, that are the foundation of all that follows. "We hold these truths to be self-evident . . ." would be a typical start for the statement of some fundamentals. Let us see how they have actually fared under constitutionalism.

There appear to be three fundamental cleavages which divide men: religious, national-cultural, and social-economic issues produce the most bitter conflicts. Assuredly religion would be acknowledged by most men to be a fundamental, if not today, then a generation ago. There has been no agreement on that fundamental under constitutional democracy. Both in Switzerland and in the United States, the two most markedly democratic constitutional governments in the world, the people have for a long time agreed to disagree on religious issues. All kinds of Protestants, Catholics, Jews, atheists, and agnostics have participated in public affairs. And yet religious issues have not been dormant. From time to time they have given rise to very sharp conflict.

RELIGIOUS DISAGREEMENT

In America, the principle of complete equality of rights for all religious views is laid down in the Constitution. This principle is, of course, not entirely carried through in practice; certain religious sects have encountered difficulties; what is more important, in many parts of the country conflict between Protestants and Catholics is intense. When Al Smith ran for president, this disagreement upon the fundamental of religion made itself felt in very sharp and bitter form. Anti-Semitism too, though usually a form of racial antagonism, at times manifests itself as religious prejudice. But in spite of all these clashes, which certainly reflect violent disagreement on this fundamental, American constitutionalism has gone forward, insisting that such dissent was wholesome and refusing to seek uniformity.

The development in England tells the same story,

though in a contrasting way. For here we find a change from agreement to disagreement as the country becomes more democratic. As long as she was a "territorial aristocracy," Catholics and nonconformists were excluded from political life. Men like Blackstone and Burke looked with the greatest apprehension upon any proposals for admitting such dissenters into the political arena. They thought it would surely have a disruptive effect, and it was only when England became democratized, at the time of the great reforms, that disagreement on religious matters became admissible.

Most democratic politicians have a horror of fundamentals. This is true in England as it is in America.[7] Within the broad framework of his party, the good politician is forever seeking to reconcile opposing viewpoints and interests. No one is more troublesome to him than the fanatic, the man of principle who refuses to compromise.[8] He wants people to come together on specific programs of action, in spite of disagreements on more general issues. Hence religion is treated with great caution by most politicians. They will cite the Bible readily enough, but prefer to remain neutral where dogmatic and ecclesiastical issues are involved.

Even in the seventeenth century there were those who desired to get away from the religious dogmatism of their time. Halifax, who played such a significant role in the Glorious Revolution, was so definitely the politician in matters of religion that his contemporaries

dubbed him "The Trimmer." He is said to have remarked that he could not digest iron like an ostrich or
swallow all that the divines sought to impose upon the
world. Once he exclaimed: "Weighty as the word ap-
peareth, no Feather has been more blown about in the
World than this word, Fundamental." It was a catch-
word of dogmatism and absolutism then, and it remains
so to this day. The politician's desire to avoid religious
issues provides an interesting confirmation of the antithesis between "fundamentals" and democracy.

In striking contrast to the democratic politician's desire to avoid the religious fundamentals stands the totalitarian conflict with the churches. Hitler personally illustrates the contrast. As long as he was a politician
operating within a democratic context, he studiously
sought to placate religious sentiment, even insisted that
his movement was going to restore religion to its rightful place.[9] But since that time, the conflict with the
Christian churches has become one of the outstanding
features of the Nazi tyranny. Men like Niemöller and
Count Galen are among the most representative figures
symbolizing the German opposition to Hitler.[10] In
short, the Nazi insistence upon agreement on fundamentals has precipitated a violent struggle.

The fundamentalists in the "Bible belt" of this country are among the most prone to adopt a fascist outlook. Thus the Reverend Mr. Winrod of Kansas City
was shown by the *Friends of Democracy* to have main-

tained close relations with well-known Nazi-dominated organizations in this country.[11] On the other hand, there has always been widespread distrust of the Catholic Church, because of its authoritarian attitude, and its insistence that it alone knows "the truth." The Catholics, like others, are of course divided on this matter. Fundamentalism in the religious sphere is the very antithesis of democracy, and we can safely conclude this part of our analysis with the statement that no agreement on religious fundamentals is either needed or wanted.

NATIONAL CULTURAL DISAGREEMENT

The second fundamental cleavage engendering bitter conflicts in our age results from national cultural differences. The Nazis have taken the position that such cleavages must be eliminated by either destroying the culturally distinct elements, such as the Jews, or subjecting such elements to ruthless domination by the master race, the Nazi Germans. The Italian Fascists, taking a similar view, insisted upon eliminating the Germans from the Southern Tyrol. In their attack upon Czechoslovakia, the Nazis continually harped upon the compound nationality structure of that country as a sure sign of its doom. They skillfully exploited the existing antagonisms, by stirring up the Slovaks and the Hungarians, as well as the Sudeten Germans. It is well known that the Nazis have done the same in Jugoslavia.

Unfortunately, in that country a dictatorial regime had previously piled up dissensions by persecuting racial minorities for many years.

The story in democratic countries is quite different. Switzerland is built upon an even more difficult nationality structure than Czechoslovakia or Jugoslavia were, since each of its component groups belongs culturally to one of the great aggressive nations of Europe: the Germans, the French, and the Italians have each contributed their share to the Swiss nation. To enhance the difficulty further, Switzerland is also divided by religious differences. We have to allow, of course, that Switzerland's three distinct cultural and nationality groups are united by a long tradition of common political customs which through centuries separated them from the surrounding monarchical regimes. But the question remains: How could they develop such a political community, since they are so deeply divided, if fundamental disagreement is incompatible with constitutional democracy? In other words, the making of modern Switzerland reinforces the proposition that constitutional democracy makes it possible for people to co-operate in spite of such disunity. Constitutional democracy has flourished in Switzerland as nowhere else in Europe, suggesting that it is peculiarly adapted to countries which are divided upon fundamentals.

The case is strengthened by looking once more at the United States, "the teeming nation of nations." Here all the nationalities of Europe have come together. Not as nationalities, to be sure, but as individuals. Archibald MacLeish sang: —

> It is a strange thing — to be an American. . . .
> America is neither a land nor a people,
> A word's shape it is, a wind's sweep —
> America is alone: many together,
> Many of one mouth, of one breath,
> Dressed as one — and none brothers among them:
> Only the taught speech and the aped tongue.
> America is alone. . . .[12]

And while they all are Americans, it would be a great mistake to think that the different nationalities embrace each other in loving affection. Far from it. As H. L. Mencken has shown in his *American Language*, Americans have coined a mass of derogatory slang words to designate these different nationalities, the wops, the chinks, the limeys, and so on *ad infinitum*. Says he: "The English have relatively few aliens in their midst, and in consequence they have developed nothing comparable to our huge repertory of opprobrious names for them." [13]

But what of Britain? It was here that the Irish Nationalist opposition so deeply disturbed the workings of parliamentary procedure. And it was the spectacle of this obstruction which influenced some of the later English theorists, and led them to adopt the view that agreement on fundamentals was essential.[14] Fundamentally, the answer is that Ireland was not represented in Parliament as if she were part of a working democracy. Ireland was not on a footing of equality with the rest of Britain, any more than the Czechs were on an equal footing with the German Austrians in the old Hapsburg Empire. If constitutional procedures are thus employed to hide the lack of democracy, rather than to provide channels for its working, can it be wondered at if they break down? And do such situations prove anything regarding the working of genuine democratic constitutionalism? For that, we have to take genuine democracies.

So, whether we consider America, or Switzerland, or yet Canada, we are once again forced to the conclusion that disagreement, rather than agreement, on fundamentals is the characteristic feature of constitutional democracy.

ECONOMIC CLASS DIVISION

But there are many who would say that neither religious nor national-cultural differences provide *fundamental* issues today. Disagreements over social outlook and philosophy, engendered by conflicting economic interests, are claimed as the cause of the deepest and most serious cleavages. Such differences are highlighted in views on property. Speaking of England, Harold Laski said that until recently, Liberals and Conservatives were "fundamentally at one," because "they did not question the private ownership of the means of production." The rise of an organized labor movement, a class-conscious proletariat, has changed all that. There can be no question that in our time men are most sharply divided in their views of property, whereas at other times other matters held the center of interest. But does it follow that such a disagreement destroys the foundation of constitutional government and democracy? That this is so may be questioned on two grounds.

For one thing, if social outlook provides the sharpest disagreement today, other matters did earlier. Since constitutionalism provided a *modus vivendi* for the ironing-out of difficulties arising from religious and national-cultural disagreements, may it not be expected to do likewise with the new fundamental disagreement? In other words, it would seem that the shift in emphasis from one problem to another would not affect the general conclusion that disagreement on fundamentals was not only compatible with constitutionalism and the belief in the common man, but that such disagreement could be effectively overcome by compromise only in a constitutional democracy.

But beyond this general argument from analogy, specific support for the contention just stated again can be derived from a survey of past disagreements on property and on social outlook generally. Such disagreements have been present right through the period of constitutional democracy. Furthermore, can there be any question that views on property have profoundly changed over the last hundred years? "The World is governed too much," the *Boston Globe* proclaimed on its masthead in Emerson's day, and he approved. If property is a bundle of rights, as has aptly been said, or a bundle of relations, that bundle is composed of different sticks from those composing it a hundred years ago. Such changes are by no means limited to a few fields of regulated industrial activity. Even farm property provides a good illustration. Rapid mass transportation has brought into existence a world market, bringing price fluctuations which cannot possibly be calculated by the individual farmer. In all the more advanced countries, the government has stepped in and developed far-flung programs of marketing regulations, price stabilizations, production controls — in short, farming as a job has become increasingly socialized. The property of the farm really is a title to engage in this job, but not in any way you want to.

These extensive changes in property rights have come about through legislation, as everyone knows. They are the result of continuous sharp disagreements as to property, reaching all the way from "rugged individualism" to "Communism." But can it be truly said that disagreements on this score have disrupted the working of constitutional democracy? These issues are amongst the most explosive of our time, and partisans on all sides

continuously proclaim that there can be no democracy
unless we follow their counsel. While some are convinced that democracy's future depends upon the maintenance of free enterprise, others are equally certain
that unless we develop "industrial" or economic democracy, political democracy will remain an empty sham.
Both groups continuously urge their view upon the
common man. This sharp conflict is by no means a
new one. From the very beginning of American history, upward surges of democratic feeling have been
coupled with social radicalism. It was so with "Jeffersonian democracy," with the issues which led to the
Civil War, with the Granger movement of the eighties,
and evidently with more recent developments. Those
great American enthusiasts for the common man, Emerson, Thoreau, Whitman, were in close touch if not
actually associated with the communist experiments of
their day. The ideas underlying Brook Farm were certainly as fundamentally at odds as anything could be
with the dominant attitude of Americans on that fundamental: private property. Nor can it be asserted that
Herbert Hoover and Robert LaFollette and the millions for whom each spoke were in fundamental agreement. We are piling Pelion on Ossa, since American
political history has been reverberating with disagreements on this score of property from generation to
generation.

What is true of America is almost equally true of

The New Image of the Common Man

England. In England, too, there has been continuous disagreement on economic and social philosophy.[15] It is interesting that Laski himself undertakes to clinch his argument rather by reference to the Irish home-rule conflict than by economic arguments. But the matter can be put into the form of a question: At what point will the continuous change in the meaning of private property by parliamentary democracy meet with violent resistance, so that a breaking point is inevitable in the transition to a more and more socialized society? Unless that question can be answered succinctly, the argument which we have been conducting falls to the ground.

Looking at the social and economic legislation of England as it evolved in the course of the last hundred years, from the factory act of 1833 to the act socializing the coal-mining industry,[16] we are forced to the conclusion that the most radical changes have never reached the point where they elicited violent resistance. For example, the "landed interest" at the beginning of the nineteenth century dominated England, politically, economically, socially. Today, their way of life and their system of property has become a dim memory, the unreality of which is reflected in many English novels, such as Hilton's *Random Harvest*. The Corn Laws of 1846 were the turning point, but the transition was a very gradual one. In the course of this transition, "fundamentals" clashed continually, but were

[170]

brought together for a concrete line of action by the very parliamentary democracy which is claimed to depend upon agreement on fundamentals.[17]

Here is still another way of looking at it. Switzerland, of all countries the most democratic, has operated its railroads as a government undertaking for many years. England and America have let them be run by private corporations under strict government regulation. Hence a proposal to operate the American railroads as the Swiss are operated is instantaneously greeted by the cry that it is Communism. Without a question, it is a proposal on which people will divide, depending upon their "fundamental" outlook concerning property. But in spite of their views on property, they will agree on some concrete way of acting, because railroads have to be operated, somehow. To discover such specific agreements for action from among common men who disagree about fundamentals — such is precisely the task and achievement of constitutional democracy.

NO DEMOCRATIC ANSWER

In spite of all the theorizing, democracy in action has functioned in communities divided by disagreement on fundamentals. It would, of course, be possible to argue that democracies — in America, Switzerland, England — still all have been Christian, all European in culture, etc. In other words, it would be possible to broaden the concept of what is fundamental to the point where nearly all folks in these communities could be said to be of a similar outlook. But such an argument, while undeniably correct, reveals at the same time the weakness in the whole argument about fundamentals. The terms in which these fundamentals are couched become increasingly vague, until finally they no longer bear any relationship to practical affairs. To illustrate: almost all mankind is united in condemning dishonesty and murder. The legal codes of people after people will show provisions against these types of antisocial behavior. But just because they are so universally agreed upon as undesirable, they do not represent any issue with which constitutional democracy, as contrasted with authoritarian forms of government, is likely to be specifically concerned. Such simple issues do not provide a problem.

It is only when qualifications of general rules, such as that against killing, are under debate that genuine "fundamentals," such as religious convictions, come into play. In a totalitarian dictatorship, the "necessity" of killing is arbitrarily determined by the dictator. When Lady Astor asked Stalin how long he would go on killing people, he is reported to have answered: "As long as it is necessary." [18] Likewise, Hitler considers himself the sole judge as to what is necessary. Such a viewpoint can and will be supported only by people whose "fundamental" outlook agrees with the dictator, whereas people with other opinions will unhesitatingly look upon the killings as murder. Under constitutional democratic conditions any exceptions to a general rule will be determined upon by compromise after discussion, usually by way of legislation. Thus, while it may be provided that a person who has murdered another will be killed, certain exceptions may be made where extenuating circumstances come into play. Recently a Virginia jury freed a woman who had killed an unwelcome suitor on the ground that "a woman has a right to defend herself in her own home." While this decision stands as far as the particular case is concerned, it may be surmised that there is considerable disagreement over such a principle; such disagreement may hark back to religious and other "fundamental" convictions.

The question as to what constitutes a fundamental cannot in a strict sense be answered democratically. Agreement upon fundamentals cannot be a prerequisite of a democracy, or of constitutionalism, because it cannot be assumed that there will be any agreement upon what is fundamental. Fundamentalism in all its various forms is antidemocratic, anticonstitutional, contrary to the spirit of freedom. All insistence upon agreement on fundamentals is basically related to the idea we have rejected as incompatible with constitutional democracy: that some persons know what is right. Even the constitution itself should not be proclaimed as a fundamental, lest we make it into a fetish. Many good men who look upon themselves as ardent believers in de-

[173]

mocracy do not realize that their counsels of perfection provide the very materials out of which the antidemocratic elite theories are forged. The common man, collectively, is presumably empowered to exercise a veto on all matters of general concern. Lofty sentiments about the public interest, about fundamentals and all the rest, are usually coupled with aristocratic or oligarchic notions about an elite which *ought* to guide the common man and his judgments. "We have to make the public-interest conception supreme in our democracy over localism, pressure politics, and class struggle," cries one of these idealists, "if democracy is to realize economic security." But how are we going to accomplish that? The very man who thus preaches will a few pages later insist that Jim Farley is right in guessing how our democracy actually works. The public-interest conception is valuable enough in providing the battle cry *for* pressure groups, classes, and regions; but no one, in a democracy, can say (as the statement implies) that he is necessarily right about what the public interest means.

WHO HAS INSISTED UPON FUNDAMENTALS?

To bring out this antidemocratic aspect more clearly, let us briefly survey the writers who have expounded the agreement upon fundamentals with vigor in the past. Burke, who started the whole argument, displays throughout his writings a vigorous contempt for the common man. "Those who would engage in great public schemes must be proof against . . . what is worst of all, the presumptuous judgment of the ignorant upon their designs." And in his enthusiasm for the elite he exclaimed elsewhere: "Nobility is a graceful ornament to the civil order. It is the Corinthian capital of polished society." [19] Carrying this strand of thought farther, Burke wrote, in his *Appeal from the New to the Old Whigs:* "I see as little of policy or utility, as there is of right, in laying down a principle that a majority of men told by the head are to be considered as the people, and that as such their will is to be law." He then goes on to proclaim as essential the social discipline by which "the wiser, the more expert, and the more opulent conduct, and by conducting enlighten and protect, the weaker, the less knowing, and the less provided with good fortune." [20] There is little here of a belief in the common man, in this first expounder of the importance of an agreement upon fundamentals.

Bagehot, likewise, is full of such judgments. The English, he thought, were happily a "deferential nation" and hence by their inbred readiness to defer to the judgments of their betters eminently qualified for representative government. "In theory it is desirable that this highest class of wealth and leisure should have an influence far out of proportion to its mere number: a perfect constitution would find for it a delicate expedient to make its fine thought tell upon the surrounding cruder thought." [21] But fortunately Bagehot does not have to worry about the English. "It has been thought strange," he wrote, "but there *are* nations in which the numerous unwiser part wishes to be ruled by the less numerous wiser part. The numerical majority is ready, is eager to delegate its power of choosing its ruler to a certain select minority. It abdicates in favor of its elite, and consents to obey whoever that elite may confide in." These statements are revealing; they actually speak of the elite. Undoubtedly, many people still agree with Bagehot, but hardly the seven-odd million voters in the Labour Party.

But one man who certainly agreed with Bagehot was Balfour. He was the third great expounder of the importance of agreement upon fundamentals; characteristically he led the conservative opposition to a reform of the House of Lords. His philosophical inclinations were altogether toward an aristocratic, Platonic position. Finally, when we turn to Harold Laski, we find him expounding the necessity of agreement upon fundamentals at a time when he had adopted the Marxist position which contains one of the leading elite doctrines of our day. In short, this argument about fundamentals apparently has a special fascination for those who are inclined toward some sort of elite doctrine.

This is not surprising in view of the fact that what is a fundamental cannot be settled democratically.[22]

IS "DEMOCRACY" A FUNDAMENTAL?

But what about the particular fundamental of "democracy" itself? Democracy, we saw, means many things to many men. Obviously, an agreement merely to use the word democracy in speaking of social convictions — which is what much "agreement on democracy" amounts to — is purely ritualistic. It has no concrete political significance at all. But there are those who would more specifically insist that we cannot have a democracy unless people "agree to disagree." Since this whole discussion is directed toward showing the importance of dissent, such a proposition is evidently correct. But are not those who advance this proposition as an argument against the importance of *dissent* engaging in a verbal quibble? Why proclaim this willingness to disagree as a fundamental? What we are dealing with here is a way of conducting oneself, a behavior pattern. To put it another way: while fundamental beliefs do not permit of exceptions, behavior does. You can say that you are more or less inclined toward a certain behavior. You are, for example, drinking more or less and are not "either a drunkard or a teetotaler." Fundamental belief is quite the opposite; for instance, you either are or are not a Christian. You cannot be a

Christian half the time and a Mohammedan the other half. You may, to be sure, behave like a Christian only half of the time. But that reinforces the argument that it is the behavior which admits of the proposition "more or less."

The same thing, of course, holds true in other situations involving democratic behavior. All behavior permits of exceptions. This is of the greatest practical consequence when one considers the so-called "fundamental rights," much more realistically called "civil liberties." Freedom of speech, freedom of assembly, and freedom of association should be treated as widely accepted behavior patterns, for if they are so considered, it means that ordinarily and under normal circumstances most of us will behave in accordance with them. You will tolerate a fellow whose views you don't like, you will let him forgather with others who feel the way he does, for example. And yet we shall act differently under exceptional conditions. If there is a war, much behavior that is admissible in peacetime is no longer tolerated. Our "fundamental" beliefs have not changed, but the conditions to which they apply have. Our civil liberties are prevailing modes of conduct which rest upon such "fundamental" beliefs. I think it is in the light of these undeniable facts that we can fully appreciate the importance, from a realistic standpoint, of realizing that these "freedoms" or "liberties" are essentially patterns of behavior. This is true altogether of the essential elements of constitutionalism. As I have attempted to show elsewhere,[23] the whole constitution is a pattern of acting or behaving. There can be more or less of it. Such behavior is not a fundamental, nor is it an absolute, in the sense in which basic beliefs in religion, culture, or social philosophy are.

An important practical consequence flows from this basing of democracy and constitutionalism on common behavior, rather than on agreement upon fundamentals. And that consequence is particularly important at the present time. The endless debates about whether we are sacrificing democracy by denying to our enemies the basic freedoms or civil liberties reflect the dilemma with which we seem to be confronted. For the conclusion seems inescapable that we must either *violate* our principles in our efforts to stop the enemy from abusing our liberties, or we must jeopardize the future of these principles, should the enemy overcome us. It is a fearful dilemma. But it exists only as long as we take the view that these are *fundamental principles*, and further that we must agree upon them if we are to be democratic. If, on the other hand, we look upon them as a behavior pattern, that is, as a pattern of human ways of acting under favorable conditions, we can without difficulty appreciate that humans will cease to act that way when the conditions are radically changed. Thus, the disposition to tolerate other views ceases to prevail when there arises a view that preaches intolerance. Yes, let us face the facts: Democracy, being a way of living and acting, will go all the way of force and violence in order to maintain itself. For life never ends until it has exhausted all the means at its disposal. The ability to put up with disagreement, though indeed central in the democratic scheme of things, prevails only up to the point of its own self-denial. Democracy is vital only when there is a sufficient sense of the vital necessity for meeting antidemocratic forces by force.

It is curious, finally, that the willingness to put up with disagreement should have been put forward so often as the ground for asserting that there must be agreement upon fundamentals. For what is the importance of being willing to put up with disagreement if there are no really important disagreements? It is improper to sidetrack this issue by shifting the ground and talking about common objectives.[24] There must, of course, be common objectives, but such common objectives are, in a democratic society, pragmatic or, to use a less controversial term, ever-changing. Democratic behavior is pragmatic in that it tends to concentrate upon practical tasks, such as defending one's country by building battleships, stabilizing distribution of income by setting up an old-age insurance scheme, or stabilizing agricultural production by one practice or another. In the realization of such practical tasks, men of very different general outlook can collaborate, particularly when the concrete aspects of the objective are emphasized. We shall elaborate this more fully in connection with our discussion of democratic planning. Here let us emphasize again that what binds a free people together is not an agreement on fundamentals, but a common way of acting in spite of disagreement on fundamentals. It might be well to illustrate the issues and difficulties involved by reference to two recent conflict situations in this country.

McWILLIAMS' CAMPAIGN OF HATE

The first is the case of Joseph E. McWilliams of the notorious Yorkville section of New York. For many years he was a speaker for the Christian Front, but he thought the Fronters were much too mild, and so he broke away and organized the Christian Mobilizers. He hoped the organization would attract the members of the German-American Bund and the more violent members of the Christian Front. In 1940 he organized the political party known as the American Destiny Party. Meetings of both the Christian Mobilizers and the American Destiny Party became very inflammatory, far more so than those of the Christian Front. Speakers openly expressed their admiration for Hitler. A few quotations from McWilliams will suffice: "I must consult with Hitler"; "Let us make this country the paradise that Hitler has made of Germany"; "We are going to win this country back for the Christians, and God pity anybody who stands in our way." [25]

Here is the way a typical McWilliams meeting would be run. A crowd would gather around a wagon at some street corner and a master of ceremonies would say, "This is a political meeting," and would quote the Bill of Rights of the Constitution. Then he would make a long speech urging the voters to send McWilliams to Congress from the Yorkville district. The moment would come when McWilliams would step onto the tailboard of the wagon and the audience — made up of German Nationalists, Social Justice people, and so on — would break into cheers. McWilliams would start off with a joke, like all American speakers; but then he would go on to make the crowd angry by telling them about some patriotic American who had been persecuted by the Jews. Next he would tell them, "Do you know that fifteen thousand Jewish refugees have landed in New York this week, and they are all going to take your jobs?" Almost always he would say, "I know there are Jewish stooges here tonight." Then everybody would begin to look around in the crowd to find a victim for the hatred the speeches had built up out of their frustration, the frustration of little men, of people with mediocre jobs. And the end of the meeting would be a riot.

You have here a case of a group of people who cited the freedom of assembly, the democratic-behavior type of guaranty, for doing what had nothing to do with democratic behavior. They cited the right pacifically to assemble as a right to hold an assembly that was not peaceful at all.

THE SAN ANTONIO CASE

A very different case is provided by an incident that occurred in San Antonio, Texas, in 1939. San Antonio is a middle-sized town with strong anti-Communist sentiment, and its mayor at that time was Maury Maverick. In August, 1939, Emma Brooks, wife of a three-times candidate for Governor of Texas for the Communist Party, sought and received permission to use a wing of the building of the municipal auditorium for a meeting. Immediately about twenty organizations, including the American Legion, the Knights of Columbus, the Baptist Ministers, the Texas Pioneers, sought revocation of the permit. With a majority of the City Council behind him, Mayor Maverick rejected these demands. Though strongly opposed to the Communists he stood his ground, citing the Supreme Court decision in the CIO–Hague case, which made the issuance of such permits mandatory.[26] The town was full of rumors that the meeting would not be held, despite the mayor's decision — threatening rumors, rumors intended to intimidate the mayor and council, such as are common in that type of setting. In answer the chief of police made detailed plans to protect the meeting.

The New Image of the Common Man

About an hour before the meeting was to convene, five thousand citizens had gathered outside the building. When the seventy-five Communists in attendance opened the meeting with the "Star-Spangled Banner," the crowd attempted to shout them down. Then bricks and stones began to fly through the windows. The Communists were forced back against the wall to avoid being hit. Policemen got the leaders out the back way, but still the crowd refused to disperse, although firemen turned two high-pressure streams of water on them and the police ineffectively used tear gas. Rumors went around that Maverick was inside with the Communists, and the mob broke the police line and forced their way into the building. They did not find Maverick, but they did find a few Communists. Once inside, the crowd was quieted by Father Marcus Valenta, who led a parade to the Alamo, where the Lord's Prayer was said. The day ended with the mayor being hanged in effigy at the City Hall. There were twenty-three casualties, of whom fifteen were policemen.[27]

What do these two cases show? They show that the holding of peaceful assemblies depends, not upon an agreement on *fundamentals* (if all agreed, the meetings would arouse little interest), but upon not upsetting certain *behaviors* that are common in a given community. McWilliams' undemocratic behavior imperiled the maintenance of this freedom of assembly as much as did the crowd hysteria in San Antonio.

The Need for Dissent

CONCLUSION

Clearly, then, the behavior that is expressed by the formula that "we agree to disagree" needs to be upheld by practicing it. Nothing is quite so inimical to the workings of democracy as shouting continuously: "Unity, unity, unity!" For unity, in the sense of agreement on fundamentals, is no sign of democratic morale. The forcing of conscience is no sign of democratic morale. But a readiness to get down to the job in hand, regardless of disagreements on fundamentals, *is* a sign of democratic morale. Why pretend that we do not fundamentally disagree with Stalin and his followers in this country? We do. But we can work with him if the task in hand is the joint one of destroying Hitlerism.

The particular kind of democratic unity we want is unity behind freely chosen leaders for the accomplishing of specific tasks. If this were not true, we could not sensibly talk of a "democratic world order." For is there any prospect of getting the peoples of the world to agree concerning religion and other "fundamental" beliefs? Obviously not. But a democratic world order does not have to wait upon such agreement, provided a basis can be found for joint action in the accomplishment of jobs to be done.

Only the readiness to agree to disagree, the pattern of constitutional democracy, can, as a universally accepted system, give us the lasting peace we are longing for. Peace is not merely the absence of war, but the state of mind which through continuous effort at mutual accommodation continually reshapes the community within which it dwells.

The demand for agreement upon fundamentals is, as we have seen, historically associated with a belief in an elite, not with the belief in the common man. It is, indeed, aristocracies which cannot long endure without an agreement upon fundamentals on the part of the ruling class or elite. Likewise, the oligarchic totalitarian systems of our time need agreement upon fundamentals amongst their party adherents. And since they cannot stand that open dissent which is so patent a part of constitutional democracies, these totalitarians go about suppressing with the most ruthless violence any sign of such dissent. That should be a warning to us — for whatever is right for Hitler is likely to be wrong for us.

Constitutional democracy is possibly the only form of government which does *not* require agreement on fundamentals. As long as there is insistence upon fundamental agreement, only force remains when people disagree. The realization that "fundamentals" are never known, demonstrably, but are matters of faith and hence unproven premises, underlies this democratic frame of mind. Free men are men who have become sufficiently mature to realize that neither they nor any leader "knows it all." They are ready to face the uncertainties of life unafraid. They are self-confident, but with moderation.

CHAPTER VI

Responsibility and the Sense of Workmanship

By their fruits ye shall know them.
— MATTHEW 7:20

T HE LATE Justice Brandeis used to tell of an experience he had after the Ballinger investigation, which he conducted. It will be recalled that this investigation led to the removal of Ballinger, then Secretary of the Interior. His successor wrote Brandeis and asked him, since they were old friends, what he would advise him to watch out for, since he had become so familiar with the Interior Department in the course of his investigation. Brandeis advised him: "Never sign a letter, unless you have read it; never sign a voucher, unless you know what it's for." He promptly received an answer from the new Secretary, thanking him for his advice, and adding: "But unfortunately, my dear friend, you are asking the impossible." This incident, to Brandeis' mind, strikingly illustrated what he called "the curse of big-ness." It was the distinguished jurist's sense of work-manship that revolted at this sort of thing. Those whose craft is administration might disagree with Brandeis, be-cause they would hold that the administrator's crafts-manship should be exercised in skillful selection of the aids who prepare the letters and vouchers for signature, rather than in reading every letter; they would heartily agree that the instinct of workmanship was essential to good management.

It is very usual for people to see an insoluble con-flict between the craftsmanlike execution of the highly complex tasks of management and the predilections of the common man. Numerous are the writers who have expanded upon the clash between the voters and the experts, between democracy and bureaucracy. If the writer didn't like what the experts were doing, he held forth about "Our Wonderland of Bureaucracy" or about "The New Despotism"; [1] if the experts seemed right to him, he would exclaim against "politicians," "demagogues," and about the "presumptuous judgment of the ignorant" upon the "designs" of the experts.

THE SENSE OF WORKMANSHIP

The tempered belief in the common man which we are developing in these pages suggests that both these views are in error. The first errs because the common man when acting through the majority exercises that instinct of workmanship negatively — he rejects those experts or uncommon men who are too far out of line. This it is that prevents our specialists from turning the government into either a wonderland or a despotism. The second view, that the expressed preferences of the majority are mostly responses to demagogic appeals, is wrong because the common man exercises his instinct of workmanship positively: he recognizes a job well done. Both these propositions are further enforced by the fact that the experts themselves are common men outside their own specialty; if they are animated by this belief they will, as I said at the end of the first chapter, recognize the limitations of their own work, and appreciate the significance of that of others.

But what is the sense of workmanship or craftsmanship? Thorstein Veblen called it an "instinct," using a somewhat obsolete psychological term. But "sense" seems more accurate and allows for development. Anyway, this appreciation of and striving for workmanship is a very important element in the tempered belief in the common man. It complements the so-called "common sense" which we have described earlier as the sense for traditional standards, values and beliefs that gives the common man's judgments stability and consistency. In *The Vested Interests and the State of the Industrial Arts* (1919), Veblen stated that "the habits of thought engendered by the machine system in industry and by the mechanically standardized organization of life under this new order, as well as by the material sciences, are of such a character as would incline the common man to rate all men and things in terms of tangible performance rather than in terms of legal title and ancient usage."

To rate all men and things in terms of tangible performance — this is the modern sense of workmanship, according to Veblen. He had developed this idea twenty or more years earlier, in lectures on "The Instinct of Workmanship and the Irksomeness of Labor." He maintained there that this "instinct of workmanship" is the "sense of merit and demerit with respect to the material furtherance or hindrance of life," and hence brings it about that "the proximate aim of all industrial improvement has been the better performance of some workmanlike task." This sense or instinct, therefore, generates standards of accomplishment, which counteract man's natural inclination toward idleness.[2] These propositions, which Veblen developed more fully later,[3] give us a firm basis from which to start.

HOW THIS SENSE WORKS

We can go beyond the foregoing analysis and apply it to the problem of the role of the common man and the expert in democratic industrialism. Standards resulting from the sense of workmanship operate essentially on a number of levels. It may be best to mark out three. The individual workman, whether farmer, painter or scientist, will apply the standard of the exceptional achievement for which he is striving. To illustrate simply (leaving aside the more esoteric realms of human effort): A dairy farmer may strive to breed a cow which will give 1000 pounds of butterfat during one lactation, and he will be the more satisfied the nearer he comes to this almost impossible achievement. The second level upon which the sense of workmanship operates is more generally applicable. Dairy farmers as a group, realizing that a cow giving 500 pounds of butterfat is doing very well, will apply the standards of usual technical achievement of the particular craft and consider a man a good farmer if his herd averages over 350 pounds (the standard set by the National Dairy Herd Improvement Association). The third level upon which the sense of workmanship is applied is that of the layman who comes into contact with the performance through use. We all argue about what is the best car or the finest lecturer and so forth. In the same way, the community at large will apply what might be called the standard of utility to the product of a farmer. His achievement must live up to it if he is to give the community milk at a reasonable price. General utility, usual technical performance, and exceptional merit are the three levels upon which the sense of workmanship operates in judging the work of an individual, a company or a public service.

These levels offer the clue to the conflict between democracy and bureaucracy.[4] They also serve to resolve the conflict. For they reveal that the sense of workmanship is at work on the level of the electorate as well as on that of the expert. The conclusion can be reinforced by another reflection. The largest part of the people have occasion to apply the sense of workmanship on all three levels in some field of activity. This helps the more thoughtful among us to appreciate the role of the craftsman in a field not our own. Nowhere is this situation more habitually recognized, of course, than in the law. The layman, the lawyer, and the judge — they clearly represent the three levels, and no higher achievement can come to the uncommon man in this field than to become Chief Justice of the Supreme Court.

Our industrial system has produced complex machinery for the satisfaction of communal needs. This machinery consists in elaborate administrative organizations, either operated or regulated in accordance with the preference of the majority. More and more people (who are part of this majority) themselves participate in the operation of these organizations by furnishing the staff.[5] Even the farmers, though still formally independent, are subject to an increasing amount of regulation by rules which have the sanction of majority approval; they too are becoming assimilated to the "bureaucracy." When looking at the development of industrialized communities from this angle, we can perceive a commonwealth of mutual servants. Each great service may have its internal controls, but these would be held together and operated in accordance with the broader perspectives of the common men collectively. In short, the work of each worker is appraised on the basis of his contribution to the communal tasks. A man's function determines his role in the society.

THE MANAGERIAL FUNCTION

This type of society, in which practically all status is the result of function, has given rise to a series of startling misinterpretations. The managerial function has often been exaggerated to the exclusion of other equally important functions. Thus a recent tour de force speaks of a "managerial revolution." By this "revolution" the author, a disillusioned Marxist,[6] wishes to designate what he considers an inevitable emergence of "the new order of managers and those who would like to be managers." It has been apparent for a long time that the core of human personnel is of decisive importance in the rise of large-scale organization. Hence there can be no question but that the managerial function is crucial. But it is merely one function.[7] The rising importance of the managerial function in our increasingly industrialized society, and the consequent blurring of the line of distinction between private and public enterprise, do not constitute a revolution in either the social or the political sense. Not in the former, because this development is purely operational and devoid of ideological content; not in the latter, because it has occurred in democracies as well as in dictatorships. The decisive question remains: *To whom* are the managers responsible? Who sets the tasks for them?

It is an amusing fact that the speculative genius of Count Saint-Simon, more than a hundred years ago, led him to believe the coming industrialism to be constructed much along the lines of a managerial society. He would have scientists and engineers with complete power to develop industry. "Everything by industry; everything for industry," he cried in 1817. He hoped to bring about a state of society where all would render voluntary obedience to benevolent captains of industry.

A modern American travesty of all this was the technocracy fad which swept America in the wake of the depression. But as captains of industry, whether benevolent or otherwise, had fought with each other, so the technocrats quarreled over who was to have the final say. That, of course, is the decisive political question. In a democracy, such as America, the majority of common men have this final say; in a totalitarian system, such as Germany, Hitler has the final say. In short, the managerial society is a mirage.

[194]

Responsibility and Sense of Workmanship

THE IMPORTANCE OF COMMUNICATION

As contrasted with these and other cranky exaggerations of the bureaucratic trend in industrialized society, the growing literature on administration — both public and business administration — is very important. Among the more recent contributions, Chester I. Barnard's *The Functions of the Executive* (1938) is particularly striking. He sees the executive's task as that of building and maintaining an organization which bears directly upon our present concerns. One is the problem of effective communication, and the other is the related problem of responsibility.

Why is communication so important? Because a working organization depends upon common purposes. Communication is the only way in which such purposes can become articulate. Hence communication must be at the heart of all organizational effort. Nowhere is this more decisively true than in the realm of public policy. In developed systems, channels of communication are publicly known. Furthermore they reach every member of the organization, indeed, everyone who belongs to the organization. Both in public and private life, important issues are raised by the question as to who "belongs" to the organization? Do the customers "belong"? Do the workers "belong" to a business enterprise? Likewise, a government agency has to face this sort of question. Do those affected immediately by its rules and regulations "belong," or does even the "general public" "belong"? In recent decades there has been a tendency in all organizations to draw the circle of those who should be communicated with more and more widely. Barnard suggests: —

. . . It appears necessary to regard as a part of an organization certain efforts of many persons not commonly considered "members," for example, customers; or those of persons that are only treated as members in special senses, for example, stockholders, who in one legal sense *are* the organization; or bondholders, who are important contributors to organization yet who at most are ordinarily viewed as only contingent members.[8]

Obviously, the nature of the communications will vary in accordance with the closeness of the relationship which exists between the organization and those who are to receive the communication. Thus, the Department of Agriculture will communicate with its officials, with farmers and with the general public who consume farm products and support its policies. Each set of communications will be distinctive.

Suppose a specific task be considered, such as increased food production. To its officials the Department of Agriculture will set forth inclusive information about steps to be taken by them in the pursuance of the task to be accomplished. To the farmers it will seek to explain the task, hoping to enlist their wholehearted co-operation. To the general public it will indicate successes in achieving the purpose of the increased production problem and explain any adverse effects which it might have upon them. In short, there can ordinarily be set down three distinct groups with whom an organization will deal in its communications: the active participants in its work, those upon whose co-operation the success of its work depends, and the public at large.[9] Only if all three are given appropriate attention can the organization be said to be conducted in a responsible fashion.[10] Which is the most important of these communication systems depends upon the nature of the organization.

RESPONSIBILITY

Responsibility is strikingly related to what we have spoken of as the sense of workmanship. "Executive responsibility, then, is that capacity of leaders by which, reflecting attitudes, ideals, hopes, derived largely from without themselves, they are compelled to bind the wills of men to the accomplishment of purposes beyond their immediate ends. . . ."[11] Such a statement of the problem stresses greatly the moral aspect of executive responsibility; it concentrates on the aspect of consistency as of primary importance. This is unsatisfactory, because too little is said about the equally important questions: Responsible to whom? Responsible for what? Within a democratic pattern, it is taken for granted that the answer to these questions is simply: the people, the majority, or the common man. But even the greatest faith in the common man cannot any longer justify a simple reliance upon the "will of the people." We have seen in our discussion of majority rule how this traditional idea has been modified. The greatly diversified mass of common men and women composing the people in a modern democracy constitutes a rather indeterminate principal. If, therefore, we had to rely upon their explicit "will" as the only sanction of responsible conduct, responsibility would remain even more fragmentary than it actually is anyway. It is especially unrealistic to think only of certain traditional devices of the electoral process, such as dependence of the cabinet upon majority support in parliament.

The sense of workmanship, working as it does upon three levels, offers the clue to the pattern of genuine responsibility. All common men respond to some extent to the standards which the sense of workmanship demands. That is why responsible conduct can be elicited on even so vast a scale as that which modern government requires. The standards resulting from a desire for exceptional potential achievement are operating within the *individual*, and hence may be left aside here, even though we all know them to be a powerful force. That leaves us the standards of technical achievement, and those of general utility. In other words, responsibility in public affairs follows a double standard which may also be called "functional" and "political." But whatever name we give them, these standards of responsibility are closely related to what we have called "the sense of workmanship." Once this is clearly recognized, it becomes possible to recognize the new forms of civic participation in public-policy formation, which have transformed the older traditional forms that rested upon an uncritical rationalistic misconception of man.[12]

ELICITED CO-OPERATION

It is the failure to understand these more recent developments which underlies a good deal of the worry of people about democracy. In the chapter on propaganda we have pointed out already how the Department of Agriculture has developed the common farmer's participation in the shaping of agricultural policy and regulation.[13] This elicited participation is completely in line with the view of modern business, which more and more includes the customers as part of the organization. If communication with all members is, as Barnard insists, the lifeblood of effective organization, then it is certainly vital to include in its membership the entire group of human beings who are vitally touched by the organization's activities. Government has been slow in following the trend of modern salesmanship according to which "the customer is always right." But improved public-relations methods are certainly one of the most striking features of the changing pattern of democratic government, especially in this country.

There has been a definite difference in approach between the Liberty Bond campaign of the last war and the Defense Bond advertising of this one. While no detailed analysis of the Liberty Bond campaign has ever been made, enough has been written about it to make it clear that the methods developed were more than doubtful. In many instances local enthusiasts fell back upon techniques of organizing community pressure which were a mockery of democracy. Statutory compulsory savings would have been much more compatible with free institutions than that sort of "voluntary" contribution.

The United States Treasury has consistently sought to avoid a recurrence of such methods this time. It would be premature, of course, to rely too heavily upon experiences prior to America's formal entry into the war. Still, the Treasury Hour on the radio, called "Billions for Defense," has been generally acknowledged as a remarkable achievement. The idea originated with a commercial sponsor who paid for the time, the Texaco Company.[14] Widely known actors and musicians, such as Laughton, Fred Allen and Grace Moore, made their talents available for the purpose of dramatizing the call to all the public to help in financing the national defense effort. The appeal was directed to the millions who listen to the radio. Here was a definite effort to enlist the public, the common men and women, through making them understand better an urgent need. But such understanding was not purely factual, but was rather definitely linked with emotional symbols and stereotypes as well.

Of course, in one respect this situation is rather unusual in that the government in this instance has something to sell, namely the bonds. But in a broader sense, "selling" is intimately bound up with much of the government's work. It is not at all necessary to take so high-and-mighty a view of the situation as did the author of the following statement: —

It is a problem for the bureaucracy to foresee a situation and evolve a solution which will break gradually upon the political consciousness and be sufficiently entrenched so that its formal adoption in the legislative chamber is not an embarcation upon an uncharted sea.

For it is very likely that some of the more immediately concerned members of the public, yes, even just plain citizens, are as apt to "foresee a situation" as these bureaucrats.

In Massachusetts, there exists the rather unusual institution that every citizen can put on paper an idea he has for remedial legislation and get it introduced into the legislature for consideration. What is more, such a proposal cannot be simply "killed in committee," but must be given a hearing. A study of this institution has shown the writer that it has been found a useful stimulant by many Massachusetts legislators through the years. But any attentive student of our legislative process knows that many civic as well as interest and pressure groups participate in "foreseeing situations." The instances are quite numerous where some citizen has succeeded, after much effort, of course, in molding such foresight into public policy.

MAIL–ORDER GOVERNMENT

It is common to look upon the informational services of government departments which are being developed in this country at the present time as largely devoted to the handing-out of routine news items to the daily press. In fields with novel policies to administer, such as Social Security or AAA, educational and promotional functions are all being recognized. But along with all this outward flow of information on emerging policies, there is an ever-increasing quantity of intake. This intake of all sorts of communicable views, opinions, facts, and criticisms is becoming a potent factor in the shaping of public policy, particularly in areas where the government is entering new or experimental ground. Often the public affected by this type of legislation will raise the most complicated technical issues. Vermont farmers inquired whether farm hands employed in sugaring were agricultural or industrial workers. The "boiling-down" of the sap, particularly when carried on in large quantities, seemed to be "industrial" in nature; much other work in connection with sugaring appeared clearly agricultural. How was this to be apportioned? Similar issues have arisen in connection with certain types of "domestic" help and dozens of other complicated issues. The informational services receiving such inquiries become important centers for policy initiation.

But even in established realms of governmental activity, new lines of approach are being pushed as a result of the activity of informational services. It is the function of the administrator to make every conceivable effort toward the enforcement of the law which he is called upon to administer. The authoritarian tradition of the past was inclined to take the attitude that it was up to the citizen to find out what the law was; if he did not, it was just too bad. Ignorance was no excuse for failure to obey the law. This conception of the government as a mere police force is quite outmoded, though undoubtedly many government offices are still administered according to such outworn notions. The modern conception of government as the largest "public service" with vast and diversified activities to administer cannot be made to work in such terms. The continuously changing pattern of our society requires that the administrator be responsive to whatever trends may be affecting his activities. Laws do not embody static and universal truths; they represent expedient policies which are subject to continuous change and must be so considered. Instead of administering according to precedent, the responsible administrator today works according to anticipation. Within the limits of existing laws, it is the function of the administrator to do everything possible to make the legislation work.

Instances of this kind are numerous. How responsive this approach has become might well be illustrated by the efforts the United States Department of Justice made to have aliens understand why they should register. All channels of communication were used to impress upon them as well as others that this registration was in the aliens' own best interest. Speeches by responsible officials, releases, radio programs and even cinema appearances were arranged. Special recordings in many foreign languages were made available to foreign-language broadcasters. The central theme of all these communications was somewhat as follows: "Please co-operate with the government in registering as this step is desirable for your own protection as well as needed for the safety of the country." In short, a determined effort was made to persuade the alien as well as the citizen that this registration was a measure necessitated by defense in which the government and those affected by it were *co-operating*. The idea of enforcing commands yields to the idea of effectuating policy. For most of the policies of a modern government, at any rate under democratic conditions, require collaboration rather than enforcement for their accomplishment.

It is very natural that policies which are novel in their creative impact upon society should elicit a great many diverse public reactions. These will flow into the administrative offices in the form of inquiries, criticisms and suggestions. Under democratic conditions, the average citizen feels entirely free to communicate with the government, because he considers it his own. According to the traditional conception of representative government, such communications would be sent to the citizen's representative in Congress or Parliament, who in turn would make them the basis of suitable action, official or unofficial inquiries, remarks in the debates of the House, and so on. A great deal of public reaction still takes this form. While elected representatives at times are inclined to feel that their mail is getting to be too much of a good thing, they would surely be agreed that the more important communications of this kind constitute an intrinsically valuable source of information and guidance.

In Great Britain, the question hour still serves this purpose fairly well. Questions constitute one of the most important tools in the hands of members of Parliament today. Questions from private members, that is members not connected with the government or the ministerial opposition bench, first intended to secure information, have become instruments for securing redress from administrative errors, as well as important occasions for embarrassing the government.[15]

In the United States much would depend upon the representative's being a member of the strategically important committees. However, the great pressure of legislative work has made it increasingly difficult for parliamentarians to attend to such matters. Moreover, a citizen, no matter how competent or well informed, would be handicapped if his views were patently different from those of his representative, whether for political or technical reasons. In these and similar situations the citizen has become more and more accustomed to turn directly to the administrator.

The Social Security Board, from its very inception, has realized the extent to which citizen-interest must be aroused and citizen–co-operation maintained in order to realize the far-flung policies which the Social Security Act embodies. Hence the Board's information service has been called upon to advise the Board and its various bureaus and the regional and field offices not only on public-relations matters but on all policy matters which affect public relations with the Board and its agents.

Indeed, there has lately developed an interesting tendency for administrative authorities to avail themselves of the large mail Congressmen receive on all sorts of questions. A Senator may just pass on to the administrator the letters he is receiving, or he may add his own comments from time to time. A representative is apt to be rather alert concerning the attitudes prevailing among his constituency; he is bound to become a specialist in public relations after a bit of experience! Hence legislators can often gauge much more accurately than an administrator what the significance of a particular communication might be. This tendency represents an interesting modern adaptation of the question hour in the House of Commons. It seems that the United States Federal Government has gone farther than any government abroad in developing such direct citizen participation in policy formation at the administrative level.

RESPONSIVENESS TO NEEDS

The whole range of activities involving constant direct contact of the administrator with the public and its problems shows that our views on responsible government are undergoing profound change. The emphasis is shifting. Instead of subserviency to "will" we look for responsiveness to commonly felt needs and wants. But there will, of course, frequently be violent disagreement as to (*a*) whether this or that need is commonly felt, (*b*) what are the means for coping with the situation. Thus, there is unquestionably a general agreement, a common feeling, that unemployment should be kept as low as possible. But there is no agreement at all as to what can be done to accomplish this purpose. A host of "schemes" have been worked out, both inside and outside the government, but their ingenuity has not, thus far, commanded widespread assent. Some of the programs are too disruptive of established folkways, others fail to convince technical experts, quite a few are just crank panaceas.

The sense of workmanship of the common man manifests itself in the reponse to these programs in two ways. First, the common man is doubtful of schemes which are rejected by quite a few experts, that is to say, by people whose workmanship is established in this field of social engineering. Second, the common man is doubtful about propositions which he cannot understand, in the sense that he cannot see how the plan as proposed would necessarily have the effect of reducing unemployment, particularly if the plan involves heavy sacrifices, such as abandoning accepted standards, beliefs, or interests. But these responses tend to make the official and the unofficial protagonist keenly interested in and desirous of anticipating the reactions of the public and its representatives. Too little attention has been given to the fact that much influence works most effectively through such anticipation of the reactions of the principal. Responsibility is linked with responsiveness through such anticipation. By way of their informational services, administrative officials have begun to tap independent sources of insight into the views and reactions of the general public, the common man.[16]

Responsibility and Sense of Workmanship

EXPERTNESS

All this, of course, is merely an expression of the fact that "will" is in many situations recognized as less important than a grasp of the social realities involved. The common man's sense of workmanship inclines him to expect from those who are responsible for the conduct of the public's business such guidance as only a real understanding of the facts can give. The common man is apt to have little patience with an administrator who attempts to excuse himself on the ground that "the majority decided that this action should be taken." He expects the responsible official to resist such majority decisions as seem to him foolish, even to the point of resigning his post. Many persons who were partly responsible for the policy of appeasement in Britain try to excuse themselves today on some such grounds. In the same way, in America, we have been treated to various excuses and subterfuges as to why we were not ready at the moment the Japanese struck at Pearl Harbor. But the public sharply objects to a workman whose sense of workmanship is so deficient that he will go on conducting the public's business badly because a misinformed majority wants him to. The public feels much the same way about this as it would about a town engineer who proceeded to build a bridge contrary to his better judgment, simply because the majority of the townsmen had demanded that he do it. In this sense, the expert is responsible for his workmanship to the rest of the citizenry. And the only standard which the common man will rest content with is that of general utility, as we have pointed out.[17]

CONCLUSION

It is clear, then, that our industrial age has brought forward a powerful support for responsible administration: the sense of workmanship. This factor has tended to counteract in many ways the dangerous tendency toward irresponsibility resulting from the vastness and technical complexity of our administrative system. This "sense of workmanship" should not, of course, ever be considered as a substitute for other controls which link up with the judgment of the common man, the voter. On the contrary, the common man can himself be seen as powerfully affected by this sense of workmanship.

In one of his tirades about heroes, Thomas Carlyle cries out that the common man "obeys those whom he esteems better than himself, wiser, braver; and will forever obey such; and even be ready and delighted to do it." That, to him, is the decisive argument against democracy. We shall have to say more about that in the next chapter. But why draw that conclusion? If the common man be so ready to recognize his superiors, why not let him determine who these superiors be? Responsible administration suggests just that: the common man, guided by his general instinct of workmanship, can be the final arbiter as to who possesses the superior workmanship in accomplishing the tasks which need accomplishing. He is to wear the shoe. When it pinches him, he will go to the cobbler, surely. Why not let him decide which cobbler is good?

CHAPTER VII

Planning for the Public Good

---

*We make plans so that we may
have plans to discard.*

— CONFUCIUS

THE INCREASING complexity of our industrial
system has been accompanied by frequent breakdowns,
crises, depressions, wars. From the very outset, these
tensions have caused men to insist that they should be
avoided, that *plans* should be evolved to anticipate and
mitigate these evils. Besides many special plans, over-all
plans have been advocated by a long list of speculative
observers of the industrial scene. Quite a few of the
critics of nineteenth-century industrialism advocated
grand designs for a regenerated or a stable society. These
various attempts were lumped together as "socialist."
Whatever their particular features, they all appear
Utopian in retrospect. Karl Marx sought to pin that
epithet on his several predecessors, the Saint-Simons, the
Fouriers, the Proudhons. It is fairly clear today that even

Planning for the Public Good

Marx and the Marxists were Utopian; like all the rest they forgot to take into account important elements of a functioning social order.

Preoccupied with the economic maladjustments, all these critics paid insufficient attention to the political, that is to say, the governmental realm. Marx, though sharply cognizant of the role of government, the "state," in the past, yet believed that a future society could be brought into existence in which administrative and political issues would disappear. In short, all these planners for the industrial society failed to face squarely the all-important question: who does the planning, and by what authority? Since they believed themselves to be in possession of the *right* plan, this failure seems understandable enough. The spectacle of the totalitarian autocracies has opened our eyes. We have been forced to recognize that a plan in the shaping of which the public has had no part is either foredoomed to remain an academic exercise, or will make of the self-appointed planner a totalitarian dictator.

WHAT IS PLANNING?

Charles E. Merriam, the distinguished Vice-Chairman of the National Resources Planning Board, has repeatedly insisted that there is a democratic form of planning.[1] "Planning is an organized effort to utilize social intelligence in the determination of national policies."

The New Image of the Common Man

To restate this a bit more broadly, we would emphasize the concept of "democratic planning," or planning for the public good — the process by which we make a continuous, organized effort to gather all the facts about and bring all the scientific insight to bear upon any problem which may require the adoption of a public policy. The problems are seen as new ones, emerging, and hence the ends and purposes are seen as changing and requiring continuous readjustment. Confucius would have approved of this approach; he always emphasized the need for continued learning and rethinking of our ideas and ways. The reason he could say: "We make plans so that we may have plans to discard" was that he felt so keenly the need for progressive self-improvement. "The things that trouble or concern me," he once said, "are the following: lest I should neglect to improve my character, lest I should neglect my studies, and lest I should fail to move forward when I see the right course, or fail to correct myself when I see my mistake." [2] Likewise we would be well advised always to keep in mind that plans may be wrong, and are usually imperfect. But they may yet be better than no plan at all. If we gather all we know about what we are thinking of doing, we are doing the obviously rational thing. If we set up organizations by which this may be done in a regular, consistent way, so that the public and its representatives may be continuously advised of all the facts and ideas bearing upon what they are about to do, we are merely extending such obviously rational methods to the realm of public policies.

Yet are we not, in considering or advocating such a course, making precisely those rationalist assumptions concerning the common man — the public — and his representatives which we have been obliged to acknowledge as untenable in the light of modern knowledge?

There can be little question that much present talk on democratic planning is couched in such rationalist terms. Against it, the totalitarians assert the need for an authoritarian procedure. One able recent analysis puts it this way: "An economy is *planned* when one central authority adopts and carries out a program designed to realize a single unquestioned end to the whole of the community over which it has jurisdiction." [3] It would seem that any "unquestioned end" is incompatible with the rule of the common man, as we have described it. In a democracy, there is no agreement on fundamentals; indeed there is not and cannot be agreement even on what constitutes a fundamental. It is the very essence of the democratic process to permit the questioning of any end at any time — unless it be the winning of the war at the time a war is on; a war situation is clearly marginal; war government borders on the totalitarian pattern. All the political processes of a functioning popular government are designed to provide for the incessant revision of all policies and all ends, no matter how basic. Evidently, an arrangement by which one central authority adopts and carries out a program related to an "unquestioned end" is incompatible with such democratic processes.

PLANNING AND THE COMMON MAN

If then we return to the conception of planning as the process by which facts and insights are gathered and brought to bear upon public policy, how can such planning be combined with a realistic view of the common man? It is the nature of the relationship or co-operation between workmen on the three levels of workmanship which helps us solve the problem which this question posits, the problem of planning in a democracy. Indeed the supposed conflict between democracy and planning is closely related to the (as we have seen) fictitious conflict between bureaucracy and democracy. It is almost a settled question in the minds of many able observers that planning is possible only under a totalitarian regime. Many who have tried to persuade the public of the desirability of their particular plans have despaired of the situation. Convinced that they knew what was right, they were ready to put the experts on top, rather than on tap. Few men seem to be able to marshal the self-denying restraint of Merriam when he writes: "An advisory agency will find that much of its advice is rejected in whole or in part. . . ."

What all the believers in authoritarian planning overlook is the simple fact that an authoritarian answer to the question *What is the public good?* can only be given by disregarding the public. This seems a very simple matter to recognize, and yet from Plato to the present day it has been neglected time and again. Bentham, we saw, came to recognize this clearly.

Have we any ground on which to share Bentham's faith that the common man will see what is good for him? Will he interest himself in the facts which bear upon the question? He will not, we may readily admit, search out all the facts. He will not, we may further concede, reach fully rational conclusions. But since public policies are adopted through a process of seeking a compromise acceptable to a majority of the public, a great many facts will, if made available, enter into the final equation. The same with insights and theories. The farmers may push some facts and principles, and the workers may insist upon others. As the planning authorities bring to light how a proposed policy affects different groups, they may shift their position in the light of these surveys. They often do.

EFFECTIVENESS AND EFFICIENCY

Democratic planning, dedicated as it must be to achieving the greatest satisfaction for as many as possible, cannot neglect the reactions of all those whom a given policy affects. Since the continued co-operation of a substantial majority of the public is needed, the common man's reaction must be considered one of the primary *facts* with which the planning will be concerned. The persistence of co-operation depends not only upon the desirability of accomplishing various purposes or ends, but upon how those involved in a process feel about the methods. There can be little question that democracy is a general term to designate all those processes by which such feelings and reactions can be gauged.

To describe the difference between the subjective satisfaction of those who are called upon to co-operate in a social program and the objective achievement of that program, it has been suggested that the terms "effective" and "efficient" be employed in a clearly differentiated sense.[4] Thus an action would be considered "effective" if it contributed toward the accomplishment of the group's or organization's purpose; while it would be considered "efficient" if it so satisfied the needs of the co-operating individuals that they did fully co-operate. An educational institution would be effective if it graduated individuals who possessed the education which the institution had been organized to give them. But it would be efficient only if these individuals, as well as those who staffed the institution, had been sufficiently satisfied to have given all of their energy and ability to teaching and learning. The use of the word "efficiency" to describe this state of affairs is a bit unusual; "efficiency" is usually seen in terms of an economical use of available resources. While this achieving of the "maximum result at minimum cost" is clearly related to staff morale and customer satisfaction, common usage makes the word "efficient" somewhat confusing in this context. For want of a better term, we shall nevertheless use the word "efficiency" in the following pages to describe a state of satisfaction among the co-operating group.

Obviously, continued operation of an organization or social group depends upon both effectiveness and efficiency. A college in which both teachers and students were very satisfied by the way things were done could yet not continue if its graduates failed to arrive at that state of education which they came to secure, and needed for later success. The failure to realize this fact has wrecked some splendid enterprises. But a college could not last, either, if faculty or student body were permanently dissatisfied, no matter how technically well-trained the students might be. In the latter case there would be too little democracy, in the former too much of it.

What is true of a college is equally true of government bodies. The conclusion can be simply stated in terms of responsibility. A responsible administration *may* fail in effectiveness, that is to say, it may fail to accomplish its purpose. Authoritarian administration is exposed to the opposite danger. It *may* fail, indeed it is often *bound to* fail, in efficiency; that is, in eliciting the continued co-operation of individuals.

PLANNING UNDER DEMOCRACY AND DICTATORSHIP

If we project the foregoing conclusion onto the broad canvas of the contrast between totalitarian autocracy and democracy, we are confronted with the startling conclusion (or shall it be called a working hypothesis?) that efficient planning is much more likely within the framework of democracy and its responsible administration. Planning in terms of a master plan, a blueprint such as the Five-Year Plan, is apt to be inefficient. As its execution progresses, it usually gets progressively out of joint. Any detailed analysis of the history of the Five-Year Plan will show this conclusion to be justified.[5] Such a conclusion does not by any means imply that the plan might not be — and in this example was — highly effective in forwarding the particular end in view, namely the industrialization of Russia and the collectivization of her agriculture. With Merriam, we conclude that "The nature of the democratic association is best adapted to management and planning; co-operation is the key to efficiency in planning. . . ."

To relate this specifically to our views concerning the judgment of the common man, the matter may be put thus: The collective judgment of the mass of men with a sense of workmanship absorbs more facts than any collection of experts would and is more likely to bring these facts to bear upon policy; the reason is that *collective* satisfactions are among the most important facts bearing upon the success of planning in the long run. We must underline, though, the truth that this observation holds only *in the long run*. For a short space of time, totalitarian methods of planning may give more satisfactory results. While the dynamism of the movement is in full swing, the enthusiasm on the part of its direct adherents may outweigh and overcome hostility on the part of the rest of the community. This is especially apt to be so if the enthusiasm is reinforced by terror. Thus a considerably higher efficiency may result than could have been obtained under a more responsible system. Why, then, does this efficiency fail to last?

Essentially, efficiency tends to break down under a totalitarian system because of the inability of such a system to shape the purpose in accordance with the needs which are felt by the community. Much thought about planning has gone astray for this reason: it assumed that in planning you start from scratch, that you can plan concerning our economy the way you can plan to build a house. This sort of assumption is the exact contrary of the fact; any planning for a developed economy is bound to be effective only so far as it is done in the light of exact knowledge as to the existing state of that economy. It is like planning the improvement of a farm that is already in operation. Existing resources and activities [6] should be utilized. This means continuous inventorying, surveying and consulting of persons concerned with the operation of these resources and the conduct of these activities.

Now, a system of terror is most undesirable as a setting for such inventorying, surveying, and consulting, as anyone will attest who has been able to observe the terror in action.[7]

The illusion of efficiency is created in both Russia and Germany by the fact that a very simple purpose, of concrete technological content, was superimposed upon the economy. In Germany it was preparation for war.[8] In Russia it was large-scale industrialization. Here it was, as we just said, not merely a matter of increasing industrial production proper, but of collectivizing, i.e., industrializing and mechanizing, Russian agriculture. Leaving aside the Nazi purpose, which obviously has no relevance to the planning purposes of America or any other democracy at peace, we may well ask: What would be the use of a Five-Year Plan in a highly industrialized country such as the United States or England? With us the peace-time problem is not one of stimulating production but of directing it into the right channels by sound public policies. It is not primarily a question of adding to production but of finding better ways and means of distributing the existing or potential produce. The need for rationalized planning in such an economy cannot be met by a blueprint for more and more production.

Russia had to "catch up" with the industrialized West. In her case it was and is essentially a matter of extending the "industrialist" spirit of rationalized production to the whole economy. It was and is an effort corresponding in many ways to what the Cecils worked for in Elizabethan England, Sully and Colbert in France: the development of a centrally directed national economy geared to give maximum production.[9] Stalinist Russia is a modernized form of mercantilism. Her great state trusts are not very different from the Elizabethan trading companies, chartered and directed by the Crown. But what good can such a program be to countries that are already highly industrialized, if not actually overdeveloped? In such countries, in which the emphasis is upon effective distribution, the customer is of paramount importance.

Effective development of such an advanced economy requires continuous adjustments in terms of customer preferences. "The greatest happiness of the greatest number" or "the largest amount of potential satisfaction" or "the largest real income for all" — or whatever you may specifically want to designate as the over-all purpose — this over-all purpose has to be broken down into concrete and immediate objectives. Such a breakdown requires testing existing policies by their effect upon the consumers, that is to say, the electorate composed of common men and women who have to "eat the pudding."

PLANNING COMMON IN AMERICAN HISTORY

Such planning is not novel. The opponents of particular planned policies are inclined to raise the cry that planning represents a radical departure, that it is "un-American." But there has always been planning on various levels in America. Indeed, the very founding of our Republic constituted one of the most far-reaching and effective planning acts. The constitution was designed and adopted by men who, confronted with widespread economic confusion and distress, "deliberately planned a way out." [10] Though governmental structure was a very important part of this plan, the primary task was, as Charles Beard showed in his *Economic Interpretation*, an economic one: interstate commerce, tariffs, currency and debts were among the primary problems for which the constitutional convention sought a solution. Such solutions were, of course, in no sense final. Periodic readjustments proved necessary, as conditions changed. Alexander Hamilton's *Report on Manufactures* (1791), Gallatin's report on internal improvements, Henry Clay's report on the "American System" of protective tariffs, the land and homestead policy (1862), the conservation program of Theodore

Roosevelt, and all the more recent efforts along similar lines represent important instances of a planned economic development. Different from these in intrinsic pattern as well as in purposive structure was, of course, the large-scale planning during the World War as well as our latest efforts to streamline mass production for war. Here the purpose was given: harnessing our industrial system for the defeat of an external enemy. But even in these, we can clearly see that over-all planning has been part and parcel of our system of government and of our developing economy.

HOW PLANNING AFFECTS THE COMMON MAN

If one traces these planning efforts, these impacts of the foresight of the few upon the economic fortunes of the many, he finds that such planning fits very well into the pattern of responsible administration which we have shown to be the basis of co-operation between the workmanship of expert and common man. Here is a rough sketch of how it functions. A need is widely felt and expresses itself in unrest and a demand for change among the public. Short-range remedies which are attempted fail to give the desired results, because a more thorough insight into conditions and trends is required. Thereupon either the government, or more often a group of specially interested and qualified persons, a civic group, at times deliberately organized for that purpose, will survey and inventory a complex field of activity, consult all the key persons at work in that field, and agree upon a far-flung policy, designed to remedy the ills or meet the needs which have given rise to the demand for planned activity.

Let me give you a rather modest, yet very characteristic illustration. One day in the late fall of 1934, Professor Curtis M. Hilliard and Mr. Frank Kiernan, President and Executive Secretary of the Massachusetts General Health Council, met for lunch. Their conversation turned to the Council. They attacked the problem of discovering some program for the Council that would make its influence felt and that would be worth while. Professor Hilliard suggested that the organization sponsor the creation of a Public Health Commission. He had been thinking of such a project for two or three years.[11] The plan was favorably received by the Central Health Council. A concrete proposal was drawn up, and steps were initiated to gain the approval of the Massachusetts State Department of Public Health and to secure the co-operation of other social agencies. The Public Health Council, composed as it is of sixteen organizations interested in public health, was strategically placed to initiate such a proposal. In spite of some vicissitudes, the Commission, whose work was financed by the Commonwealth Fund, was set up. In due time this commission, composed of key persons in the field, presented an extensive report to the Legislature, containing fifty-eight concrete proposals for legislation. Numerous social agencies, affected by the report's recommendations, took up the cudgels for one or another of them. Special-interest groups who felt their interests threatened by the proposals likewise became active in opposing them. Since the report covered a very wide field, ranging from smoke pollution to the sanitation of shellfish, diverse organizations such as the Associated Industries of Massachusetts and the Massachusetts Fish and Game Association came out against certain bills. The problem of "local autonomy" played a strong role in the opposition to two proposals which the Boston Board of Public Health disliked.

But after all is said and done, it is possible to say in retrospect today that the Commission worked well as a "planning" device. Of its fifty-eight proposals, seventeen have become law in the six years since it went into effect, and others will undoubtedly follow.[12]

This case of "planning" public-health measures is valuable in that it shows, in a comparatively neutral field, the way in which governmental officials and specialists, civic and interested pressure groups, are brought together through planning. They enable the legislatures and the public to act more effectively in an important field of public policy.

The New Image of the Common Man

THE CASE OF AGRICULTURE

You may consider this a very cumbersome method, and so it is. But as our industrial society becomes more complex, it is more important to avoid errors which may multiply the tensions. Secondary and tertiary effects often have far-reaching and disastrous consequences. Planning is not a theoretical undertaking, unrelated to the human beings involved. It is not the blueprint of some bureaucrat behind his desk. It is more and more definitely being related to the public. The Department of Agriculture's planning is today carried on in continuous consultation with farmers throughout the country. Long before war came to this country elaborate surveys and inventories were made by the experts in the Department. They reached the conclusion that a substantial increase in agricultural production would be necessary. How did they go about securing that increase? Did they, like bureaucrats in Germany and Russia, commandeer the farmers to put out the additional percentages? Did we threaten those who would not obey with concentration camps? Not at all. All over the country, the county planning committees were summoned, and discussions were held as to how such a purpose as a certain percentage of increase in the production of milk could be achieved. Such discussions went into great detail, naturally; for farmers think in concrete practical terms. Labor supply, grain prices, possible overproduction after the defense emergency had passed — all these and many others constituted part of the "planning" on this county level. Having listened to some of these discussions, I would not pretend that they were as good or as searching as they might have been. Visiting officials often seem to lack any genuine interest in what such committeemen have to say. This is perhaps natural, when one considers that these officials usually have to go to meeting after meeting, explaining the same ideas and listening to the same arguments.

But whatever the shortcomings today, there can be little doubt that these planning committees and the procedures of consultation represent a most important forward step in the direction of bringing the planning at the center into continuous live contact with the thought and the reactions of the public. If the procedures could be inspired by a bit more realism concerning the common man's way of thinking, if they could be a little less based upon the eighteenth-century ideas of a rationalist man, they would provide a definite solution. For the results of all these discussions go back to headquarters in Washington, and are digested and related to the overall plan.[13] The sense of workmanship is here operating on the two craftsman levels of highest and intermediary workmanship. Farmers and agricultural experts are seen co-operating in evolving the national policies in the field of their technical competence.

But what of the rest of the public? What about those

millions who consume agricultural produce every day, but cannot "tell the tail-end from the front-end of a cow"? There is a very real problem here, not only in planning, but in execution as well. Only beginnings have been made. Maybe the war will bring significant progress. The Department is now developing nutrition centers as the latest addition to our large-scale program of planning agriculture the democratic way. These centers will of course reach out to the ultimate consumer, more especially the housewife. We have, to date, relied upon our traditional machinery of representation, implemented by the newer informational services which I have described in the previous chapter, to give us that responsiveness to popular needs which responsible administration implies. But there is no reason why this may not be further extended by eliciting consumer responses on the part of the mass of common men and women throughout the United States. For such has already been the practice under the Food Stamp Plan of distributing surplus agricultural produce to the needy.

FOREIGN PARALLELS

While progress toward special forms of democratic planning has been noteworthy in American agriculture, other countries, relying upon more conventional techniques, have been successful in planning agricultural production, especially the Scandinavian countries and

Planning for the Public Good

Switzerland. The Swiss, who experienced near-famine conditions during World War I, when their grain supplies were throttled by the Allied blockade, decided upon a program of planning against the recurrence of such an emergency. Both in grain and in dairy products they evolved an ingenious system of increasing production without unduly increasing prices of agricultural foodstuffs. Though technical experts were at odds concerning the value of the system, the Swiss farmer and consumer had found a working compromise. This compromise, basically, amounted to distributing through taxes the cost of this national plan to the public at large, rather than levying it upon the poorest class through artificial price increases.

Britain likewise has had fair results with a conventional technique of fact-finding and projecting concerning a proposed public policy. It is the employment of Royal Commissions of Inquiry. Many of these Commissions have been of the greatest importance in laying the basis for "planning" in some important areas of public policy. Many years usually elapse before the reforms recommended by these Commissions find their way onto the statute books. This is at least in part because the "facts" which the particular Commission has brought out take a long time to penetrate the public thinking on that subject. But they decidedly affect public opinion, and as soon as a large enough part of the public recognizes the findings as applicable to the "jam" in hand, policy is formulated to deal with the need as recognized. Indeed, the efficacy of these Commissions has in recent years given rise to the demand that our own Congressional Investigating Committees might be similarly utilized. The Temporary National Economic Committee suggests the possible use of such Committees.[14]

PRESSURE GROUPS AND PLANNING

Experience both here and abroad suggests that "pressure groups," so-called, have a great deal to do with democratic planning. They seem to be both initiators of large-scale over-all plans, and destroyers of such plans. The Massachusetts public-health program affords as good an illustration here as the agricultural programs. This is perfectly natural in view of the vital role which pressure groups have come to play in the life of popular governments. It is very popular, and has been for some time, to fasten attention upon the negative aspect, and to decry such pressure groups as "the end of democracy." It is forgotten that there are few measures of lasting public importance the history of which could be written without giving extended attention to one or more pressure groups. The adoption as well as the abolition of prohibition, social insurance, labor legislation, public health and water power, and lately national defense — wherever one looks, he sees the dynamic impact of pressure groups upon public policy.

Planning for the Public Good

Can anyone who knows the story doubt that we would be without an army to defend our country, had it not been for the ceaseless, devoted activity of the National Emergency Committee of the Military Training Camps Association? If certain men had not banded together, raised the funds, and gone to Congress and the public with the idea, how could the idea have been popularized? The pressure groups, taken as a whole, are the channel through which the common man today makes himself felt. They form the means by which the public becomes articulate.[15]

Civic and interest groups operating in the field of their special concern collect all those citizens, those common men and women who, for one reason or another, have acquired greater knowledge of the facts than the rest of the community. They become so many self-propelled centers of "planning," that is, of "an organized effort to gather the facts, bring scientific insight upon any problem that may require the adoption of a public policy." In any complex field of policy, many different groups, in co-operation and conflict, will be seen participating in the task of arousing civic interest to the point where the common man becomes vitally concerned and ready to participate. Those who thunder against these groups, on account of their divisive effect, forget that only when intensely interested will a group of common men devote the time and energy which is required for understanding the facts of a given situation.

The New Image of the Common Man

They forget that most men will develop such interest only if the matter in hand is vitally related to their life. How can it be so related without touching upon those interests which are peculiarly theirs? A realistic conception of the common man shows that he will contribute his time and energy to those causes which touch his interest, not only his material interests, but his ideal ones as well. Some men will lean more in one direction, and some more in the other. But it is through membership in pressure groups that the common man participates in the planning and shaping of public policy.

A GLANCE AT THE WORLD

If planning in terms of a flexible end requires the continued participation of civic groups on a national level, this is even more true on the international level. The idea that international planning could be carried forward by the orders of a totalitarian dictator lacks all concrete content. It might be extraordinarily difficult to create machinery which would channel the preferences of common men throughout a world-wide organization, and to provide for the workable compromises. It is impossible to conceive of an efficient world economy planned according to a fixed and uniform end, such as is implied in totalitarian planning — or rather, the only possible conception is the organized exploitation of the peoples of the earth by the "planners," the master race to come.

[234]

Planning for the Public Good

Weighty arguments have been advanced in support of the contention that any planning at all is inconceivable on a world-wide scale.[16] Conservative economic thought has sought comfort in the reflection that national economic planning must fail, because all the major economic problems are international in scope, and yet international planning cannot be conceived because no world-wide authority of sufficient power can be expected to arise or be established within the foreseeable future. However, if instead of this totalitarian concept of planning, a democratic concept is established, if planning is seen as arising from the continued, organized effort to utilize social "technique in the determination of policy," why then international planning can definitely be envisaged within any framework of peoples who are effectively united through a common union government. Nations, indeed, would operate somewhat in the way in which pressure groups function within the national context.[17]

CONCLUSION

The common man is ready enough to co-operate with even the most far-sighted planning for use. If the broad underlying conception of a policy is sound, in the sense of being meaningfully related to vital needs, he is either participating through special groups of which he is a member, or he is inclined to leave the details to the workman in the field. For he knows that if he himself were the workman, he would want to be recognized as knowing a bit better than the other fellow how to do his own job. Why expostulate about the conflict between democracy and planning, when planning really depends upon a functioning democracy? The future depends upon the gradual solution of problems whose complexity makes it essential to plan for their solution.

The industrial system within which we live has come to stay, for better or worse. The lives of all of us depend upon it. We have lost the charming eighteenth-century faith that all will be well if you "leave well enough alone." The pre-established harmony of "this best of all possible worlds" is no more. A realistic analysis of the conditions at the time when people believed in such natural harmony has revealed that it did not exist even then. It does not make sense now. The sense of workmanship that is the precious possession of every common man who has to earn his living by the labor of his faculties, has taught him that if you want something to grow you have to plant it, and that if you want to plant it, you have to prepare the seed-bed, and that if you want to prepare the seed-bed, you have to have manure to put onto it, and so forth ad infinitum through the seasons. Planning is good husbandry, and good husbandry presupposes a knowledge of a lot of things.

Such knowledge is needed on many different levels

and in many different assignments. Every useful member of society is a good workman in some field of activity. There is no room for any elite of self-appointed supermen who concoct blueprints and master plans without regard to the thinking and the knowledge of all those who are concerned in the plan. The broader the plan, the broader must be the basis of planning. Planning for the public good depends upon setting it up in such a way that the public can participate in determining what is good.

CHAPTER VIII

The Elite

---

*Universal history . . . is at the
bottom the history of the great
men who have worked here . . .*

— CARLYLE

WILLIAM JAMES was very fond of telling a
certain story on himself — an encounter he once had
with a neighbor up at Lake Chocorua. James was mending his stone wall, or trying to, and for some time had
been fussing over a stone that he could not seem to fit
into place. Whichever way he put it in, it came sliding
down, or it wiggled. Finally, his farmer neighbor (who
evidently had been watching him for some time) offered
to help him. They exchanged the usual remarks about
the weather while the man, with one or two deft moves,
put the rock down so that it sat as if it had been there
since eternity. James complimented him upon his skill,
and with a twinkle in his eye the farmer replied, "Glad
to help you, Professor. This kind of work takes brains,

you know." James was, of course, a philosopher of the free society. As one commentator has summed up his viewpoint: "Nations, arts, religions, science itself, are all given direction and character by the free initiative, the effort and activity of individuals. Give individuality a chance, enable initiative and freedom, and life and growth are assured to society." [1]

As contrasted with this generous outlook, men like Carlyle have asserted the view that most human achievements are the creations of great men. These theories extolling the select few have exercised a profound influence not only in Europe, but in America. They have not only furnished welcome rationalizations for antidemocratic sentiments from the Federalists to the present day, but provided the basis for much fascist ideology. These ideas are rooted in reaction against democratic equality, and hence are endemic in democratic society. Men whose intellectual achievements command respect have in recent years been led astray, especially by Pareto's extraordinary conceit.

Obviously, many of these writers and thinkers are not fascists — far from it. The absurdities of the traditional rationalist conception of democracy and of the common man have been responsible for much of this antidemocratic sentiment. Only a realistically balanced concept of the common man can be the basis for a sound view. Such a sound view sees human group life as oscillating between two patterns: the pattern in which co-operation of the members is mostly elicited, and the pattern in which such co-operation is forced upon them by a self-appointed group or elite. It is, of course, the latter view which is propagated by the totalitarian philosophies.

THE NINETEENTH CENTURY

Throughout the nineteenth century, doctrines extolling the role of the select few were popular. Indeed, there was a continuous succession of elite doctrines. We saw earlier how Burke and Bagehot and Balfour, insisting upon agreement on fundamentals, each expounded an elite doctrine, according to which "the highest class of wealth and leisure should have an influence far out of proportion to its mere number." Such views, with advocates in all countries, represent the intellectualist reaction against the forward march of democratization. As the belief in the common man spread, the belief in the uncommon man was advocated with renewed ardor by poets and philosophers, historians and sociologists, revolutionaries and reactionaries.

Apprehensions concerning the common man have given rise to elite doctrines in this country from the very beginning. The Federalists continually harped on the wisdom of the educated classes. In his monumental *Main Currents in American Thought*, Vernon L. Parrington has traced the interweaving of this theme with the broadening currents of democratic outlook. The belief in the aristocracy has, after all, deep roots in the Calvinist conception of the elect under predestination. Speaking of the Puritans, Parrington says: "Their Utopia must be a close-knit church-state, with authority reserved to the aristocracy of Christian talent." The self-interest of the lay and clerical leaders found a perfect expression in the doctrine of an elite of successful servants of the Lord, the type so vividly portrayed in *The House of the Seven Gables*.

This glance backward shows us that here, as in Europe, elite ideas come first and common-man ideas afterwards. All that the forward march of democracy did was to bring these elite ideas more fully out into the open, as they were adapted to successive stages in the evolution of an expanding industrial society. The shaping and molding of these elite theories, both here and in Europe, occur in response to two distinct stimuli: ideology and experience — experience, that is, with the actual workings of democracy, party machines, and the rest. While the two stimuli continuously reinforce each other, they are nevertheless distinct and distinguishable in the development of elite *theories*. As was pointed out in the beginning of these pages, certain ideological forces — Marxism, Freudianism, and the rest — undermined the eighteenth-century rationalism upon which the traditional belief in the common man rested. In doing so, they provided ideological points of departure for new elite theories. Thus Marxism stands at the cradle of the elite theories of Mosca and Pareto.

PARETO'S ANTIRATIONALISM

What such ideologues usually fail to take into account is the fact that the antirationalist "discoveries" of the class struggle, or the subconscious drive, undermine the belief in the uncommon man as much as they undermine the belief in the common man. Pareto's obscurantist terminology hides, but cannot eliminate, the fact that elites vary greatly in importance in different social bodies. Yet Pareto does not address himself to the very urgent problem of determining the conditions under which elites play these varying roles. Instead, he treats us, with a great display of "scientific" haughtiness, to a lot of platitudes. In every society, he says, there are some people who are better than others at certain jobs. Indeed, he defines a member of an elite as one who is better at a job.[2] But his real spite (and Pareto was a very spiteful man) comes to light in his assertion that popular representation is a fiction: "Poppycock grinds no flour." "Everywhere one finds a governing class of relatively few individuals that keeps itself in power partly by force, and partly by the consent of the subject class."[3] This sentence is an almost verbatim repetition of Mosca's statement concerning the ruling class: "In all societies two classes of people appear, a class that rules and a class that is ruled." [4] The propagandist slant of both is anti-democratic. They both identify democracy and plutocracy — a view which has become odious to many of us, since it serves as one of Gayda's and Goebbels' propaganda slogans. While there is a good deal that is sound in their analysis of plutocratic government, the "realistic" dissection of what pretended to be democracy in France or Italy in or around 1900 hardly settles the general problem of democracy.

Pareto himself might have conceded this; for in one of his frequent "asides" he asserts that "the best government now in existence . . . is the government of Switzerland, especially in the forms it takes on in the small cantons — forms of direct democracy." Some kind of normative ideal seems here implied, in spite of the fact that Pareto has just exclaimed against normative ideals. He insists that the statement "a government is best" has no meaning, "unless some explanation is given of the term 'best.'" Pareto amplifies that objection to the idea of a "best government" by saying that such a notion alludes in a very indefinite way to the various individual and social utilities. [5]

Almost the central concern of Pareto's thought is to show that nonlogical conduct is prevalent in society. Pareto makes a tremendous effort to prove that humans do not act logically. He is plainly preoccupied with traditional eighteenth-century rationalism. This rationalism confronted him in two powerful currents: The political phraseology of the French Revolution, and the verbiage of the so-called "classical" economists, more especially in the shape of that rationalist homunculus known as "the economic man." As a Franco-Swiss economist, he was engulfed by these two currents and he struggled all his life to free himself from their outlook by combating their extreme rationalism. But in thus asserting the persistence of nonlogical conduct, Pareto considered himself much more original than he actually was. Few historians or philosophers had adopted this outlook; at the very moment he was ponderously demolishing the straw man he had set up, antirationalism was already celebrating its most extreme triumphs in the Nietzschean philosophy of the superman. Interestingly enough, Nietzsche's inspiration came from another Swiss, the historian-philosopher Jakob Burckhardt, who in his *Culture of the Renaissance* and other works had given expression to his dislike of the democratic age.

These ramifications, which could be indefinitely extended, show vividly how these elite theories, these antidemocratic currents, are not limited to any one country, but occurred all over Europe and America. It is important to insist upon this fact at the present time, because there has been a lamentable tendency of late to confuse our thought by injecting the propagandist notion that certain ideas are peculiar to certain peoples. Antirationalist and elite theories are at least as common in democratic countries as elsewhere. They constitute, as we said, a reaction to both democratic ideology and democratic reality. Thus Mencken's bitter and sarcastic views of democracy which dominated the "lost generation" were inspired by disappointment over the workings of democracy no less than by the reading of Nietzsche or Bernard Shaw. And the outburst of academic enthusiasm for Marx on one side and for Pareto on the other was similarly conditioned.

ELITE DOCTRINES WIDESPREAD

When we look over the field of political writing of the last hundred years, we find a veritable avalanche of writers extolling the virtues of the few who are wise, if not virtuous, as contrasted with the low-brow belief in the common man. In fact, so imposing is the list of writers that we are forced to the conclusion that it simply was not smart to do otherwise than praise the upper class and its merits. With Bentham, we might sardonically remark that "as long as wealth and government have had existence, the powers of poetry and oratory have been employed in singing the praises of the powerful, the dignified, and the wealthy." To poetry and oratory, the nineteenth century added the social "sciences." Here are just a few names out of the long parade: In England we have Carlyle, Ruskin, Arnold, Maine, Lecky, and Macaulay; in America John

The New Image of the Common Man

Adams, Fisher Ames, John Calhoun, and Irving Babbitt; in France Stendhal, Taine, and Maurras; in Germany Marx, Engels, Nietzsche, and Treitschke; in Italy Mosca; in Switzerland Burckhardt and Pareto; in Spain Ortega y Gasset and Unamuno. Besides, much official Catholic thought, including a number of papal bulls, falls into the same category. Obviously, it would require more than a volume to deal with all these extraordinary thinkers adequately. The history of anti-democratic elite doctrines is a dominant theme in the history of Western thought in the last three generations.

I do not pretend to claim that in isolating and dissecting their elite theories I have dealt with them adequately or even "fairly." Indeed, the merits of these writers are so well known that their adherence to these elite doctrines merely illustrates the formidable array of intellect which the believer in the common man has to cope with today. Since these men believed in an elite, they did not believe in the common man; that much is obvious. He who does believe in the common man will be well advised to scrutinize with care anything these gentlemen offer in the way of "self-evident" truths.

Both Marx and Pareto assure us, of course, that their views are strictly "scientific" and devoid of bias of any kind. Whoever disagrees with them is simply engaging in unscientific "value judgments." It is a peculiar paradox of nineteenth-century thinking that this naïve unawareness of the unproven major premises of "science" itself is found most commonly in writers who insist that all human beings are motivated primarily by irrational factors. Thus Marx and Engels insist upon economic self-interest, Pareto upon residues (sentiments); but they failed to analyze their own conduct in such terms.[6]

WHO EXTOLS THE ELITE?

This vainglorious wiser-than-thou attitude is also characteristic of other believers in the elite, such as Carlyle and Nietzsche. Are we then confronted with a common psychological condition? Is the elite an escape for men who have been unable to take their turn in the line of common men — who were indisposed to wait until the barber said, "Who's next?"

It is a well-known fact that the intellectual is apt to be maladjusted in childhood and youth. Frequently he is ridiculed and even persecuted by his more normal schoolmates. His superior mind becomes the avenue of escape from this hostile environment. Often the teacher — the ostensible authority maintaining law and order — has to intervene to protect such an "ugly duckling" against his equals. It is evident that that kind of childhood begets a sense of frustration and a disposition to frown upon the common crowd.

Whether the particular individual turns toward revolution or reaction, it is very natural for him to think of himself as part of a select group which, when supported by authority, will constitute a class destined to direct the crowd of common men. As most individuals of this type develop a distinct intellectual aptitude, a professional craftsmanship, they will increasingly associate with others of their kind. These associations confirm them in their natural proclivity to look upon themselves as different and apart. Normally, such individuals have rationalized their personal experience and projected it into their intellectual work. Whether as historians or sociologists, philosophers or poets, such men have helped to build and perpetuate the idea of the elite. These intellectuals, being themselves members of a select group, were especially affected individuals — men who had felt with particular vehemence their apartness from the common men.

THOMAS CARLYLE

Just one hundred years ago, Thomas Carlyle published *Heroes, Hero-worship and the Heroic in History*. He here sounded the shrill, almost agonized, call for the superman which Friedrich Nietzsche was to magnify about fifty years later in *Thus Spake Zarathustra* (1883–1885). "Universal history . . . is at bottom the history of the great men who have worked here. They were the leaders of men, these great ones; the modelers, patterns, in a wide sense creators, of whatsoever the general mass of men contrived to attain." They may be prophets, priests, poets, or men of letters; but — "The commander over men; he to whose will our wills are to be subordinated, and loyally surrender themselves, and find their welfare in doing so, may be reckoned the most important of great men." Thus Carlyle. And why? Because "He is practically the summary for us of *all* the various figures of heroism . . . He is called Rex, Regulator, Roi: our own name is still better: King, König . . ." Two years later he pushed these thoughts further in the direction of an elite; in *Past and Present* (1843) he envisages an aristocracy of talent. "Democracy, which means despair of finding any heroes to govern you, and contented putting up with the want of them," makes it "a dire necessity of Nature's to bring in her Aristocracies, her best, even by forcible methods." The common man is incapable of taking care of himself; liberty consists in doing what is right; the common man has a right to demand that he be compelled to do the right. "Whatsoever forwards him in that, let it come to him even in the shape of blows and spurnings, is liberty: whatsoever hinders him, were it wardmotes, open-vestries, pollbooths, tremendous cheers, rivers of heavy-wet, is slavery." To do the right thing is liberty, Carlyle seems to shout; but if you ask who is to say what is right, his answer is "your Real Superiors." The capitals, we may surmise, are to indicate the emphasis of our desperate hero-worshiper. "The toiling millions of mankind," he cries, "are in most vital need and passionate instinctive desire of Guidance." And to round out this fantastic sermon, Carlyle adds that "the smallest item of human Slavery is the oppression of man by his Mock-Superiors." The lucky son of mid-Victorian England is not likely to get more than a wry smile from his fellow men of the age of Hitler.[7]

And who are these Real Superiors going to be? The "Leaders of Industry." They, Carlyle proclaims, "are virtually the Captains of the World; if there is no nobleness in them, there will never be an Aristocracy more." Poor old Thyssen; he, protagonist of a fancied managerial revolution, will surely be moved to tears by Carlyle's prophetic vision of the world-governing elite. That Carlyle should address himself to the captains of industry as the future noblemen, the emerging elite, is one of the strangest features of his strange and turgid protest against the ravages of industrialism. With Goethe's Faust a common man might well exclaim: "*Mir wird bei alledem so dumm, als ging mir ein Mühlrad im Kopf herum* (I feel as stupid after all you have said as if a miller's wheel were whirling in my head)."

NIETZSCHE'S SUPERMAN

Nietzsche, longing with equal passion for a new dawn and an age of supermen, took a view less practical but bolder yet. He foresaw favorable conditions for more comprehensive control structures. ". . . I am writing for a genus of human beings who are not yet here: for the lords of the world, Britains, Americans, Russians. . . ." These future lords of the world, Nietzsche thought, might be bred in international families which would make it their purpose to breed such a master race — a new, stupendous aristocracy — a higher type of human being. These men, due to their superiority of will, knowledge, wealth, and influence, would utilize a democratic Europe as a most pliable tool for seizing the world. Their ultimate purpose: to mold "man" himself. The time is coming, he said, for a new kind of politics.[8] But unlike Carlyle, Nietzsche envisages the highest type of man as a philosopher-lawgiver, a man who has the will and the ability to educate mankind. With Plato, he envisages the philosopher as king.[9]

All elitists, but more especially Carlyle and Nietzsche, resound with Platonism. Indeed, the elite is a modern version of Plato's guardian class. This is significant not only because of the Greek foundation of the state-church idolatry but more especially because Plato's political thought is itself directed against "democracy."

THE CULT OF VIOLENCE

Nietzsche shows with particular vividness that his deeper impulse is purely emotional, reactive, irrational; he never states in any but the vaguest terms what need or purpose these philosopher-lawgivers, these supermen, are to serve. His formula for the ultimate purpose "to mold man" is obviously devoid of content. For what is the mold? That, precisely, is the question. Like Hitler, he seems to shout: "Give them power, and they will show you." The fact that Nietzsche and Carlyle would probably be revolted by the terror of the masters of the totalitarian slave states must not mislead us; the sensitive intellectual is apt to recoil from the concrete application of his ideas. But both Carlyle and Nietzsche are so full of outbursts about how these "leaders" must and will be hard, cold, icy, brutal, and the rest, that their title to being prophets of fascism must remain undisputed. If Goering, commenting upon the brutalities of the concentration camp, said, "Where one planes, shavings fall," Nietzsche wrote, "From wars one must learn to sacrifice many and to take one's cause seriously enough, so as not to care about human lives"; and finally Carlyle proclaimed life to be "a battle and a march, a warfare with principalities and powers." Characteristically, he loves the "conquerors, Romans, Normans, Russians, Indo-English; founders of what we call Aristocracies." Such men of steel have a "divine right" to found such governments, seeing that they are truly the bravest, the best, "and conquering characteristically a confused rabble of the worst." And why do they have this divine right? Because they have been tried in the "greatest Law-Court known," namely, history.

It is within this setting of ideas that Carlyle's demand

for an elite must be seen: "That Europe requires a real Aristocracy, a real Priesthood, or it cannot continue to exist." "Aristocracy and Priesthood, a Governing Class and a Teaching Class: these two, sometimes separate, and endeavoring to harmonize themselves, sometimes conjoined as one, and the King a Pontiff-King: — there did no Society exist without these two vital elements, there will none exist." It is absolutely essential to contemplate these phrases in their original form, to ponder them in their excited violence: for it is in this smithy that the crisis of democracy was forged.

"The Wiser, Braver: these, a virtual Aristocracy everywhere and everywhen, do in all Societies that reach any articulate shape, develop themselves into a ruling class, and Actual Aristocracy, with settled modes of operating." [10] In this statement, Carlyle affirms what at other times seems more nearly an overwhelming need. This uncertainty as to whether to speak of an elite as a norm, an imperative, or an actuality, is present in all writers on the subject. Naturally; for practically any generalizations concerning man or society can be put in either the imperative or the indicative mood.

There is nevertheless a significant difference here between Carlyle, Nietzsche, and other writers of a certain type on one hand, and Marx or Pareto on the other. The elitists are really, if we look further into this difference of emphasis, of two kinds. The man who is disgusted with the shallow materialism of the nineteenth century cries out against it and insists upon an emotional spiritualism. Both Carlyle and Nietzsche are acknowledged as great moral challengers. They see the elite as the carriers of the new spirit, indeed of all spirit. Very different is the inspiration of the other kind of elitist. Men like Marx and Pareto are disgusted that so much emotionalism and prejudice are still left in a supposedly rational world. They sternly demand that these irrational factors be recognized for what they are. To them the elite consists in the keen intellects who "tear away the masks" — a favorite expression of Pareto's.

THE COMMUNIST ELITE

Karl Marx's doctrine [11] of the elite is rather inexplicit, but nevertheless of central importance. It forms part and parcel of his class concept. In every class, but more especially in the proletarian class, he believes there will be found men, uncommon men, who possess a sharper than usual sense of historical necessities, and who possess the courage and will power to act upon their insight. In the *Communist Manifesto* a whole section is devoted to a discussion of the relation between the Communists and the proletariat. The Communists are described as the active, forward-driving, class-conscious element of the proletariat — in short, as its predestined leaders. "They are ahead of the rest of the mass of proletariat in their comprehension of the conditions, the development, and the general results of the proletarian movement." "They represent the future of the movement." The idea of the elite as a ruling class is, of course, implied in Marx's doctrine of the state as the executive committee of the entire bourgeois class.

Altogether, the class character of society was being increasingly recognized about a hundred years ago. The problems of class conflict had been brought out into the open by the French Revolution. The writings of Burke and other defenders of the *status quo* had further emphasized this aspect, as we have seen, and Lorenz von Stein's epochal *History of Social Movements in France* (1847) had given these generalizations a solid factual foundation. Much of de Tocqueville's philosophizing about American democracy was concerned with what might be the results of a classless society or, to speak more accurately, of a society with a fluid class structure; de Tocqueville, too, posed the question as to whether there might not arise a new aristocracy of wealth, and he warned Americans to be on the lookout for it. If such an aristocracy should become stratified, it might have serious consequences. Fifty years later, Thorstein Veblen saw such a class firmly established: the leisure class. But these general class theories frequently confused, rather than clarified, the problem of an elite. In Marx's doctrine the Communists are clearly envisaged as the elite. They are the select part of the proletarian class, which does not own the means of production.

In other class theorists the question as to who constitutes the elite remains obscure.

THE RULING CLASS AS ELITE

The problem was squarely faced, however, by Gaetano Mosca and Vilfredo Pareto. Indeed, Pareto's and Mosca's thought revolves around the elite problem. This was clearly expressed in the title of Mosca's book: *The Ruling Class*. Pareto, who systematized and developed Mosca's ideas, sought, however, to give the idea a broader sociological basis.

The relationship of the two writers is somewhat controversial.[12] Since Pareto's elite theory is of broader scope and rests, as we have already seen, upon an explicit criticism of the rationalist concept of man, we shall concentrate upon it here, in spite of the fact that it is wrapped up in the weird vocabulary by which Pareto chose to obscure his ideas.[13] The elite, as we have seen, consists of the people who have the highest indices in their branch of activity. Thus, an exceptional thief is said to be a member of Pareto's elite. This is no parody, but an actual illustration given by Pareto. This kind of elite concept, then, pretends to be purely functional, and simply means the best in every kind of activity in a given society. That Pareto is here making one of his typical displays of much greater objectivity than he actually possesses is shown by the fact that a few sections later he speaks of the elite as the "upper stratum of society." [14] He has no intention of making earnest with a genuinely functional concept of leadership; it would lead him toward democracy. It is, of course, impossible to deny the fact that there are exceptional painters, plumbers, writers, and scientists — in short, that there exist great differences in functional excellence. But this patent fact proves little unless it can be shown that these persons together constitute a separate and distinct group.

No attempt is made by Pareto to show that the "elite," as defined by him, possesses a distinct group character; if he had made it, it would, no doubt, have failed, for these several exceptional persons do not constitute a cohesive group. Why, then, assert that there are such exceptional persons? Essentially, I believe, in order to provide an unobjectionable starting point for the ideas which Pareto wishes to set forth concerning the "governing elite."

Who, then, is comprised within this governing elite? "Individuals who directly or indirectly play some considerable part in government," Pareto answers.[15] We do not learn much more about it. The argument remains tautological, just as in Mosca the ruling class is said to consist of the class of people who rule. Both writers smuggle in as an unproven assumption or major premise what is the most problematical part of all elite doctrines, namely, (a) that those who play a role in the government constitute a coherent group, and (*b*) that they possess distinguishing characteristics. The second of these is, of course, implied in Pareto's general definition of an "elite," of which the "governing elite" is supposed to be a part.

As we said, it is undoubtedly true that we can classify each functional set, such as lawyers, into effective, ineffective, and indifferent, because of the technological standards involved. Yet it is the very contention of the critical view of government which has given rise to democracy to assert that such a classification cannot be undertaken with reference to the function of "governing" or "ruling." That is the reason why it is considered *least unsatisfactory* to let the common man decide periodically whether he wants to go on with the particular crowd that is in or "turn the rascals out." In short, we must reject Pareto's trick of putting over on us the assumption that there are such valid standards of what is an effective performance of the task of governing, by saying that there is, under democracy, no such thing as a "governing elite," although there are superiorities. In view of the false implications it seems, however, undesirable to call these functionally superior persons an "elite." This is not to deny that in other than democratic societies, from which most of Pareto's and Mosca's examples are drawn, there may indeed be a governing elite. Just as we said that there is at times "a state" and "a sovereign," but not always, so now we say that there exists at times "a governing elite," but not always. We reject the proposition that there must always be a governing elite, or a ruling class.

The foregoing conclusion is strikingly reinforced by once more asking: Do those who play a role in the government constitute a coherent group? Neither Pareto nor Mosca offer any but historical evidence, drawn mostly from nondemocratic societies. Mosca could consequently classify political societies into various kinds of aristocracies: military and priestly, hereditary and land-owning aristocracies, aristocracies of liquid wealth and aristocracies of merit. The last is, of course, the concession of Mosca to democratic verbiage as it was current at the time. But the use of such an expression as "aristocracy" or "elite" obscures rather than elucidates the situation under genuinely democratic conditions. For those possessing "merit" must be divided into those who possess the capacity for workmanship in a given field of activity (whatever that field may be), and those called upon to formulate public policies because their general outlook coincides with that of the majority, and they possess merit only in that they are "representative." Pareto's remark about representation being poppycock is a poor substitute for a realistic analysis of this phenomenon — one of the most important in the whole field of politics.[16]

In the light of the continuous *changes* in the composition of the majority, it is not possible to say, under conditions such as prevail in a functioning democracy, that those who play some considerable part in government constitute a cohesive group. The "facts" which Pareto and Mosca adduce in support of their contention are highly questionable. They are on the one hand drawn from such journalistic accounts of pre-World-War French politics as de Jouvenel's smarty *La République des Camarades*, and on the other from Marxist and anarchist interpretations of English and American society as "plutocracies." Even granting for the moment that the "facts" were correct, this would merely argue that democratization was incomplete, or, in the light of de Tocqueville's warning, on the retreat.

REVOLUTION

Having constructed their erroneous (because too universal) ruling-class or elite doctrine, both Mosca and Pareto proceeded to devote a good deal of attention to the problem of the circulation of such classes or elites. This idea of class circulation had become increasingly popular in the decades following Marx's enunciation of the doctrine of the class struggle. The various forms which it took all represent attempts to correct the Marxist view by a more adequate generalization of the facts of history. Theories of class circulation are in a sense the political birthmark of all these elaborate bourgeois sociologies — they all reveal the deeper propagandistic intention to "disprove" Marxism. It was certainly a gain to have the propaganda virus of the doctrine of the class struggle thus counteracted. But in the process a Fascist position was adopted, just as in the practical realm Fascism followed the Communist revolution. By going back to history, these writers brought forward categories which generalized conditions in the past, and then insisted that these must be true for the future.

Now there is no question that in search of antirevolutionary, that is to say, reactionary formulas Pareto and others brought together many enlightening insights concerning the nature of social change. Thus, Pareto's theory of revolutions [17] is not without value. But through their insistence that past experience covered all experience, these theorists obscured the one-directional creative change in human society.

To put the matter succinctly with reference to the elite doctrine of Pareto: where there is an elite or ruling class, it will change or circulate, but all the facts of history showing how such elites have circulated proves nothing concerning the kind of society in which no such elite can be shown to exist.

ELITISM A REACTION

It would seem, then, that scientific elite theorists assume what they should attempt to prove — namely, that there exists necessarily an elite in every society. A strictly empirical and inductive attempt to show that such elites have existed in the past does not prove that. The delight with which Pareto dwells upon historical examples of actual elites, asserting that they confirm his theory, simply reveals his bias in favor of such an elite. Is it not curious, anyway, that the very writers, such as Pareto, who continually emphasize the role of the non-logical in human conduct, should at the same time exhibit such a decided interest in any kind of empirical evidence? That is what they think of as "positive" proof, as "scientifically" conclusive. Yet does not all the evidence concerning human society show that past experience "proves" little about the future? Could anyone, in the year 1600, by examining the evidence to date, have given an adequate description of the economy or government two hundred years later — of parliamentary government in Britain, or the Constitution of the United States?

Elite theorists, then, exaggerate the rationality of human society. Even when they thunder against rationalism they build their appeal upon attacks on the obsolete foundations of the eighteenth-century belief in the common man. Yet in either interpreting society as molded by an inevitable sequence of social forces, or picturing man as an inevitable result of psychic drives, these writers unwittingly destroyed as well the foundations for the belief in uncommon men, in an elite.

The Elite

The same exaggerated rationalism which inspired the now obsolete concept of the common man is central in these elite theories. The positivistic radicalism of Marx and Pareto seeks to apply to all social phenomena the mechanistic and quantitative view of man and society which French politics and English economics espoused throughout the nineteenth century. But those who fled from this type of super-rationalism to such views as were expounded by Carlyle and Nietzsche likewise exaggerated the importance of rationalism. The frantic re-assertion of the importance of emotions, sentiments, and values stems from an overemphasis upon the same mechanistic and quantitative view. In this respect Marx and Pareto on the one hand and Carlyle and Nietzsche on the other represent opposite poles in their approach to the problems of man and society. This difference in their reaction to the industrial reality has obscured for many observers their common inclination to overstress either the extent to which the human relationship in our society is rationalized, *or* the extent to which it could be.

REACTION: FEUDAL AND BUREAUCRATIC

In this overemphasis they resemble each other strikingly, as they also do in their subconscious inclination to reach back to an older pattern of society. This older pattern of an authoritarian hierarchy, feudal and/or bureaucratic, forms their common background. They are all offspring of a society containing as yet many feudal remnants. This is important, for no man is thoroughly rational, but is motivated in his thought and action and in his creative impulses by the traditions and modes of behavior prevalent in the society within which he is placed. The elite theorists are no exception to this general rule. Disturbed by the state of society in which they find themselves, in seeking for a remedy they fall back upon feudal and bureaucratic ideas which have dominated an earlier phase and are still influential. Bolshevism and Fascism are practical applications of these elite theories. Stalinism seeks to bureaucratize society, whereas Fascism attempts to refeudalize it.[18]

These attempts to return to a preceding pattern of society and political organization are in spite of their vast scope psychologically similar to a recurrent feature of individual human behavior. When confronted with a difficult situation growing out of a novel undertaking, one falls back upon older habits. The offended bride will rush back to weep on her mother's shoulder, if formerly she depended upon her maternal parent for protection and guidance. "Restorations" are attempted after revolutionary upheavals. Rationalized industrialism has confronted western man with a range of difficulties commensurate with its revolutionary impact upon all phases of life. Impatient with the slow process of gradual adjustment and of universal education, men revert to

The Elite

an older, less mature pattern of social ordering in which the conquering few, convinced of their superiority, monopolized the task of deciding what needed to be done. Out of the very bowels of industrialism there are, then, recruited individuals who will hark back to ways of thinking which may have been preserved in forgotten corners, such as the harsh paternal rule of Carlyle's Calvinist boyhood, the Prussian school in which Karl Marx sat, or the deferential peasants on estates of large landowners in Sicily where Mosca's cradle stood. Although all these were social institutions on the wane, they embodied ways of thinking sharply contrasting with the expanding industrialism and with the broadening democracy.

The concepts of the "elite" and the "ruling class" are useful only in analyzing and describing the non-co-operative patterns of society. The new concept of the common man, as here presented, provides the central idea for analyzing and describing the co-operative pattern. We have seen that responsible leadership rests upon the common man's recognition of the superior workmanship of some members of the society in performing particular functional tasks. The basic, commonly felt needs permit the common man through his own sense of workmanship to evaluate a workmanlike performance without especial intellectual equipment. Everyone knows when the shoe no longer pinches.

The New Image of the Common Man

PUBLIC–OPINION POLLS

A striking development of recent years has been the public-opinion polls developed by market-research technicians. These polls apply highly specialized methods of testing and sampling to the common man. The purpose is to ascertain the opinions of the public about issues of the day. Interestingly enough, these polls have been attacked again and again on the ground that they endanger representative government. These arguments usually take forms very similar to those which were advanced by antidemocratic elite theorists from Burke to Balfour.[19] As a pioneer in this field of activity has stated emphatically, "There has always been a fear of the majority at the back of the minds of many intelligent critics of the polls." While this is true of quite a few who do indeed distrust the common man and do not want to hear what his opinions are, it is not true of all. For there has always been a quite opposite opinion to the effect that these polls create a false impression by the way the questions are asked and the results presented — indeed, some people have charged conscious manipulation. But even after discarding some unproven accusations, an unresolved element of doubt remains.

The public-opinion polls base their claims to authority and reliability upon their results in elections. These claims are all right as far as they go. Elections present clear-cut alternatives and the questions asked of those interviewed present little difficulty of interpretation. It is always a matter of asking *Are you for Roosevelt or Willkie? Whom do you favor?* — and so forth. The reliability of the polls in dealing with questions of this type proves little regarding their reliability in polling the public on issues of a general nature. When a poll asks *Should women replacing men in defense industries receive the same pay?* you get one result. If you ask *Is it practicable for women to receive the same pay?* you get another. If you ask *Are women likely to receive the same pay?* you get still another. Illustrations of this kind are provided by practically every poll. The extremely interesting results of the *Fortune* poll published in December, 1941 — concerning the attitudes of Americans toward postwar problems — are subject to a variety of interpretations.

It is in the selection and phrasing of issues to be presented to the public that we face the most doubtful aspect of public-opinion polls. The only answer seems to lie in providing a sufficient number of polls. The recent establishment of the Public Opinion Research Center at the University of Denver is a desirable development from this standpoint. Backed by a national foundation, this organization will be ready to make test polls for any civic or scientific organization that requires such services, on a cost basis. The government has also been developing special polls. Such polls are well adapted to guide service departments in learning the reaction of sections of the public who are affected by their activities. In short, just as in the case of propaganda, the answer to those who fear the effect of polls upon public opinion is that the remedy for polls is more polls. "The best guarantee for the maintenance of a vigorous democratic life lies not in concealing what people think . . ." "The real tyranny in America will not come from a better knowledge of how majorities feel about questions of the day. . . . Tyranny comes from ignorance of the power and wants of the opposition." [20] We do not want an elite doctrine to stop us from knowing what the common man thinks. Neither do we want the elite idea to inject itself into the thinking about the polls themselves: that only certain people, whether they be commercial organizations, civic groups, or even the government, are qualified to carry on such polls.

CONCLUSION

The underlying reason for all the argument about an elite is the uncertainty of the future. No matter how intense is the quest for certainty, we can never know whether we took the best course of action. In the political field above all, we can never know what might have happened had we adopted another course than the one we took. It is this never-ending argument about what might have been which lends fascination

to the study of the past. That is why it is a matter
ultimately of belief. Carlyle and other elitists thought
that great men shape history. Democracy's belief is in
the common man. We believe that he knows best what
job should be done next. That decision sets the stage
for the operation of the expert and the specialist, the
manager and the administrator. With the community's
resources limited, the basic decisions are forever concerned with what to do first, what second, and so forth.
It is, most of the time, a matter of ranking the jobs to
be done in their order of urgency. These decisions,
forever controversial, are arrived at by a continuous
battle between various individuals and groups who seek
to convince the common men that their preferences are
the right ones. Through such efforts such individuals
achieve leadership.[21] But they cannot stabilize their position, because their "solutions" are likely to be judged
inadequate after a trial, while their opponents will make
the best of any errors committed. What is correct about
"ruling classes" according to Mosca, namely that "they
tend to become hereditary in fact, if not in law," cannot be true concerning such leaders; they come and go
in continuous succession. Indeed, the most striking
thing about such leadership is that it is most usually
recruited from among the common men.

Possibly the greatest of all American Presidents was
Abraham Lincoln. He is the common man incarnate.
He belonged to no ruling class; he belonged to no

elite. He came from common folk, and the people who fancied themselves the elite in America laughed at him. Carl Sandburg has depicted him for us as he groped his way through the seething hatreds of the Civil War. He possessed in superb degree that quality of judgment which is felt urgency, not figured calculation or argument. "A people cannot long endure half-slave and half-free . . . "; "The Union must be preserved . . . " — these were the judgments of the majority of the common men and women of America. He was their leader because he represented them — men of better brains and of all the other adornments did not.

I know whereof I speak, for I myself have been converted in these past twenty years to a belief in the common man, after being surrounded by the belief in the elite. But till now, it has been a belief in the common man here in America. Can we deepen and strengthen our new belief to the point where it will embrace the majority of mankind? Where we can truly say, with Schiller and Beethoven: "Be embraced, all ye millions . . . "? Can we make world-wide the kind of society where no class rules, no elite appears? Only such societies are free.

CHAPTER IX

The Future Citizen

*How can we expect a harvest
of thought who have not had
a seed-time of character?*
— HENRY DAVID THOREAU

THE AMERICAN answer to the arguments of the elitists was universal education. Such universal education was to give every child in the land the minimum of mental equipment to participate *intelligently* in the life of the community. The emphasis was upon mental equipment, and upon rational faculties. German and other European ideas reinforced this outlook. It was at first largely a matter of offering to the masses what had been the privilege of the educated classes. It was an educational and cultural ideal meant for an "elite." Few asked to what extent it might be adapted to the needs of the common man. Practical educators were, of course, bound to be troubled by the incongruities, but much of the discussion was carried on in other terms.

The New Image of the Common Man

To clarify the issue it would have been necessary to probe deeply into the social as well as the individual psychological views of the traditional humanism which democratic educators inherited from the past. The age of individualism had little inclination for that sort of thing. Most educational thought, that is to say, most conscious pedagogy, revolved around the problems of the individual to be educated, and the "raising of the general level of intelligence." It was rarely asked, except by anti-common-man conservatives, whether such a plan as raising the general level of intelligence was at all within the realm of the possible.

NATIONAL CULTURE

There was one further aspect of universal education that was not entirely thought-out and intentional. This was the predominantly *national*, not to say *nationalist*, character of most public education. In a series of revealing studies, Professor Merriam and a group of associates have traced the making of citizens as a central goal of educational effort throughout the nineteenth century.[1] The humanist emphasis upon language was reinforced by the romantic ideas about language as the expression of a people's soul (*Volksgeist*). This twist gave to humanism a turn which was quite at variance with its original cosmopolitanism. It reintroduced the notion that a man to be truly human depended upon his cultural setting, an idea equally potent in the French Revolution and in the nationalist counter-movements which Napoleonic imperialism brought on. A profound enthusiasm for one's own people, its language and linguistic culture, associated itself all too readily with feelings of national pride and a sense of superiority. Such enthusiasts often looked down upon people speaking another tongue the refinements of which they did not appreciate.

Ideas of national cultural superiority have been a potent factor in the common man's feeling throughout the period of rising democracy. Indeed, certain writers insisted that nationalism and democracy went together. People were "naturally" nationalistic, it was asserted. Throughout the period culture was taken as something God-given, something that always was there. Having accepted a given set of cultural traditions writers then proceeded to explore their effects without any regard to the possibility of changing the cultural conditions themselves. Much of the writing on national character, for example, was based on this kind of *petitio principii*.

The only large country in which there was a measure of general appreciation for the diversity of national cultural backgrounds was the United States. Indeed, it is one of the most striking features of American intellectual history in the nineteenth century that maturing minds moved from nationalism to cosmopolitanism. The autobiography of Henry Adams is an outstanding document for this reason alone. Nothing comparable to *The Education of Henry Adams* could have been written in England, France or Germany. Only the small nations of Europe showed a similarity to the United States in this respect. This, incidentally, is the reason why they are such natural collaborators for America in the rebuilding of the world.

In *Walden*, Henry Thoreau remarks: "It is something to be able to paint a particular picture, or to carve a statue, and so to make a few objects beautiful; but it is far more glorious to carve and paint the very atmosphere and medium through which we look. . . ."[2] What is this new atmosphere which we must seek to paint? It is the atmosphere of a realist democracy. We are confronted with the most far-reaching educational task that any generation has had to face.

HUMANISM IN EDUCATION

In our democracy, there have been prevalent three educational outlooks, or predominant atmospheres. Besides the authoritarian view of the Catholic and other church bodies, there is the humanist and the pragmatic or realist approach. The humanist conception stresses languages, especially the classics, and mathematics. The realist or pragmatic view stresses understanding of things, science, social environment. I am myself a product of humanist education, and hence quite ready to defend its achievements, but I have become intensely opposed to the classical tradition of an intellectual elite which that education fosters in so many imperceptible ways. But what would constitute a sound education for free men?

We have come a long way from the sixteenth-century humanists who developed the educational philosophy of the emphasis on classics, and we are remote even from their nineteenth-century protagonists in England and Germany. It may be well to remind ourselves at this crisis that the humanist educational outlook was shaped in opposition to the dogmatic religious conception of Catholic, and later of Protestant, church authorities. In a nutshell, the adherents of the classical tradition are rationalists, believers in the mind. Plato and Aristotle and Cicero are the lodestars of their heaven. Hence, humanist education stresses the development of the logical faculties, that is to say, of speech. Hence, the emphasis upon language, and more especially Latin, with the superbly logical structure of its grammar. Culture, they thought, is first and foremost linguistic culture, and the high value they placed upon esthetic form manifests itself specifically in the stress upon poetry. Here the unique beauty of the Greek language provided a welcome balance to the more prosaic Latin. The cult of linguistic and poetic form made intellectual discipline an inescapable principle of this school.

The New Image of the Common Man

THE REALIST APPROACH

Neither industrialism nor the American frontier were especially favorable settings for this educational ideal. And although it has been persuasively argued that modern science, and hence modern industry, are the products of this humanist cult of the rational, disciplined mind, it is equally true that the expansion of modern industry and of pioneering and colonizing both at home and abroad gave birth to a new spirit of realism. It is curious and yet a highly characteristic thing to find Thoreau, the Harvard-trained lover of Greek poetry, outlining educational reforms which a succeeding generation embraced with alacrity (though rarely, if ever, referring to the arch-individualist craftsman of Walden Pond). In discussing what was wrong with Harvard College (a favorite pastime, even in his day), he wrote: "How could youths better learn to live than by at once trying the experiment of living? Methinks this would exercise their minds as much as mathematics. . . . Which would have advanced the most at the end of a month — the boy who had made his own jackknife from the ore which he had dug and smelted, reading as much as would be necessary for this — or the boy who had attended the lectures on metallurgy at the Institute in the meanwhile, and had received a Rodgers penknife from his father? Which would be most likely to cut his fingers?" [3]

The Future Citizen

Anyone will recognize the "realist" educational philosophy here; even the standard of utility is brought forth in the final interrogation. The educational inspiration is not esthetic form, but useful knowledge. As part of this outlook, the adherents of realism stress the development of personality, particularly the more recent "progressive" representatives of this outlook.

THE "PROGRESSIVE" TREND

Some years ago, in a piece for the *Atlantic Monthly*, I tried to spell out what seemed to me as a student of politics the curious paradoxes of American educational trends. Since the article bore the provocative title "This Progressive Education," it brought down a storm of protest and praise from all kinds of partisans. In the turmoil, my major point got lost. This was, Does progressive education, so-called, bear any definite relationship to what appears to be the dominant (progressive) trends of our society — the changes that are taking place whether you call them progress or not? It was (and still is) my impression that progressive education does so only in part. In many respects it seems an outlook born of leisure-class needs under an individualistic economy.

It is commonly recognized by intelligent people everywhere that large-scale organization of work is on the increase in all walks of life, even if actual government control is not established. The Clinic of the Mayo Brothers in Rochester, Minnesota, in the medical field, Stone and Webster, of Boston, in the engineering line, are only two extreme examples of what is in fact a very general development. Big universities, co-operative research organizations, large law offices, and so forth, are the order of the day. Everywhere and all around us it becomes increasingly difficult to "start out on your own." An ever greater percentage of men and women in professional life enter private and government organizations for a "career."

Now it is the general characteristic of all these organizations, whether public or private, to be in a measure bureaucratic. Harvard University and the Bell Telephone System, the Pennsylvania Railroad and the United States Geodetic Survey — all have their little bureaucracy. That means for the individual member a rather rigid system of *subordination*. Willingness and ability to take orders and instructions, and to carry them out faithfully even when you disagree — this is a habit pattern without which success in modern life is well-nigh impossible. We have all become soldiers in a huge army of workers, though a few among us still kid ourselves into thinking we are independent. This is not to say that we are *merely* cogs in a machine. But we are in part such cogs. In my opinion, the ideal attitude under these conditions is the attitude usually achieved by the good soldier: he cheerfully accepts the need for subordination, and yet retains a sufficient detachment from it to safeguard his inner personality. And such an attitude is best developed under a system of schooling which approaches the authoritative pattern to some extent.

There was a paradox in people who considered themselves progressive organizing a kind of school calculated to hinder rather than help the development of children destined to carry on our progressive industrial society, of would-be socialists who trained their children for a golden pastoral age. Perhaps our changed outlook is due to our having become accustomed to a more and more collectivist society. We do not shudder at the thought of the Soviet Union; but we also do not consider it the golden age. At any rate, people have to work hard in Communist Russia. And the habit patterns of professional or craft competence, or moral and intellectual discipline, of subordination and courage, are as necessary there as they have ever been anywhere in the world.

This recognition of a disciplined pattern of student-teacher relationship is quite compatible with the realistic insistence upon making the student's relationship to his environment meaningful. The capacity to establish such meaningful relationships is related to spontaneity. This spontaneous enthusiasm for one or another realm of things is utilized to provide an outlet for intellectual development. Typically, some schools have gone into the country and have built their teaching around a farm, so that farming could become the center of the learning process. There is no reason why the same might not be done with factories, as it has been in colleges like Antioch. The cult of the real as felt sense impression makes "self-expression" an obvious principle of this outlook — as naturally a part of it as self-discipline is of the humanist outlook.

THE NEW SYNTHESIS

In the public schools of this country the two outlooks have been slowly merging. Their gradual convergence has given rise to a new synthesis. From humanism this new outlook inherits the emphasis upon co-operative discipline and upon a sense of values that is explicit and rational. From realism and progressivism has come the insistence upon acquiring a vivid sense of our social environment. The crisis has greatly speeded a crystallizing of this new outlook which may be called "civics." This is misleading, since the word "civics" was used in the past to designate a certain type of high-school course now largely discredited. Perhaps it should be called "democratics." Its concern is with democracy in the ethical as well as in the functional sense. All the explorations into particular phases of the environment became meaningful as part of an over-all pattern: democracy. The problem is why democracy leads into

[280]

values. To make the rational real requires disciplined thinking.

Recently this trend has become vocal in an educational program which is of great importance for the new belief in the common man.[4] The task of a democratic education is clearly faced as in sharp contrast with totalitarian education. In spite of a torrent of familiar high-sounding phrases with which these "educators" overwhelm the reader, the core of their argument is very up-to-date. They recognize that democracy is something else besides institutions and a "way of life." They call it a "great social faith." By this they mean that democracy is "a question of the values and ideas to be applied to life." This sounds a bit like the "agreement on fundamentals." It is too broad and vague. But it is nevertheless valuable, because it leads to a recognition that education is concerned with what is believed to be right. Values are central.

But are such values rational? Are they necessarily embodied in formulas that can be stated in so many words? We have at the very outset insisted upon the importance of character in the common man, the moral vigor or firmness acquired through self-discipline. A man of character is a man who knows his values, or at least senses his values and sticks by them, we said. It is the primary task of education to inculcate such a sense of values. In contrasting education with propaganda we showed how education is concerned with

[281]

shaping human beings in the light of a believed-in ideal. But such an ideal need not consist in a set of abstract rules or principles. Werner Jaeger has vividly shown how the Greek human ideal evolved slowly over a long period of time. An ideal may express itself in many detailed rules of conduct, such as were embodied in the Chinese tradition, or in the codes of chivalry of medieval Europe. Indeed, ethical ideals have ranged all the way from explicit formal rules to broad conceptions of virtue.[5]

But whatever may be the particular embodiment of the human values, whether they be rational principles, rituals, felt preferences, or customs and folkways, genuine education will be preoccupied with them. That is the reason the home is of such importance in shaping the character. That is also a reason why there has been so much confusion in educational judgments. The schools have been asked to do the whole job. Not only a declining church influence, but also a disintegrating family setting have left a void which the schools have been slow to fill. Yet the nature of modern industrial society is such that it is essential that the schools do step in. There are supplementary forces at work. The 4-H Clubs have made some strides in implementing home and community in shaping the character of young farmers along with teaching them technical skills. Boy Scouts and Girl Scouts have likewise stepped into the breach. Healthy as such efforts are where the leadership is good, they are not sufficient. A community of free men may only at its peril neglect the education of its future citizens. Certain modes of behavior are so essential to the conduct of its civic affairs that it will have to mold as many young people into that pattern as possible. Only the schools provide the appropriate, because continuous, setting for the accomplishment of this task. They have been rightly called "the churches of democracy." Symbolically, as one drives through small New England towns, he finds again and again that the most impressive, the most substantial building is the school.

LIMITATIONS OF PRINCIPLE

It is extremely difficult, if not impossible, to formulate in abstract terms what constitutes the rational framework of such modes of behavior. Since there is no agreement on fundamentals in a living democracy, different schools of thought will rationalize in different terms the modes of behavior which they all practice. It has, for example, been stated authoritatively that "the individual human being is of surpassing worth." Yet are free men who conduct themselves democratically willing to say that "this individual human being, Adolf Hitler, is of surpassing worth"? Or that "those individual human beings, the Japanese military clans, are of surpassing worth"? We know they are not so willing. What is more, we see no reason why they should be.

The New Image of the Common Man

Again, it has been asserted that "the earth and human culture belong to all men." Such a principle looks innocuous enough, until you make the practical application to the Nazis and their kind. Why should a believer in democracy be willing to concede any part of the earth and its culture to them?

These limitations of principle may be explained in many ways. Their disregard under certain conditions may be convincingly rationalized. Ultimately we come back to what we pointed out earlier, namely that we are dealing here not with abstract principles, but with a communal way of doing things, with a common mode of behavior or conduct. Any men who do not act in accordance with that common mode are outside the community, and hence are subject to quite different methods of treatment. It is, therefore, better not to state such modes of conduct as absolute principles or articles of faith. We thus avoid getting ourselves entangled in contradictions whenever we are faced with people who do not act as we do.

A breakdown in values and standards of conduct may occur within a democratic community just as it does in other communities. A continuous effort is needed to maintain the community's democratic behavior intact. A group of industrialists, in the late depression, were angrily arguing about various violations in a gentlemen's agreement to which they had all subscribed in better times. Finally, one of them dryly remarked: "The trouble is that in times like these there simply aren't any gentlemen left." A mode of behavior once readily accepted by all had given way under the stress and strain of altered conditions. We all know that this happens. Social conditions are forever changing, and the disintegration of one kind of standard will be followed by the emergence of another.

CONFLICT OF LOYALTIES

Once we recognize the nonrational needs of human beings and the necessity of founding conduct upon feelings or sentiments rather than upon mere thoughts, we find ourselves compelled to place great emphasis upon loyalties. Loyalty is *felt attachment*, based on living experience. If no loyalties are firmly implanted, there can be no cohesion in the community. Different people might stress different loyalties, but since they are based on experience through living, they will unite men who share a common pattern of life. Thus, the loyalty which consists in respect for and appreciation of talent, training and excellence in all fields of socially useful endeavor develops naturally out of the sense of workmanship with which we have dealt at an earlier point.

But the real problem here is not an enumeration of a list of loyalties, but an indication of which loyalty comes first, i.e., how they are stacked. It is the conflict of loyalties that presents the ethically serious issues. When Jesus says: "Leave thy father and mother and follow me," he demands of his followers that they face this issue squarely. Catalogues of loyalties are no better than catalogues of virtues.[6] The rationalists answered this problem by an "appeal to reason." Supernaturalists answer it by an "appeal to revelation." But whatever his answer, anyone who wants to live as a free man among the free will recognize that there is no acceptable way of forcing his answer upon others. No group of common men is in a position to decide these matters uniformly, and no elite is wanted to do it for them.

THE NEED FOR DISCIPLINE

If ways of conduct are stressed and their value insisted upon, as the crux of educational endeavor, discipline must necessarily play its role. It is, therefore, only natural that we should find the new educational program for free men containing an explicit recognition of the need for discipline. Knowledge and loyalty are not enough. The behavior of the mass of common men has to be molded by a measure of discipline. But there is a world of difference between the discipline of free men and that of totalitarian states.

"Every society or group must achieve an appropriate discipline or perish." The essential difference lies in the ultimate objective: authoritarian discipline aims at obedience, while the free man's discipline aims at self-discipline. One seeks to develop the self, while the other seeks to vanquish it. One believes in the common man's character and capacity for self-improvement, the other in the need for direction by an elite. For these reasons, the belief in the common man leads to the conclusion that "the discipline of free men cannot be achieved by subjecting the young for a period of years to the regimen of the slave." It is less certain that they will all agree that "neither can the discipline of free men be achieved by allowing the young to follow their own impulses and take over the process of education." [7]

We are here confronted with a very difficult problem — a problem which is not even clearly understood. How does an external discipline become converted into an internal one? How does discipline imposed by others become self-discipline? It is a very old problem, and for the education of free men it is indeed crucial.

A great part of the answer depends upon one's view of man. If human nature is assumed to be good, as the optimists of the eighteenth and nineteenth centuries maintained — and "good" in this context meant "sociable," "friendly," "co-operative" — then all that is needed is to let it develop according to its inclination. If contrariwise it is maintained, as by most supporters of authoritarian doctrines, that man is bad, or evil, or depraved — that is to say, selfish and un-co-operative

The New Image of the Common Man

— why then rules of conduct have to be imposed by external authority and force. Now, as a matter of fact, neither of these views is in accordance with the findings of psychology, sociology and political science, or with the new belief in the common man built upon them. For all these fields of study have gone to show that man is neither evil nor good by nature. The degree of sociability varies greatly among individual persons, and so do other psychic inclinations that may be comprised under such general terms as "good" or "bad." And insofar as these words refer to some such general proposition as "behaves according to or contrary to standards," evidently men become "good" or "bad" as they grow to maturity, depending upon whether they acquire the capacity to maintain such standards — either by self-discipline, *or* by obedience to authority. There was a great deal of value, from the viewpoint of freedom, in insisting, as the rationalists and romantics did, that man is not by nature depraved; but it did not follow, as they were inclined to assume, that man can therefore get along without standards, or find them all by himself, or maintain them without having acquired self-discipline.

Discipline, a hateful word! And yet, is it so very surprising that a civilization built by men and women whose stern religious convictions revolved around the idea of discipline, should demand of its active leaders that very quality which animated its builders? Obviously not. We may have lost the stern religious faith of our forebears, but the house which we live in is their house, and its management requires their qualities.

What we have said about the requirements of modern professional life is the inexorable consequence of the initial conception of our industrial civilization. And, though we may yearn for the happy-go-lucky ways of a pastoral society, bringing up our children in such a spirit merely means putting them out of the society into which they are born. If we can leave them enough to enable them to live the life of the charming amateur, the harm may not be personally apparent, though the loss to the community must inevitably be great. But if we are ourselves professional people, unable to amass a fortune, or if we are convinced that such fortunes will melt away under the hot sun of the fiscal burden which mounting social legislation imposes, then we had better take heed, and look for an education which is progressive in the direction in which our society is progressing.

SELF–DISCIPLINE

How can such moral and intellectual self-discipline be achieved? If we apply the teachings of modern psychology, we should say that it is basically a matter of conditioning children in such a way that certain situations call forth certain reactions. What are these situations, and what are the corresponding reactions? In other words, what are the habit patterns involved in self-discipline?

This we can answer most simply by looking at a self-disciplined person. A doctor who responded to calls from patients, no matter at what hour of the day or night, would be considered self-disciplined; while another doctor who instructed his secretary to tell callers that he was out on an emergency call, when in fact he was playing golf, would not be so considered. The old-fashioned religious way of talking about this difference was to say that one of these doctors had a sense of duty, while the other was devoid of it. But since there is no convincing foundation for a "sense of duty" except in terms of religious convictions, and since religious convictions are the exception rather than the rule among scientifically trained, professional persons today, the only other fairly secure foundation for such habit patterns as are desirable from the community's point of view is the right kind of education.

Now, would an education built upon the quest for ego-satisfaction procure the habit pattern we are looking for? There are those who claim that it would; that the vivid realization of the distressed mother's worry would elicit a feeling of distinct unhappiness in the doctor, and would therefore lead him to respond to her call. Unfortunately, this argument presupposes in the doctor high sensitivity and a vivid imagination, two qualities which are notable by their absence in the generality of mankind. Balancing the beckonings of such imaginative sympathy for the sufferings of unknown fellow beings are the siren calls of callous sophistry, which argue: "She can get another doctor. I hate to be interrupted in my golf. People make a lot of fuss over nothing most of the time, anyway. I ought to have some rest."

If, however, the childhood education has been of such a nature that indifference, sloth, carelessness, have invariably, in school and at home, brought down unhappy consequences, even if merely a scolding, then there settles upon such a person the habit pattern of feeling uneasy at the neglect of duties. And as, in later life, such a person discovers that attending to one's appointed tasks brings the gratification of success and fulfillment, you are more likely to make such a man or woman happy and contented than if you let him discover by the painful process of trial and error that life is hard, and ruthlessly destroys those who do not fulfill the expectations of their fellow men.

If the habit pattern of moral self-discipline is set by the child's being disciplined when small, it is the same with intellectual self-discipline. Not to rest content until an experiment, a term paper, or a case study is as perfect as it can possibly be made (in one's own view) is a habit which develops slowly under the guidance of teachers who so insist at the time when the natural inclination of a child is to drop a matter when it gets hard. Everything gets boring after a while, and yet no technique is ever acquired without constant application, least of all the ability to think clearly. There are many tools for clear thinking which are hard to acquire, and it is almost impossible to acquire them after a certain age. Latin, for example, develops the abstract logical faculty to an unsurpassed extent, because of the rigidity of its grammar. The playing of musical instruments provides, of course, a striking analogy. Few are the people who have learned the playing of anything but the radio after maturity. Many regret that their parents did not insist upon their continuing to practice, when more exciting things beckoned.

But we are told that children are not happy learning Latin. I suggest that this is a question of relative merit. They are not *as* happy as they would be playing in the yard, but happier than if weeding a vegetable garden. And this shows us that the problem of successful habit patterning of the intellectual and the moral side of a personality go hand in hand. To object to this in terms of such rhetorical questions as "Must we have the hickory-stick?" is unfair. There are much better ways of maintaining discipline. But if we acquire in early childhood a sense of order and fitting-in as being innate to a workroom, we shall later find ourselves less appalled by laboratory, library, and court, not to speak of modern factories.[8]

This recognition of the need for external discipline

serves purely the function of promoting self-discipline. Hence all genuinely progressive education for free men will seek to expand the range of responsibility as rapidly as the development of believed-in standards permits. As the capacity for self-discipline expands, youth grows into maturity. In spite of many failures, this is the goal. It is a never-ending task. Reflecting upon it, one perceives clearly why democracy is never finished, never static, never at rest.

Since it is through lived experience that desirable behavior becomes established and elicits the necessary loyalty, youth is organized deliberately both at home and in school to give it the experience in democratic living which will aid it in learning to subordinate the self to group needs, while participating in the determination of what these group needs are.

The task of home and school is greatly complicated by the influence of magazines, movies and the radio. Few, if any, of those who operate these media recognize any but negative standards. Their approach is largely in terms of entertainment. In order to entertain they incline to coddle and cajole their audience. This is as true for the children as for the adults. We must recognize this situation as a potent part of our environment, regardless of whether we feel that it could or should be changed. It may be that, like bacteria threatening the health of people, these programs presenting us with a distorted outlook on life are inevitably with us. Maybe we have to accept them, along with all the fine things we get from magazines, radio and movies, just as we have to accept the bacteria along with our food.

The home shares with the school the responsibility for shaping the future citizen — and it is a difficult responsibility to discharge. But it can be accomplished, if one thing is clearly recognized: we need standards and values to provide us with that consistency which is the essence of character.

CONCLUSION

Both the man-always-bad view and the man-always-good view are mistaken and unrealistic in their excessive generalizations. Our regard for the facts, our inclination to doubt, our vastly increased knowledge of cultural diversity between individuals and groups — they all have made us ready to take a more tempered view of the common child. It is seen as perfectible, as capable of improvement; but this improvement is not seen as reaching perfection. We distrust the perfectionist as a species of inverted misanthrope. We know from experience that perfectionist counsels only too readily turn into counsels of despair. We do not want either to overestimate or to underestimate the range of possible change and improvement. We are reasonably sure, on the evidence, that human beings can be made to fit, to a varying degree, into a co-operative pattern of free men. The disagreement is really not so much over *what man is,* as it is over *how man becomes* what he needs to be to participate effectively in communal life. It is the nature of this participation which determines to a large extent what man needs to be for this purpose. The new democratic outlook stresses *ethics* as the central task of education, because we have come to realize that the emphasis needs to be on character. The cultivation of mind and personality, which preceding humanist and naturalist conceptions have stressed, is not neglected, by any means. But it is subordinated to that of character. *Character,* the consistent loyalty to believed standards, is accepted as the basis of education for free men. It is part and parcel of the new belief in the common man.

CHAPTER X

Pan-Humanism

How beautiful upon the moun-
tains are the feet of him that
bringeth good tidings, that pub-
lisheth peace . . .

— ISAIAH 52:7

Eᴀᴄʜ passing day makes it more abundantly clear
that the world of the past is dead and gone, that we
are moving on into a new world. If it is not to be Hitler's, it will be ours. What do we want it to be? Unless
we want to take on Hitler's job and become the world's
masters, imposing on it our own conceptions of life,
liberty, and the pursuit of happiness, we are confronted
with a gigantic problem. Upon what common ground
can mankind meet? What principles, values, standards
are common to a majority of mankind? A majority! For
it would plainly be absurd to ask for unanimity. But
even a majority presents us with a problem of the first
magnitude.

THE FOUR FREEDOMS

We want to live in a world where law and order reign. Right. But upon what common ground are such law and order to be erected? When speaking of our own constitution, we used to use the language of the eighteenth century. We talked of a "Bill of Rights." It was the right of a man to his *property* that loomed large in those words. In more recent years, *civil liberties* have taken the place of those rights. It has been the liberty of the *person* that has seemed most important in the age of individualism. Now comes a further step. On January 6, 1941, President Roosevelt proclaimed four *freedoms* as essential to a democratic world. Freedom of speech, freedom of religion, freedom from want, and freedom from fear — these four freedoms he insisted upon as essential.

They were meant as a challenge and they are a challenge. Whom were they meant to challenge? Americans heard the message with a brief flurry of enthusiasm, but they were perplexed. "Those are fine words," they seemed to say, "but what do they mean?" "Are we going to make the world safe for democracy once more?" sneered the men who disliked the President's foreign policy. There were many others, men and women firmly convinced of the urgency of defeating Hitlerism, who also were left wondering. The words seemed to echo an old battle cry — they stirred up uneasy memories of a crusade that had left them stranded.

Why this anxious questioning, this uncertainty about the meaning of these freedoms?

It cannot be a question of words, for the words are clear. Under the two freedoms of speech and of religion are comprised all those rights associated with a man's personal self-expression. Free press and free, peaceful assembly, and latterly the freedom of peaceful association, are covered by the first of these freedoms. Freedom of conscience and all that goes with it are taken care of by the second. We here in America find little difficulty in understanding the imperatives which these two freedoms of speech and of religion embody. What bothers us is the suspicion that we are far from having realized these aspirations.

OUR OWN SHORTCOMINGS

Any reader of literature on civil liberties [1] will hesitate to consider freedom of expression a reality even in America. Only the thoughtless will forget the man who was put in jail for several years because he ventured to discuss peace problems in 1918. To speak of these high aspirations in the face of the treatment meted out to our colored people makes most of us feel ill at ease. Have we been able to make these freedoms secure to our own citizens? Yet after all is said and done, an impressive residue of really achieved freedom is left, as any refugee from Hitler will gladly testify.

Pan-Humanism

Is there any immediate prospect of eliminating want from America, let alone from wide areas of the earth's surface? Freedom from want means first and foremost freedom from unemployment. Yet unemployment remains an unsolved problem right here in America. Want is, of course, a flexible term, but an equal standard of living should be the ultimate goal, although the President did not make it clear to what extent he meant to imply an equalizing of living standards throughout the world. Surely we do not wish to hide under a different set of words what Hitler brutally proclaims as his aim: to make the Nazi master race benefit from the toil of the rest of the world. At the same time, how can we hope even to approximate freedom from want? How many of our people are willing to share their real income with other peoples? How many of our people have been willing to admit that the equalizing of living standards even within the United States is necessary?

Probably the most important single item in the whole creed is freedom from fear. The right of *habeas corpus*, secured through centuries of hard struggle, is the freedom from arbitrary arrest. Its lack is the most bitterly felt loss of all those who have fallen under the domination of the Nazis. The terror of the totalitarian tyranny is quintessentially opposed to this freedom. Almost equally important nowadays is some kind of provision for protection against mob violence. Have we been able to provide it? Even on paper, we have not succeeded in outlawing lynchings. How is such freedom, then, to be brought to the suffering millions of poor bloody humanity?

WORLD PROBLEMS

It does not seem sensible for us to proclaim as a goal for the whole world what we have not been prepared to attempt at home. How can we become the pioneers of a new world order, a free co-operative world order, unless we seek to bring these high-sounding phrases down to earth? But even assuming that we have to some extent succeeded, how are we to secure adherence to all these freedoms on the part of other people?

Eighty million Germans, a hundred and fifty million Russians, tens of millions of other Slavic peoples, well over three hundred million Indians, between four and five hundred million Chinese and Japanese, not to speak of the numerous other peoples in the Near and the Far East, in all probably three fourths of the earth's population, have been living under social and political conditions where freedom of speech, of the press, and of assembly are almost meaningless phrases.

And as for freedom of religion — and of education? Do not many of these people acknowledge faith in a religion which dogmatically denies the desirability of tolerating other creeds? Can we force them to accept toleration? The British troubles in India furnish a striking object lesson; Mohammedan and Hindu have persecuted each other with relentless ferocity. The profound sympathy which any free man must feel for Indian demands is badly shattered by the discovery that, like the New England Puritans, they often seem to seek freedom the better to suppress their dissenting neighbors.

President Wilson was unable to secure adoption of an article guaranteeing the freedom of religious worship into the Covenant of the League of Nations. The Japanese dislike for such an article was intense; but in order to bring home their view they adopted the very telling device of suggesting that the Covenant contain an article guaranteeing all peoples under the Covenant against discrimination. The Australians, as hostile as America toward Japanese immigration, secured the rejection of this proposal, and so religious freedom was also abandoned. It is such conflicts that the advocate of a democratic world has to face; a readiness to make compromises upon one's own fundamental premises seems to be required at the very outset. Yet, to what extent can such a readiness be expected in others? This is in many respects a pure question of fact, but one with regard to which we lack the most elementary knowledge.

It was wise and helpful of the President to have the long and involved Bill of Rights of our constitution thus made more compact. It was bold and imaginative to bring the idea of the pursuit of happiness face to face with a twentieth-century reality: unemployment. And yet I know people of real ability and insight who are filled with enthusiasm for the world order, but who would not be the least happy over a tax increase that would help to banish want from our own country, to say nothing of China.

THE PUBLIC'S REACTION

Shall we then do nothing? Shall we allow things to drift? This also seems impossible. The four freedoms *are* the great symbols we are fighting for. But neither here nor abroad has the declaration of the four freedoms met with the enthusiasm to which its high idealism entitled it. Why? Wherein does it fail to rouse us — and more particularly the younger generation? Obviously a vast educational crusade is called for. Extensive conversations with all kinds of people, students and workers, farmers and businessmen, doctors and preachers, housewives and schoolboys, will convince anyone that the statement of these freedoms lacks that peculiar something which gives to an idea its representative, its symbolic value.

The spirit of the common man in America is practical and realistic. Though deeply attached to ideals, he wants to see them meaningfully related to what he knows about the world. He feels himself freer and more nearly in possession of what the four freedoms proclaim than most other people are. Yet he knows that we are far from any realization of these freedoms. He wants to know what is to be done about them.

Can we say that Americans in the mass are behind these four freedoms, not only for themselves but for China or Poland? Or do they look upon the idea of freeing the majority of mankind from want and fear as utterly chimeric? A survey has convinced me that the general feeling is one of great uncertainty. "How do I know what's good for China?" "I never met a Hindu, so I can't tell whether they would go along." The plain fact of the matter is that we have little or no idea, most of us, of what are the basic beliefs, values, standards of the majority of mankind. Here is the greatest stumbling-block to that "new world" which we seek to achieve.

THE WORLD CITIZEN

There can be no democratic world order without a democratic world citizen, any more than there can be a democratic American order without a democratic American citizen. What is more, we cannot be the protagonists of such a democratic world order if we are not prepared to be such world citizens ourselves. This will involve very great efforts and sacrifices on our own part. These sacrifices are part of establishing the world order we want to live in. The only basis on which we can ask other people to share the four freedoms and to be willing to accept their guarantees through effective world government is our own use of them. This means that our own policies and commitments must be such as to help other people to prosper. Carl Schurz once said: "If you want to be free, there is but one way: it is to guarantee an equally full measure of liberty to all your neighbors. There is no other." [2]

We cannot hope to go forward by ourselves, either materially or spiritually, on this planet. And when we say this, we are not thinking of this year or next year, but of the generation now in the making. The citizen of the past was a national citizen. It was a question of turning folks from many lands into Americans. The citizen of the future will be a world citizen, or there will be no democratic world order. Frankly, I believe that this building of world citizenship has to begin right here in America.

Undoubtedly there will be great difficulties in establishing this world consciousness abroad, especially where totalitarianism has been rampant. On the other hand there may be a violent reaction against totalitarianism after it collapses. That is what happened last time, and such a reaction may well be even more far-reaching this time. Quite a few of those who have lived for years under Hitler know more about the beauty of freedom than we do. From the little countries that have been overwhelmed by the Nazi war machine come persistent voices that proclaim the end of national sovereignty. Out of Germany come demands of a similar nature.

We have indulged ourselves in much self-criticism. I feel that there has been too much talk about the purely organizational side of things, about the League and whether it would all have been different if we had gone in — or had we never espoused it in the first place. Every thoughtful American is agreed that that must not happen again. Americans are afraid of the ideals which inspired them then, because they found themselves confronted with tasks from which they recoiled. Why did they? Primarily, it seems to me, because Americans had assumed that making the world safe for democracy required nothing of them but to defeat the Kaiser. They did not realize that they, too, had to become something new, something almost unheard of — world citizens. Not quite unheard of, though. For at the very beginning of our democracy, there were a few world citizens: Tom Paine, Thomas Jefferson, Benjamin Franklin, Lafayette.

It was admittedly this failure of ours to mold ourselves in the spirit of our own professed idealism which left us stranded. We do not want to be so stranded again. Can we escape the job then of looking beyond our immediate responsibilities? Of facing the task of becoming ready for world citizenship ourselves? Obviously not. Well, what does that imply?

The New Image of the Common Man

MANKIND'S COMMON GROUND

Our most intensive efforts must be shaped to meet this challenge in the years to come. Blueprints of world organization, economic programs, and social institutions are important, to be sure, but among the things to come, the most basic is the new man. Democratically speaking, we cannot have a new world without him. Yet this is no call for Utopia, no demand for changing basic human nature. But in a changed environment human nature can be brought to respond to different ideals and different needs. There will be balanced men and reckless adventurers, brilliant minds and reliable souls of pedestrian imagination, honest men and crooks — but unless their strivings and doings can be given a world orientation, America cannot assume leadership in world government.

There are such basic human facts — experiences which provide a starting point for understanding. Women of all nations can talk with each other about childbirth and children, no matter how diverse their background. These are feelings and interests common to all of them. Almost all mankind seems to be agreed that the mother has first claim on her infant. All of the questions large and small which grow out of this basic right are readily understood by women the world over. It is from simple facts such as these that we can start.

I do not feel at all ready myself to be dogmatic in

formulating fundamental human rights of a cosmopolitan civilization. I do not feel that I have much to work with that would give me sympathetic understanding of the ethical aspirations of mankind. We have read a little Confucius, and we have a very vague idea of Buddhism and Mohammedanism, but our grasp of the ethical implications of their teachings leaves us uncertain. What *behavior* do we have in common with them? The group of writers known as "the Humanists," notably Irving Babbitt and Walter Lippmann, strove toward such a broad base, but their efforts were in the prefatory mood. They were too concerned with pointing out the shallowness of their contemporaries to make an attempt at being practical. "And so the mature man would take the world as it comes, and within himself remain quite unperturbed," Lippmann wrote in the *Preface to Morals*.[3] It appears that he has lately — and quite rightly — ceased to be such a mature man and has become quite perturbed once more. It is right and proper that this should be so. It is just as true of the rest of us. The moralist, that old-fashioned creature who takes ideals seriously, is turning to and becoming practical. In doing so, let's start at home.

AN EDUCATIONAL TASK

For if we ourselves are in no sense ready to become citizens of a new world order, neither are our children.

The New Image of the Common Man

Whether they go to bad schools or to good schools, they are brought up to think of themselves as American citizens. All schools have gone in for civics, but civics in the past has tended toward a shallow nationalism. Cheap patrioteering has found more of a place in courses of this kind than any good educator could accept. The mere fact that America has been a democracy longer than any other large country seems to foster smugness. Fortunately, educators are more and more aware of this pitfall. Recent programs, such as that set forth in *The Education of Free Men in American Democracy*, candidly insist that American democracy is far from fulfilling its ideal. While a knowledge of the resources, achievements, and promise of American democracy is considered essential, an understanding of our weaknesses is declared to be equally so by this program.

But this self-critical attitude is not enough. There is need for a generous reaching out towards others. The democratic creed contains the seeds for a broader flowering. Our insistence upon tolerance is being broadened into respect and appreciation for peoples with a different culture from our own. But to date, we have thought too much in terms of minorities, racial, cultural and religious. In the emerging world order it is not merely a matter of minorities, but of the majority of mankind. Let us become familiar with the long struggle to liberate the human mind and civilize the human heart.

It was one of the strong points of humanist education

that it conveyed a real feeling for another culture and its concrete aspirations. It provided a window out into another world. I shall never forget the glowing enthusiasm with which I wrote my graduation essay: "What the Greeks Mean to Us Today," even though I have long lost that sense of intimacy with Homer and Sophocles which inspired it.

The realistic trend of recent education, while admirable in its insistence upon making the teaching meaningful for the present, has tended toward a "spiritual provincialism." Our children may learn much about history, they may acquire wider knowledge of the broad sweep of civilization and yet fail to reach down to the core of understanding, for this can only be achieved through wrestling intensely with different conceptions of what is good and what is beautiful. The value judgments upon which culture rests are the decisive understanding of their inner springs. For it is in terms of these that they unfolded their colorful creative detail.

If this is a task too difficult for the school perhaps it should be attempted in the home. But how equipped are we, as parents, to handle this task? Suppose your eight-year-old girl comes to you, as mine did recently, and wants to know: "Are the Russians on our side?" How ready are you to help her to understand the broader issue of democracy versus Communism? I found it extremely difficult to get across to her the reasons why we must help the Russian people against the Nazis, and yet must also work for a more democratic union. I told her that they are not exactly on our side, but that we have a common enemy; still, I found myself handicapped by a sense of failure, an inability to present the ethical issue simply and clearly.

Education for free men in a democracy is confronted, then, with a new task of far-reaching consequences. If this is true at home, it is even more true at school. Out of a realistic approach to the problems of democracy, we are faced with the need for what may be an entirely new curriculum. It's not a matter of going back to the old literary humanism. To that the realist might well retort that such acquaintance lacked vital relationship to our own problems. One of their number, referring to Walter Lippmann's comments in a column entitled "On Being Too Current," recently exclaimed: "Seriously, does Mr. Lippmann think that young people of 1941 can be insulated, sterilized, wrapped in cotton batting, fed only on what was written and what happened before 1800, and at the age of twenty-one spring full-armed from the brain of Jove as responsible citizens of the world's greatest democracy?" I greatly sympathize with the protest, but I should like to add that probably no single educational task is of greater importance today than to ensure that these youngsters shall become ready for a citizenship wider than that of American democracy.

Pan-Humanism

COMMON ETHICAL ASPIRATIONS

The new ethical realism, closely tied as it is to a realistic conception of the common man, provides the general approach. Rather than just proclaiming the principles of tolerance, an attempt should be made to bring clearly into focus the common ethical aspirations of mankind, to show that certain basic patterns of behavior are common to the vast majority of mankind, whether they be Christians or Buddhists, Mohammedans or Jews, Confucians or secular humanists. The elimination of special religious instruction from our schools, in keeping with the separation of church and state, has removed from the classroom the most essential of all subjects — namely the ethical aspirations of man. In this our age of maturity it should be possible to return to it in the spirit of a new fellowship of man. That is the prime educational task, and it certainly is not an easy one. But if we don't start this effort, who will?

Beyond this educational task lies a political one. Politics in a democracy is adult education, at least half of the time. We may not think of it that way, but the educational value of a free discussion of public affairs is nevertheless one of the most important arguments in favor of democracy. John Stuart Mill put it very well in his *Representative Government*. Arguing against the Greek philosophers, especially Plato, he pointed out that the notion of an ideal king is bad, because the more benevolent his rule, the more enervating its effect in the long run. "Their minds are formed by, and consenting to, this abdication of their own energies." [4] It is this active participation which makes of democratic politics a school for adults. How can this participation be elicited? How can we rouse ourselves to facing the same issues which the schools are groping toward in their work with our children?

A CONCRETE PROPOSAL

What might be done to give us a democratic basis for proceeding with the task that the presidential declaration opened up? Might we not gather forthwith, under either governmental or civic auspices, a world convention of men and women of thought rather than action, who could represent *a majority of mankind?* These representatives should not scatter before they have agreed to a more specific formulation of the ideals of the four freedoms in conformity with the great religions which mankind professes. It need not be a vast group of men; a gathering the size of our original Constitutional Convention would probably be quite adequate. One for each 75,000,000–150,000,000 population among the peoples should be sufficient.

It is probably foolhardy to guess as to some of their conclusions, but it may serve to arouse disagreement and thereby promote discussion.

Pan-Humanism

In spite of vast differences in theology, all the great religions have in common, first of all, what we have already been implying: a belief in ethics as such. In practice, this means the recognition of personal responsibility. It means that elemental realm of freedom which in our culture is institutionally protected by the freedom of religious worship. But it is this device of a written constitution, rather than the idea itself, which is peculiar to our own ways. In the Mohammedan world, as well as in China and elsewhere, a considerable measure of this freedom has been accepted for a long time. The Turkish Empire was the marvel of Europe in this respect in the sixteenth century. While the bitter religious wars were raging in England, France and Germany, men pleading for toleration time and again pointed to the Turks' willingness to live and let live so far as the realm of conscience was concerned.

Where a measure of religious freedom has been denied, it has usually been denied in the name of religion. It remained for the totalitarians of our own day to deny religious freedom out of a nihilistic denial of all religion. To be sure, they proclaimed their own, anti-ethical doctrines in pseudo-religious terms, but that does not alter the fact that they denied freedom of conscience to all but those who agreed with their particular version of determinism and materialism. In doing this, they attacked the *human* core of civilization. Human beings were asked to become something worse than slaves: robots. For the human being who is deprived of a belief in his responsibilities becomes an automaton executing the irresistible commands of social forces, biological drives, and the rest.

The universal recognition, then, of a belief in ethics and personal responsibility would be the first freedom that the pan-humanist congress would, I believe, agree upon.

An interesting confirmation comes from Professor Toynbee, whose comparative interpretation of world civilizations entitles him to great respect in a matter of this kind. "There can be no international ethos without a religious basis," he wrote, pointing out at the same time that this basis need not be necessarily Christian, and that religious elements in Islam, Hinduism, Buddhism and other religions offer hope of reaching such an ethos.[5]

Freedom of conscience and of religious worship depends, in the world of hard facts, upon the right to one's physical person. In our own culture, in the English-speaking countries, this has found institutional expression in the right of *habeas corpus*. It has been discussed before. Protection against arbitrary searches and seizures, against being detained without being charged with a legally determinate crime, would be a first and foremost function of world government. Any local authorities unable to guarantee this protection to the inhabitants of their territory would forfeit the right to continue in office; it would be prima-facie evidence that that territory was not yet ready to govern itself. Such a condition may well be found in many parts of Europe after the collapse of the Nazis' rule of terror. If so, the other nations will find themselves saddled with the job of administering such countries for a transition period. For it is my second guess that a pan-humanist congress would agree upon what corresponds to the right of *habeas corpus* as the second universal imperative. It embodies the quintessence of freedom from fear. Without it, the common man as we understand him cannot come into action on a world-wide basis any more than he can on a national one. Even his collective judgment, fallible as it is, cannot come into play if the common man is terrorized.

PAN–HUMANISM

Is all this Utopia? Or is it the shape of things to come? All that mortals can do is to embrace the future with faith in the creative possibilities of mankind. What I hope I have shown is that a solid foundation for a free world is to be found only in a universal common man, a world public. The four freedoms, or indeed any other constitutional guarantees, are of little avail unless they give us that universal common man.

A French skeptic, looking at America in the early nineteenth century, wrote: —

The New Image of the Common Man

It is immensely difficult to create a country out of states without any community of religion and interests, states which have been peopled by different stocks, and are living on varied soils and under diverse climates. What link is there between a Frenchman of Louisiana, a Spaniard of Florida, a German of New York, an Englishman of New England, Carolina, Georgia — all considered Americans? . . . How many centuries will be needed to make these elements homogeneous? [6]

What Chateaubriand overlooked was that they were all *men*, common men united in the allegiance to those freedoms which they had come to live under. After their escape from the despotism, benevolent and otherwise, which they left behind them in Europe, they had become primarily human rather than English, French, German or Spanish. They came first, and the collectivity lived only in and through them.

We have had Pan-Slavism and Pan-Germanism, Pan-Europeanism and Pan-Americanism. All these are expressions of a dying nationalism. Pan-Europa and Pan-America are lame attempts to rescue this moribund force by putting it on a continental basis. The belief in the common man, tempered and restrained by modern knowledge of man and society, gives rise to Pan-Humanism. It is the banner of the future.

The proclamation of the four freedoms has opened a great debate: What are the common patterns of conduct that will enable the world's common men to join forces in solving their common problems? Is there a basis for a world community?

On the answer to this question hinges the future of peace and of a democratic world order.

Looking Backward and Forward

---

*Practical reason provides us with an ir-
resistible veto: there shall not be war.*
                                    — KANT

PREDICTION AND PROPHECY

ON OCTOBER 27, 1941, shortly after the preceding chapters were completed, Hadley Cantril approached
about fifty social scientists and other students of man
and society with the request that they write out in a
couple of pages what they thought the world might be
like in 1951. He was interested in prediction and what
went into it, and he published the results in a much ab-
breviated form,[1] not disclosing the authorship of the different predictions. Here is what I wrote:

Over-all predictions of the developments in human society are not possible. This for one very definite reason, and
that is the <u>unpredictability</u> of creative effort. We cannot

[318]

know what new ideas, inventions, leadership, etc., will make their appearance, and therefore we cannot know who will achieve leadership, who will win battles and, being victorious, will determine the future condition of society. Nor can we know when creative efforts will fail. Nobody has yet been able to fathom the hidden recess of the womb of life. All prediction is premised on things remaining as they are — and we know from experience that things do not remain as they are.

With this general caution in mind, I'd say that, barring unforeseen creations, there are three primary possibilities of the things to come. First, there is the possibility that we may still be at war, second that we will have been defeated by the Axis, and third that we will have won the war. I consider the third the most likely of the three possibilities.

If the third has happened, and if it has happened, say in 1944, I should be inclined to think that the world would be divided between the Anglo-American and the Soviet Russian sphere of influence — unless England, too, had gone communist (which is conceivable, though not too likely). The efforts to establish effective world government will, I am afraid, have proved difficult of achievement, due to this conflict of two world outlooks. A considerable number of peoples, in the Americas and Western Europe, probably will be clustered around the United States, while a good part of Asia and Eastern Europe will be grouped around Moscow. Possibly, though not probably, the two systems will each have assimilated some of the political, economic, and social traits of the other. I do not consider it out of the question that the Soviet Union might have become somewhat more "democratic" and even more likely that the United States somewhat more socialistic. Germany may have become divided between an Eastern part, inclined more or less toward Moscow, and a Western and Southern part, tending toward the opposite pole. Both Germans and Japanese will, at any rate, be "invalid peoples" with a definitely pathological (though possibly a reconvalescent) psychology.

Economically, the world outlook will be confused. The devastations of the war will have only very partially been repaired, and the birth rate will have continued to fall, except at the center of the Slavic and Mongol (Chinese) center of expanding industrialism.

In the sphere of moral standards, there will be continued confusion and uncertainty as the ideas of different peoples and cultures are clashing in the melting pot of an emerging world society. A certain penchant toward religious revivals, in most of the areas of the several world religions, will increase this Babylon of conflicting voices, as each will intensify the belief that its particular gospel is vital for the future of mankind . . . Whether a new religion transcending all the others will make its appearance is one of those questions which are unpredictable, depending upon new creative achievement.

The polarity of outlook between Moscow and Washington will be reflected in internal tensions everywhere, giving rise to civil war situations in marginal territories. Maybe in one of these new territories a new religion will be born. It seems doubtful, though, in view of the declining vitality of human beings, all over.

Looking Backward and Forward

Japan, which is possibly one such marginal area, may have been shaken by a most violent social revolution. Whether at the end she will turn in the direction of Sovietism or American constitutionalism is very difficult to say. I'd be inclined toward expecting the former alternative.

I believe my reply was the only one which questioned, for human affairs, the possibility of prediction in any scientific sense. The creative innovation which in fact altered the situation of mankind in the intervening years is, of course, the atom bomb. Fortunately for me, the impact of this particular innovation reinforced the divisive forces upon which my prediction was based. Some would even say that it was primarily responsible for the divisions which rend the world today. Having deceived themselves about the realities of totalitarian dictatorship, such people would presumably do it a third time, if the atomic potentialities of future warfare did not force the issues out into the open.

If we look retrospectively, then, upon the past ten years, we perceive pretty clearly that they brought three primary developments related to the future of democracy and totalitarian dictatorship — that is to say, to the future of the common man. First, the defeat of Fascist totalitarianism by the combined forces of democracy and Soviet totalitarianism; second, the polarization and division of the world into the totalitarian camp of the Soviet Union, China, and other satellites, and the constitutional camp of the United States, Britain, and their allies and associates; and, third, the development of atomic and related weapons of universal destruction. The third of these developments belongs, properly speaking, in the area of unpredictable creative effort; for appearances' sake, it was lucky that this new factor happened to reinforce, rather than controvert, the predictions I ventured upon in 1941; it may yet, in another few years, have the opposite effect.

The other two developments were predictable, and occurred as predicted. But in connection with both, a vital element was the extent to which America's belief in the common man — that is in democracy of the constitutional kind — would be able to mold the outcome. Internationally and for America's allies and friends, that issue revolved around the establishment of an effective world organization for the maintenance of peace, giving the common man, everyman, freedom from fear in the future. With regard to America herself and the peoples who might be or might come under her control, it raised the issue of "democratization." Democratization, in this broadest sense, would be any extension of the democratic process; it presupposes a realization that democracy is not a fixed and static condition, but a lodestar toward which even a society which has been democratic for some time is forever striving as a high ideal. Unfortunately, it is often forgotten that peoples in various stages of democratization share this task, and that the more democratic peoples might well show their more advanced state by a greater understanding of this basic problem. Even more unfortunate it is that we Americans have been retrogressing in certain essentials of democratic constitutionalism at the very time that we have been urging democratization upon the peoples we conquered. This problem will be considered a little later, because it is generally linked to the "cold war" and often excused by it.

DEMOCRATIZATION: *PRO AND CON*

In any case, after some hesitation, democratization was made the major positive objective of military government following the war. After the end of fighting, the restoration of law and order is bound to assume primary importance. It expanded into the establishing of constitutional democracy. It is fair to say that constitutional democracy is presumed by most Americans to be the only sound basis for law and order. The inclination of Americans and Britishers to look upon democratization in this light was encouraged by the complete absence of the rule of law in the fascist and militarist regimes; that a comparable lack of attachment to the rule of law was characteristic of the Soviet Union was glossed over. Yet this divergence in outlook made the whole democratization policy highly problematic. Since there was not, and is not now, held in the Soviet Union any image of the common man resembling that in English-speaking countries, the term "democratization" had divergent meanings for the Western Allies and the Soviet Union. No sentimentalizing about the gallant Russian soldier (and he was a good fighter) and about "Mother Russia" could alter this basic fact. Agreements, such as the Potsdam Agreement of 1945, embodying the term "democratization" were therefore in reality no more than compromises on a word or formula. Events were bound to prove, as soon as concrete implementation was attempted, that the divergent conceptions of democracy were in a number of vital respects mutually exclusive.

It is difficult to accept the now often heard excuse that Western policy makers had to learn by experience that this was going to be so. The contrasting and mutually exclusive conceptions of democracy were a matter of full and well-established record. If the right emphasis had been placed at the outset upon the distinguishing criteria of a constitutional as compared with a Soviet system of government, if the system of free elections and rival parties had been adequately faced, true agreement might have been achieved on something perhaps less imposing than democratization, but more nearly in keeping with the facts than these empty formulas.

The controversy over democratization has not, however, been confined to disagreement between the Western powers and the Soviet Union. Democratization has also been a bone of contention among the Western Allies and among their citizens. The occupation of Germany, especially, has been bedeviled by the fact that each democratic nation inclines to identify its own outlook with democracy as such. Hence, throughout this period, the free market economy, the compatibility of socialism with a free society, the position of the civil service, and similar issues have been the focal point of controversy. Behind these specific economic and governmental issues lurks the broader problem suggested by the belief in the common man. Neither the British nor the French share the American conviction that, given adequate opportunity to develop, the common man will come to the fore in all nations and assert his rights and utilize his opportunities. Ancient national rivalries, frozen into rigid superstitions about the "character" of nations, tend to reinforce this lack of faith in the common man — everywhere.[2] Thus the experience with military government after World War II is replete with difficult situations and breakdowns resulting from disagreements over what democratization calls for. Whenever the United States, Britain, and France deal with denazification, decartelization, re-education, or any one of a great array of vital concerns, the same basic issue reappears. It continues to plague all concerned.

Constitutionalism, and more especially democracy, presupposes an active group of citizens who are ready to assume responsibility. Too many Americans neglected this basic condition of constitutionalism and democracy in planning for democratizing the occupied peoples. Fortunately for all concerned, such groups of citizens did exist in Italy, in Austria, in Germany, even in Japan. Their hard core was the trade unions with their millions of members. They had a grasp of the dangers inherent in our American approach to constitutionalism and democracy, since in many minds it was so vague as not to enable them to perceive distinctly the non-democratic nature of the Soviet Union and its partisans in other countries.

It thus happened that decisive actions had to be taken by German elements in Berlin at a time when the official Allied policy was still one of "trusting the Russians." In fact, top policy makers refused to acknowledge the patent acts of totalitarian dictatorship in the Soviet Zone of Germany in early 1946, when moves began which resulted in the forcible absorption of such Social Democrats as would allow themselves to be coerced into the Socialist Unity Party. There was then one area in which the Communist claims that such a merger was desired by the membership of the Social Democratic Party could be tested — and that was Berlin, and more specifically the Western sectors. In these sectors the party membership flatly refused and overwhelmingly rejected the proposed merger; in the sequel they gave a substantial majority to the Social Democrats and roundly defeated the Communists. It is clear that these votes were taken with a reasonably definite understanding of what they implied in the way of hostile acts by the Soviet

Union, and of the resulting sacrifices to be expected by the German democratic elements.

It thus came to pass that the common man asserted himself in the most dramatic fashion at the very center of the totalitarian maelstrom. This is the more noteworthy, since a real test of this common man came two years later, when the Soviet Union imposed the blockade. Had the common man in Berlin not been a true image of the reality, as seen by the Americans, it would have been impossible to carry out the airlift. None other than General Clay has made it emphatically clear that that magnificent British-American operation could never have succeeded had it not been for the ardent support of the people of free Berlin, from Mayor Reuter to the overtime worker, from the students and professors leaving the Soviet sector and founding the Free University to women who "kept things going." Another test is happening as Communist demonstrations in Western Berlin are being planned; these too will fail, and again upon the rock of the common man's resistance.

It would lead too far afield to trace the wide ramifications of the democratization issue. Thoughtful Americans have frequently been assailed by grave doubts concerning the "democratic" quality of this effort. The role of coercion is so considerable in any occupation regime, the authoritarian character of such a regime is so palpable, the role of the military in politics is so contrary to democratic traditions, that these efforts have to many seemed more akin to dictatorship than to democracy. Some forget that democracy had its start in England during the Civil War and its aftermath, and that the military played a rather momentous role in the winning of American independence which led to the establishment of the first great constitutional democracy in the world. What is more, they fail to realize that the holding down of anti-democratic elements — indeed their very destruction — may be vitally important in giving the comman man his chance. The trouble with countries like Germany and Japan was that the entrenched classes of militarists, bureaucrats, and big landowners were able to prevent the democratic groups from achieving a majority. Such negative activity may, therefore, be of decisive importance, because it produces the conditions under which the common man, according to the image we have sketched, may emerge and become predominant.

After all, this has been a long struggle everywhere. A young German told me in the summer of 1946 when our repressive policies were still being applied without much discrimination: "You Americans may refuse to admit that you have come as liberators, and pride yourselves on being conquerors, but you have liberated us just the same." He was profoundly right; for liberation, in the democratic and constitutional tradition, means helping people achieve constitutional freedom by combating and defeating those who would deny this freedom to them. To look back three hundred years — did not the Scots, when they made war upon Charles, Strafford, and Laud in 1638, liberate the English constitutional forces? They were feted as liberators in the London of the Long Parliament.

UNPRECEDENTED WORLD SITUATION

When the Scots took up arms to repel the tyranny of Charles Stuart, as they saw it, the European system of nation-states was just coming into being. Within a few years, the Treaty of Westphalia established this system which was to last for almost three hundred years. Perhaps we can now, in retrospect, see that it ended in 1910; but until the conclusion of the Second World War brought the polarization of East and West, it was not generally realized that the system of European nation-states predominant in the world had come to an end. That system revolved around four centers of power: Britannia, France, Russia, and the German complex — in which the Hapsburgs predominated until the nineteenth century, when Prussia took over that role. Balanced, though occasionally disturbed by imperial ambitions, this system rested upon the predominant position of Europe throughout the world, as embodied in the colonial empires of France, England, and lesser powers.

What has today taken the place of this system? I

suggest that it is something entirely unprecedented. History knows balanced systems of several states. History knows universal empires. But history does not know the polarity of two giant continental powers with peculiar opportunities for defense and autonomy. But what is more unusual yet is that each of these two powers rests upon a creed. Each resembles a church and shares with churches the wish to convert everyone to their creed. They are missionary, and cannot help being missionary.[3] A man can *become* a citizen of the United States or of the Soviet Union in a much more comprehensive, thoroughgoing sense than is possible elsewhere. The convert can, and at times *does*, become a better American than the native. Why? Because he has a more vital belief in the convictions upon which America is based. The core of the great communities is the view of man, of society and government, which they represent.

This inherent desire to become *the* universal order, to see the world organized in their image, has often been taken to mean that a sanguinary conflict between the U.S. and the U.S.S.R. is unavoidable. Expressions like Lincoln's famous dictum that a community cannot remain half slave and half free are applied to this situation. It is often overlooked that Lincoln's remark applies — correctly — to a country living under one government. It contains, besides, a somewhat loosely phrased metaphor which is suggestive of an incompatibility of social organization. It is paradoxical in that the U.S. *had* in fact lived "half slave and half free" for more than two generations; many of us would be quite content, if the absence of war could be made secure for that length of time. But the United Nations, while structured somewhat in the image of the United States, is actually a confederation in which at least those powers that possess the veto continue as "sovereign" in all essential respects. That is the reason why it would be — in our understanding of the new image of the common man — quite incorrect to describe the United Nations as the organization of the "common man everywhere," although this is often done in political oratory and pamphleteering. The reason is the simple one which our entire foregoing analysis has developed: neither in education and propaganda, nor in political dissent, nor in public service and planning, are the human beings of a large number of the member states able to develop in the image of the common man and act accordingly.

It is therefore only natural that the representatives of the Soviet Union and its associates should continually protest. To meet their requirements and to correspond to their image of the mass-man, an entirely different kind of organization of the world would be appropriate: an organization modeled upon the pattern of the Cominform, which is the pattern of the Soviet Union. Immanuel Kant, in his celebrated essay *On Eternal Peace* first developed the principle that a lasting peace organization must consist of states which are built upon the governmental principles of constitutionalism. Prophetically, Kant pointed out that one would have to be careful in organizing the world, not to arrive at a universal despotism. Such a world tyranny would, he felt, be a dubious alternative indeed to the anarchy of recurrent wars. Some of us would still agree with him, even in face of the threat of atomic warfare, while others seem more and more inclined to sacrifice liberty to security, if necessary.

It is increasingly clear that the demand for a world organization in the image of the Soviet Union, even though it appears in the garb of Marxism, is in fact the demand for a world empire of universal scope. There are comparable voices in the United States, and while they represent a minority, they are gaining in influence. Even though its author may not have so intended it, the formula of the "American century" was often understood in this way. The *Pax Americana* in analogy to the *Pax Romana* would be the establishment of peace upon the basis of American power. Such a conception is quite incompatible with the American belief in the common man and the structuring of American constitutional democracy which rests upon it. The belief in the common man does not halt at the borders of the United States. It is in its very nature applicable to all peoples; for it is built, as we have seen, upon that common humanity which unites all nations. Policies will often fall short of this conception, but it remains as a permanent guide and criterion. Unless the United States is therefore transformed into some kind of dictatorship, it is apparent that efforts will continue to universalize the kind of order in which the common man is supreme. The United States will, it seems, sacrifice considerable material interests in order to forward such a policy which is conceived in terms of making secure a lasting peace.

In point of fact this policy conjures up, as most people realize — even those who favor it — the very greatest danger of a war with the Soviet Union. This danger arises from the progressive deterioration of relationships, even if both powers pursue what to them appears a policy of peace, avoiding outright aggression and provocation. It is, however, not beyond the realm of possibility that these tendencies will be checked by the development of balancing centers of power. Whereas at the present time the British Commonwealth is so closely tied to the United States as to constitute no genuine balance, the emergent European Union holds out a propect for a basic improvement. For this Union, even though it is being promoted by the United States, displays a decided preference for playing an independent role. Such a role would enable a United Europe to mediate between the Soviet Union and the United States, not in terms of the old balance-of-power game of trying to gain ascendancy over both, but primarily for the purpose of maintaining peace. For the common man throughout the length and breadth of Europe realizes today that the fate of Europe may be that of providing a battlefield for the two contenders for world supremacy. That prospect, coupled as it is with that of occupation by the Red Army at the outset, has no appeal to any but a few hotheads.

In short, the unprecedented world situation may before too long return to a more conventional pattern in which at least four great centers of power hold each other in check. No one who knows the history of Europe can deceive himself into thinking that such an arrangement would provide any sure guarantee of peace; but it appears to many a more promising road than the present contest of a "cold war" between East and West.

PEACE AND WAR

The cold war to many means the "failure" of the United Nations. To them it seems that the fond hope of President Roosevelt lies dashed to the ground — his hope that by agreeing on a world security organization the recurrence of war could be prevented. The common man in America seems perfectly willing to have his government support the United Nations, to make patient attempts at enabling it to work; yet, at the same time, he seems convinced that another war is "inevitable." It is extraordinary how the belief in the inevitability of war has grown; it is really a disbelief in the avoidability of war. "There have always been wars, and there always will be" is one of the most usual comments heard today throughout the Western world, especially in America. And yet, this apparent resignation is in fact the expression of a deep-seated anxiety.

Robert Sherwood in *There Shall Be No Night* — played and published in 1940 at the time of the Soviet war against Finland — had his Doctor Kaarlo, in a memorable discussion he and his friends held in the face of death, answer a comrade who thought that "the light was going out" in these words:

It is just beginning to burn with a healthy flame. I know this, because I have seen it. I have seen it in all kinds of men, of all races, and all varieties of faith. They are coming to consciousness. Look at the millions of men now under arms, and all those fearful that arms may be thrust upon them. Are there any illusions of glory among them? None whatever. Is not that progress?

And to the objection that it makes no difference, he replies:

There is all the difference. Because those illusions . . . are devitalized by the conviction of futility. But grim resignation that makes a man say, "This is an evil job — but I have to do it," . . . that is consciousness. And for the first time in history, consciousness is not just the privilege of a few secluded philosophers. It is free for all.

The New Image of the Common Man

The common man, the thoughtful part of humanity, has largely lost the belief in war as an agency for the achievement of any good.[4] He is even inclined to overlook the negative good that consists in resisting the enemies of what he believes in: democracy and freedom. The common acceptance of the inevitability of war therefore is paradoxical. Like most such paradoxes, it arises from an ideological perplexity. This ideological "jam" results from the belief that conflicting ideas if they touch the basis of society cannot be resolved except by violence. It seems to me that we have here a secular equivalent to what brought about the wars of religion. Then it was believed that men's souls could not be saved except through a particular faith, and hence it was held to be the essence of Christian charity to convert them by force to the "true" faith. Now the secular order, and especially the economy, is invested with a similar halo. But the facts speak too loudly against any sanguine belief in forcible conversion; thus each party to the conflict imputes to the other the "aggressive design" of wanting to go to war for its scheme of secular salvation. And both sides mockingly "laugh off" the other's protestations to the contrary as nothing but propaganda. As we said earlier, both the U.S. and the U.S.S.R. are convinced that what they are aiming at is a reign of universal peace, of "the most perfect democracy." [5]

This persistent belief in a reign of universal peace as the desirable end-state of human development had, of course, been the theme of Immanuel Kant, not only in the essay *On Eternal Peace* (1795), but throughout his philosophical works and more especially in his sketch of a philosophy of history "with a cosmopolitan intent." When the framing of the United Nations charter coincided with the sesquicentennial of Kant's celebrated essay, I was moved to attempt a study of the work, its background and setting within the Western tradition. For although this essay has often been treated as an afterthought of Kant's old age, peace is actually the one theme to which Kant returned again and again. It is Kant's central problem. And it is one of the central problems of Western society. Deeply embedded in the Judaeo-Christian tradition, in the message of the prophets of peace and of the prince of peace, universal peace has been one of the dominant preoccupations of the Western mind. Indeed, Kant pleaded that universal peace was "inevitable." He concluded the essay thus:

If it is a duty, and if at the same time there is well-founded hope, that we may realize a state of public law [i.e. peaceful world organization], even if only in an infinitely gradual approximation, then the *eternal peace* which will take the place of the peacemakings, falsely so-called because they are really just truces, is no empty idea, but a task which, gradually solved, steadily approaches its end . . .[6]

This inevitability is not a mechanical and deterministic dependency, but rooted in the moral aspirations of man.

The New Image of the Common Man

It was Kant's belief in the common man, understood as these moral aspirations, as the natural "good will" of man, that this inevitability — the confidence in the "inevitable peace" — grows out of. "Nothing can be conceived in the world, or even out of it, which can be called good without qualification, except a good will" — with this extraordinary statement, Kant aligns himself with what has been shown to be one of the central tenets of the image of the common man. "Intelligence, wit, judgment, and the other *talents* of the mind, however they may be named, or courage, resolution, perseverance, as qualities of temperament, are undoubtedly good and desirable in many respects. But these gifts of nature may also become extremely bad and mischievous if the will . . . called character, is not good." Kant totally rejects intellectualist elitism:

I myself am by inclination a seeker after truth. . . . There was a time when I thought that this alone could constitute the honor of mankind and *I despised the common man* who knows nothing. Rousseau set me right. This blind prejudice vanished; I learned to respect human nature, and I should consider myself far more worthless than the ordinary workingman if I did not believe that this view [his philosophical one] could give worth to all others to establish the rights of man.[7]

Thus, the belief in the common man is firmly anchored in the most penetrating thought that the English,

[338]

the French, and the American revolutions produced. It is a belief shared by the Socialist thinkers and writers who followed, and is given at least general recognition by Karl Marx for the period after the dictatorship of the proletariat might be established. This is of considerable importance when one considers the presumed "inevitability" of war, resulting from ideological differences. It means that the Marxists do not "believe in war" in the sense in which the Fascists do. They do not glorify war as such. Unfortunately, this ray of hope is considerably dimmed by their glorification of class war, and the consequent glorification of violence as a means towards achieving the eventual reign of universal peace. In mocking at the idea that the bourgeois state could possibly wither away through gradual reforms in a socialist direction, as the evolutionary school of Kautsky had suggested, Lenin wrote:

Engels' historical analysis of [the revolution's] role becomes a veritable panegyric on violent revolution. . . . Here is Engels' argument: ". . . force plays . . . a revolutionary role . . . it is the instrument by the aid of which the social movement forces its way through and shatters the dead, fossilized political forms . . . the immense moral and spiritual impetus that has resulted from every victorious revolution . . ."

Ideas similar to these are the stock in trade of Communists everywhere. It can be called the doctrine of "peace through class war." [8] If this outlook were not tempered by the belief in the inevitability of historical evolution as indicated in the materialist conception of history, as well as the exigencies of Russia's resources and the preparedness of the West, it would have to be considered almost the equivalent of the familiar glorification of war by the Fascists, especially by Hitler.

MINUTE MAN AND COMMON MAN

Every spring, on the 19th of April, the towns of Concord and Lexington celebrate the "shot that was heard 'round the world," as Emerson put it. On the site of the "battle of Concord" stands the well-known statue of the Minute Man — who is the common man in arms. He is the non-professional soldier, the liberty-loving freeman facing the "experts." In the spring of 1944, while everyone was waiting with bated breath for the news of our landing across the English Channel, the town of Concord asked me to make the annual talk that is given at the battleground, in the shadow of the monument, after a rider impersonating Dr. Prescott has delivered his message to the Selectmen. Here is part of what I said:

"The balls whistled well." Or so it seemed to Corporal Amos Barrett. He was one of the Minute Men who stood their ground under Buttrick one hundred and sixty-nine years ago. . . . Before the day was done, an amazing thing had happened: a greatly outnumbered, ill-equipped and untrained bunch of free farmers had inflicted defeat upon a regular army unit of a great empire . . .

The capacity of free men to rise to their defense and to display unexpected capacity in improvising successful warfare has been this country's salvation even in this war. Caught desperately unprepared, we yet succeeded in converting our peace economy into the most gigantic machine of production for war the world has ever seen and within the short span of three years converted a small service force into a fighting force of 11,300,000. Only the student of organization can perhaps fully appreciate the stupendous achievement which the building of the United States war production and military forces between 1941 and 1944 represents. We can be sure of one thing: no dictatorship ever did it. Just as no regimentation could ever have gotten these farmers here into the battle within a few hours of their hearing of the coming of the enemy.

Those men were battling the reactionary forces of imperialism and privilege just as we today are battling the reactionary forces of nationalist ambition and racial conceit. Is it too much to hope that there will grow a United World out of this great world revolutionary conflict just as our United States grew out of their stolid stand? . . .

Is it too much to hope that enmities of today will be resolved in a higher fellowship just as the enmities of that time have been? King George, to be sure, was no Hitler. And deep bonds of common language, common tradition in law and government bound the colonists to their British forebears, as they bind us today. But is there not perhaps a higher humanity which binds us all?

The New Image of the Common Man

These are our hopes. These are the goals we are fighting for. But the bitter experience of man's long struggle has taught us that freedom is not secure until it is firmly protected by established government. Only a union of the free can erect a lasting peace. There is no wisdom in sentimental optimism. The coming of freedom is the reward of protracted effort. The prospects are anything but rosy. The United States will find herself in a world full of totalitarian forces. Like little Switzerland she will have to face up to these forces. The prophets of gloom proclaim that this will mean the end of democracy and freedom in the United States. They do not know that the Swiss have grown to be the stoutest democrats with guns in hand. They do not realize that the Swiss have ever been mindful of the importance of each man's having a share in the defense of freedom. They do not realize that such a conception of military service can be a positive contribution to the education for citizenship.

It was a small crowd that gathered by this bridge on April 19, 1775. But it was the fountain of a mighty stream. It is a stream that is still swelling . . . The road ahead is hard. It is full of pitfalls. But a United World will be ours in the end.

At the time, most Americans hoped that this stream might "sweep into its mighty current the Chinese, the Russians." I myself expressed this hope. I still do. But it would have been a miracle — one which I could hardly say I expected to occur at the end of World War II — to have the Soviet Union under its present masters permit such a thing to happen. The fanaticism which they must cultivate, the suppression of the common man in favor of the mass-man which they celebrate as the "perfect democracy," the glorification of class war and revolutionary violence under a self-appointed elite — all these stand in the way of such a miracle. Yet, the image of the common man here outlined has its counterpart among the Russian people; given a chance to develop, the common man would come into being there as anywhere. There *is* a common humanity.

This common humanity tends, at times, to get lost, in the long perspective of history, under the variegated cloak of diverse cultures. One of the most striking indications of a widespread sense of doom is the response of the Western mind to "philosophies of history" which pretend to plot the course of man throughout the ages past and thereby claim to provide a lodestar of the future. Spengler and Toynbee are only the most ambitious philosophers of this kind. Against these prophets of doom, the new image of the common man is set as a vigorous reassertion of the capacity of man to play a role in shaping his future.[9] It is distilled from the American tradition; but it must not be identified with the "cult of the average man" which has been described as ·the "dominant American political philosophy," in terms of a cult of the common man, i.e. that "the common man would think and act rationally." It is vital that this "cult" be deprived of its "cultist" aspects through a restatement of its basic view of man. Even now, I urge the acceptance of this restatement.[10]

SMALL TOWN

The vigor and vitality of small-town life which expressed itself in the spontaneous response of the Minute Men seems a far cry from the millions who have to be organized for the common defense of the United States today. Yet, in the last analysis, the human resources of a great society are dependent upon the communal life of the small towns comprised within it. The mechanistic abstractness of the great society, and the loneliness of the human beings who are part of it, have, in recent years, led to a considerable searching for ways of reviving the local community. Following the challenge by John Dewey in *The Public and Its Problems*, and the morphological portrait of *Middletown* by John and Helen Lynd,[11] further work in this field by anthropologists and sociologists has produced interesting, but by no means consistent, results. Lloyd Warner's *Yankee City* series was originally undertaken with an economic bias; the fundamental structure of American society which controls — even dominates — the thought and action of the American people was assumed to be economic, and hence the common man's values were considered as predominantly economic and related to an economic order. But preliminary inquiry disproved this working hypothesis. As a result, Warner and his associates substituted a broader "class" concept which they defined in terms of subjective opinions concerning the prestige of different individuals: "[By] class is meant two or more orders of people who are *believed* to be, and are accordingly ranked by the members of the community, in socially superior and inferior positions" (italics mine). Clark Wissler (James West) produced a divergent view in his *Plainville, U.S.A.*, which is in keeping with his earlier culture analysis.

The striking feature of these studies is the extent to which they confirm the new image of the common man that it has been our concern to delineate. This result is the more significant, since no such intention was part of the undertaking of these analyses. In fact, they were somewhat influenced by the conceit of being "free of value" and for that reason "scientific" and "objective." The extent to which they reveal value judgments to be at work in structuring the communities which were being studied indirectly confirms the new image of the common man as primarily a man of character rather than of intellect.

But perhaps the most striking series of portraits of the common man as here mirrored is contained in Granville Hicks' remarkable *Small Town*. Devoid of the ambitious apparatus, methodological and conceptual, which characterizes the studies just referred to, it nevertheless brings to light the essential factors — indeed, does so with greater vividness. Hicks himself, a one-time Marxist and therefore intellectualist elitist, is still much troubled by the role of the intellectual in "Roxborough" (presumably Grafton, N.Y., where he lives). But his very earnest and persistent effort to participate effectively in the life of that small town forced Hicks to abandon his former intellectualist preconceptions. Once he had faced the problems of effective communication, of communication so designed as to achieve social action, he could not help but discover the true image of the "common man." It was an exciting experience for me to read Hicks' account of this discovery, because it paralleled so closely my own observations and difficulties. Hicks, however, carried the effort so much farther, committed himself to so much more thorough a participation, that his experience possesses broader evidential value than my own encounters.

At the heart of his analysis, we find him insisting upon the importance of the small community in spite of all its limitations:

There is a good deal of talk these days about the common people and the grass roots, much of it being done by individuals who recommend measures that would inevitably concentrate power in the hands of a small minority. . . . The very difficulty of that problem [the problem of democracy in a complex society] makes me all the more certain that people should have as much power as possible over the things that directly affect their lives.[12]

Looking Backward and Forward

The reason for this insistence upon the importance of people's having as much power as possible over the issues that directly affect their lives is that "it is a practical school of democracy." Hicks has no more illusions than I have about the realities of small-town politics. But it is this very lack of illusions which feeds the new image of the common man. Various socio-psychological studies have confirmed what stands at the center of this conviction — namely, that in neighborhood and group there is an informal leadership which rests upon the weight which certain persons carry among the human beings composing that group. As often as not, the particular individual may not enjoy a special status at all, but, as Hicks observes, and so vividly illustrates from his own experience, "somehow authority attaches itself to his words, and this personal authority is more persuasive than the prestige of any radio commentator or newspaper columnist." Here we have the image of the common man.

The problem of the rebirth of the small town today confronts the United States (as well as other countries) not only in terms of the federal government, as is the usual view, but also and more insidiously in terms of the growth of the metropolitan areas. In fact, at least one school of analysis of urban problems is convinced that the United States at present has become a congeries of metropolitan regions, with the urban cores and their hinterlands covering most of the land area of the nation.

The New Image of the Common Man

Curiously enough, the discussion of the metropolitan region has been largely carried on in terms of the "rotting urban core." Such a project as the Greater Boston Plan [13] has been predominantly focused upon solving Boston's problems. It seems to me at least as urgent a problem how to keep the economically dependent smaller communities effective and alive. The plan which I had the good fortune to help in framing centered therefore upon the federal solution. Federalism is the democratic device for the solution of complex patterns of community organization. For it is built upon the recognition of levels of interest and participation.

Thus the role of the common man — and more especially the informal leadership characteristic of the small town — would be effectively continued. Unhappily, it is the opposition of the small-townsman which is thwarting this solution. Like the small-country politicians in Europe between the two world wars, they insist upon their local independence and autonomy in disregard of all economic and ecological realities, and may continue to do so until disaster overtakes them. The sense of regional community has not yet asserted itself.

1984

It is the withering away of the informal leadership, which is in no way conscious of status or prestige, which blurs and eventually blots out the image of the common man under totalitarian dictatorship. No vague, general oratory about the people, the masses and the classless society should be allowed to obscure this crucial disaster. The "authoritarian man" takes the place of the common man. The endemic danger to a functioning free society is the emergence of this mass-man in sufficient numbers to achieve ascendancy over the common man. At the present time, this danger is highlighted in the United States by the hysterical witch-hunt by mass-man for any "deviations" from the supposed orthodoxy of "patriotism." As a consequence, the noblest symbols of America's tradition of freedom are once again being perverted to the use of obscurantism and oppression. Dr. Johnson's famous dictum that "patriotism is the last refuge of a scoundrel" is becoming applicable.

The sound sense of the common man which tells him that a "party" which acknowledges ties with a great foreign power is suspect in a free society is being reinforced by the anxiety occasioned by the particular outlook of that foreign power, with its belief in class war and the fifth-column activities connected with it. The resulting issues of how to maintain a free society free, and yet prevent its enemies from using that freedom to destroy it, are probably the toughest problems which constitutional democracy has yet encountered, in its brief history. The new constitutions which have been adopted in France, Italy, and Germany seek to develop novel protective devices to cope with this situation; it

cannot be said that they have been especially successful.[14] Rather they epitomize the fact that everywhere
constitutional democracies are at present in danger of
developing totalitarian patterns of their own.

The resulting sense of despair has found its most mor-
dant expression in George Orwell's *Nineteen Eighty-
Four*. In the center of this nightmare-England that has
become totalitarian under the sign of Ingsoc (or English
Socialism), there moves, suffers, and eventually is
snuffed out a typical common-man-in-the-making. He
is not in any way a remarkable fellow, this small official
in a branch of the Ministry of Truth. But the nature of
his task, the rewriting of past records to make them fit
into the shifting party line, rekindles in his mind a glim-
mer of independent thought. This thought-crime in its
ramifications, including a "genuine" love affair, engulfs
and destroys him.

The terrifying impact of this story is largely the result of the fact that the features of this England in 1984
are discernible in the England and America of today.
This aspect of the story is more significant than its resemblance to the reality of the Soviet Union and the
Fascist dictatorships, though the resemblance of the
book's portrayal had been anticipated in such books as
The Seventh Cross and *A Room on the Route*. Considering what the present system of mass communications already does to the independent thought of mass-
man, it seems not too far-fetched to read of Room 101

in the Ministry of Love, where the remnants of an independent spirit are broken until a man believes that
black is white, that two plus two equals five, and — as
the party's slogan has it — that "war is peace, freedom is
slavery, ignorance is strength."

But what kind of 1984 does the new image of the
common man allow us to set against such a persuasive
counsel of despair? Shall we assume with one English
critic of Orwell's that the catastrophe of a vast war of
totalitarian and semi-totalitarian powers is inescapable,
but will be a blessing in the end? This critic writes:

The suffering of such a catastrophe would be so enormous
that no one would dare to wish for it or to work for it. But
it is the probability that it is this which awaits us, that in a
compelled return to simplicity we shall find again a release
for those creative impulses for which tyranny and large-
scale industrialism have failed to find a place and that in the
long run such a catastrophe will prove to be a blessing.[15]

As an escape from the three totalitarian systems which
George Orwell envisages, I agree that such a prophecy
still represents a lingering belief in man. But the new
image of the common man calls forth a different vision
altogether. Not, to be sure, the unbelievable and self-
righteous vision of a world satisfied with becoming what
the United States is now. But a world which, as long as
it manages to avoid bloody fighting, converts the war-
ring into a heated struggle over the issues of the future
values of humanity.

[351]

The New Image of the Common Man

As I tried to indicate in Chapter 10, "Pan-Human-ism," very difficult and perplexing tasks confront mankind. The patterns of belief which have been the basis of judgments as to "good and evil" are not merely a matter of theology or philosophy; they are living and creative forces. "Living law," "Living art," and related slogans epitomize a vast area of unresolved tasks which in a sense are never-to-be-resolved tasks. For it is the peculiar and inescapable destiny of finite minds that any solution of a given task is likewise finite, and consequently begets new tasks in turn. The new image of the common man is rooted in this recognition of limits — as well as potentialities.

THE PATHOS OF PATIENCE

The aging Milton, blind and weighed down by the defeat of the "good old cause" which was yet the bright cause of the future once wrote:

> But patience is more oft the exercise
> Of saints, the trial of their fortitude,
> Making them each his own Deliverer
> And victor over all
> That tyrannie or fortune can inflict.

Against the revolutionary violence and the fanaticism of the totalitarian doctrinaire, the common man in the free countries has only the defense of patience, of which the poet speaks. It is no good clamoring for a "burning faith" in democracy; the true democrat knows too well how short of ideal standards the actual performance falls even under favorable conditions. If there is one difference between the old and the new image of the common man which is more important than any other, it is the mode of the new image and the moderation of its beholders. As they look into the mirror they see themselves but "through a glass, darkly." But this very moderation is, as we undertook to show, the great strength of this "new" belief which is as old as man's aspiration for freedom under law.

To conclude, the common man is neither the mass-man nor the average man. He is the personal symbol, the embodiment and image of what all have in common when they personally participate in communal tasks and civic duties. That this is only a small part of every one should be obvious to any sensible observer. Even those with a genuine civic conscience devote only a limited amount of their thought, time, and energy to public affairs; but it is in these limited periods that everyman becomes the common man. At least, this is the image of the active common man. As a passive recipient, his image merges with that of everyman. But it is the common active man with whom the functioning of democracy is concerned. He is the human, the personal agent upon whose vitality and integrity the life of a democratic nation and of a democratic world order depends. The new image of the common man salvages from the on-slaught of the irrationalist revolt those elements in the older doctrine which are essential to democratic politics. It seeks a middle ground between the extreme rationalistic ideas of an earlier day and the denial of all rationality by those who were disappointed over the limitations of the common man's wisdom and prudence. What these irritated critics overlooked was the role of patience in human affairs, whether domestic or world-wide. Patience may be the beggar's virtue but

> Patience, my lord! Why 't is the soul of peace;
> Of all the virtues, 't is near'st kin to Heaven.
> It makes men look like gods.

So sang the irrepressible Thomas Dekker, born in want, reared in poverty, yet a happy spirit. The world of *The Shoemaker's Holiday* (1603) is the world of the common man in the making.

Notes

PROLOGUE

[1] *The Century of the Common Man* (1942). How general this condescension is was unwittingly proved by one of Wallace's admirers, Frank Kingdon, who in 1945 published a book about him entitled *An Uncommon Man — Henry Wallace*. No indication here of the fact that Henry Wallace is, and wants to be, very much the common man, in spite of his uncommon achievements and qualities.

[2] Translation as given by George A. Morgan Jr., *What Nietzsche Means*. Chapter IV, entitled "Man," of this remarkable book is very important for the problem of this Prologue.

[3] Recently, H. A. Overstreet has offered a catechism of what men can do to achieve "the image of adulthood." In his *The Mature Mind* (1949) he urges his readers to become "mature" by responding to the "image of maturity" which he sketches. I can best indicate the broad area of agreement by saying that anyone who realizes this "image of maturity" would qualify himself for the role of common man according to the image I have in mind.

[4] See pp. 323 ff.

[5] Published in German in 1936; in English in 1940.

[6] Mannheim, pp. 81 ff.

[7] See pp. 256 ff.

Notes

CHAPTER I

1. See B. E. Lippincott, *Victorian Critics of Democracy* (1938).

2. The French had a great body of rationalist doctrine of their own, of course. Both Paine and Bentham were in close touch with it. Emphasis on national traditions has distorted the history of ideas and has barred a comprehension of the evolution of the mind of Europe.

3. See É. Halévy, *The Growth of Philosophic Radicalism* (1928), pp. 168 f., 172 ff. This excellent work was published in French in 1904.

4. These passages are from *Rights of Man*. I have quoted from the special edition published in 1925 by the Thomas Paine National Historical Association, and edited by William M. Van der Weyde, Vol. VI, pp. 240 ff.

5. See *Works* (ed. Bowring), Edinburgh, 1843, Vol. IX, p. 5. Of the first book, pp. 1–10 and 95–114 are particularly relevant here. An interesting contrast is afforded by George Cornwall Lewis, *The Influence of Authority in Matters of Opinion* (1848).

6. See R. H. Gabriel, *The Course of American Democratic Thought* (1940); Henry Adams, *History of the United States under the Administration of Thomas Jefferson*, Vol. I, ch. vi, and V. L. Parrington, *Main Currents in American Thought* (1927–1930).

7. This rather unusual book by an unusual author was described by Samuel E. Morison as one of the few historical novels that were good history. It is based upon a careful study of local material by Bellamy himself, who was a resident in

Notes

that part of the Berkshires for many years. Although all general histories of the period refer to this popular uprising (usually in somewhat partisan terms), we have no thorough historical study of this important phase of American history.

8. J. C. Miller, *Sam Adams* (1936), p. 390.

9. See Herbert Agar, *The Land of the Free* (1935), ch. 5.

10. F. O. Matthiessen, *American Renaissance* (1941), p. 78.

11. Matthiessen, *op. cit.*, p. 632. See also text, pp. 248–250, 252–253 for Carlyle.

12. Further confirmation may be found in Thoreau's respect for and interest in the *skills* of common craftsmen. "It is now clear," Matthiessen writes, "that his revolt was bound up with a determination to do all he could to prevent the dignity of common labor from being degraded by the idle tastes of the rich." *Op. cit.*, p. 173.

13. *The Pulse of Democracy* (1940).

14. V. L. Parrington, in the book already cited, gives many striking instances, e.g., Vol. II, pp. 275 ff., 451 ff.

15. This is the real purport of Ortega y Gasset's book by that name. Unfortunately, it provided antidemocratic, even fascist, formulas for many who read it superficially.

CHAPTER II

1. The famous definition comes in Bodin's *De Republica Libri* (Paris, 1576, Latin translation by the author, 1586), Book I, ch. viii, and reads: "*Majestas est summa in cives ac subditos legibusque soluta potestas.*" Later on he adds the important stipulation that *summa* means that *majestas* recognizes no earthly superior, which shows that the definition was politically directed against the authority of Pope and Emperor. Bodin also insists that *majestas* is *potestas perpetua*, thereby excluding all temporary grants of power, no matter how comprehensive.

Notes

2. See more especially Johannes Althusius, and the author's introduction to a new edition of his *Politica* (1932).

3. Rupert Emerson, *State and Sovereignty in Modern Germany* (1928).

4. See *Encyclopedia of the Social Sciences*, Vol. XII, p. 173.

5. For Laski's pluralist view, see *A Grammar of Politics* (1925).

6. See above, p. 19.

7. This view is more extensively examined in Chapter VI.

8. See, e.g., R. M. MacIver, *The Modern State* (1926).

9. F. M. Watkins, *The State as a Concept of Political Science* (1934).

10. For an elaboration of this, see the author's *Constitutional Government and Democracy* (1941), chapters i and vii–ix. MacIver's view is really similar, once it is stripped of the words "state" and "sovereignty." He definitely contrasts the present "state" which he calls democracy and an older state which was "the organization of a class." It is confusing, to say the least, to have the same word for two distinct phenomena.

11. Watkins, *op. cit.*, p. 66.

12. This distinction was very popular in the seventeenth century and before. Althusius and other defenders of the people against monarchical sovereignty tried to construct the concept of popular sovereignty in these terms: *cives universi* versus *cives singuli*. Obviously the people *singuli* are still part of the association.

13. The writer prefers *consent* and *constraint* to *persuasion* and *coercion*, because they emphasize the common man's rather than the government's part in the relationship. Besides, persuasion postulates, in many instances, more than can be rightly asserted, e.g., when a member of a college faculty or of any group "goes along" when rules are altered, although he may not be the least "persuaded." Yet it would be erroneous to consider him "coerced." Acquiescence is an important ele-

Notes

ment in consent; it is also an element in constraint. Only an examination of the persons concerned can, in particular instances, determine whether acquiescence is the result of one or the other.

14. See Chapter IV.

15. See Chapter X.

16. See Charles E. Merriam, *The Making of Citizens* (1931), and the other books of the series "Studies in the Making of Citizens."

17. See Chapter VII.

18. Compare A. D. Nock, *Conversion* (1933).

19. Here is how George C. Robertson summed up Hobbes's position: "The sovereign power, if it will maintain itself at all and be able to provide for the safety and well-being of its subjects, cannot choose but take in hand the regulation of their whole life, *religious as well as secular.* . . . The State must be at the same time church, if it is to remain State . . . See his *Hobbes* (1886), p. 154.

20. For a further elaboration of this point see the author piece in *The Review of Politics*, Vol. I, No. 1, p. 26.

21. These points have been more fully developed in a recen study by William M. McGovern, *From Luther to Hitle* (Houghton Mifflin Company, 1941). In spite of the misleadin title, McGovern says: —

"Hobbes is undoubtedly the greatest, the clearest, and th most logical of all the advocates of absolute monarchy, a though he lived at the time and the place where absolu monarchy was resisted and overcome. Absolute monarch was to persist in most European countries until the end of th eighteenth century. It was only in England that democrac was able to secure public recognition in the seventeenth ce tury. However, none of the countries in which royalism ha undisputed sway produced a work in favor of royalism ha as convincing as that of the English Hobbes, who wrote o defense of monarchy when Charles, the English king, was

Notes

prisoner, and the other in 1651, two years after King Charles had been decapitated.

"To many contemporary English observers, it seemed as if Hobbes, with his belief that kings should be allowed to rule as they see fit, was 'behind the times,' a relic of a bygone age. Hobbes' real glory and fame started a century after he was dead, in the nineteenth century, the era of democracy; and it was Bentham and his fellow utilitarians, the most radical advocates of democracy, who did the most to revive Hobbes' popularity.

"The utilitarians, to be sure, disagreed with Hobbes' conclusions even though they adopted his methods. They were sure that these conclusions were entirely outmoded. Yet a century later, in our own generation, we find a revival of the principles which Hobbes defended and the utilitarians rejected. In fact we can best understand Hobbes if we regard him, not as a singer of the swan song of the Stuarts, but as the prophet of a system which was to be carried out nearly three centuries later by Mussolini and Hitler." *Absolutism v. Tota*

22. See G. P. Gooch and H. Laski, *English Democratic Ideas in the Seventeenth Century* (1927); C. J. Friedrich, *Johannes Althusius' Politica* (1932), and the literature cited here.

CHAPTER III

1. See *Public Opinion* (1922), Part III. Lippmann, it should noted, did not leave the problem on that skeptical note.
2. See p. 34.
. See pp. 25 ff. where *The Public and Its Problems* (1927) discussed.

. A very intelligent recent survey of psychological definition of propaganda by Jerome S. Bruner culminated in the following definition: "Propaganda is that aspect of com-

Notes

munications which maintains or changes the susceptibility of an individual or group of individuals to some particular social movement. . . . Propaganda may take effect through influencing the emotions, reason, or any mental process of which the human organism can boast." See his unprinted dissertation, *Psychological Analysis of International Broadcasts by Various Nations* (1941), in the Widener Library. It is clear that this definition, whatever its utility for the psychological purposes in hand, is much too broad to provide a basis for distinguishing, even roughly, between propaganda and education or propaganda and information.

5. See the *New York Times*, October 24, 1936, p. 1, and subsequent issues for the full story.

6. Details may be found in the *New York Herald Tribune*, May 23, 1941, p. 11.

7. There is a definite similarity between propaganda and so-called "institutional advertising."

8. From a folder issued by the Council for Democracy. In the first sentence quoted it would have been more accurate to have said, "is reported to have spent."

9. *Propaganda* (1938), p. 12.

10. See the articles in the *Atlantic Monthly* for August, September, and October, 1940.

11. "Politics under democracy consists almost wholly of the discovery, chase and scotching of bugaboos. The statesman becomes, in the last analysis, a mere witch-hunter, a glorified smeller and snooper, eternally chanting 'Fe, Fi, Fo, Fum!' " *Notes on Democracy* (1926), p. 22.

12. For a more elaborate examination of elite theories, see Chapter VIII.

13. Sandburg, *Abraham Lincoln: the War Years* (1939), Vol. III, p. 384.

14. By making available to us the colorful, if rather baroque, panorama of his *Abraham Lincoln*, Carl Sandburg has greatly

Notes

aided this insight. At the same time, we must remember that Sandburg's achievement is itself the outcome of the new spirit of which we are speaking.

15. See, for further aspects of this matter, Chapter VI.

16. Published by W. W. Norton in 1938, just before Munich, this book showed why war was inescapable.

17. See Chapter X.

CHAPTER IV

1. Parts of the argument of this chapter were first published in an article entitled "One Majority Against Another: *Populus Sempervirens*," in the *Southern Review*, Vol. V, No. 1 (Summer 1939), and in *Constitutional Government and Democracy* (1941), chapters vii–ix. Lewis, *op. cit.*, ch. vii, has a discussion of the majority principle.

2. See, e.g., Max Lerner's able but one-sided statement in "Minority Rule and the Constitutional Tradition" in *The Constitution Reconsidered* (1938), pp. 191 ff.

3. See, e.g., *The Majority of the People: A Grammar of Democracy* (1941), by Edwin Mims, Jr., and the interesting unprinted thesis by William N. Chambers *In Their Defense* (1939), which deals with "Theories of Minority Rule in Three American Political Struggles — 1787–1939."

4. See, e.g., McIlwain's thoughtful, but also one-sided, statement in "The Fundamental Law Behind the Constitution of the United States," *The Constitution Reconsidered, op. cit.*, pp. 33 ff.

5. Mims, *op. cit.*, p. 33.

6. Willmoore Kendall, "The Majority Principle and the Scientific Elite," the *Southern Review*, Vol. IV, No. 3 (Winter 1939), p. 463.

7. *Social Contract*, Book IV, ch. ii.

Notes

8. See C. J. Friedrich, *Constitutional Government and Democracy* (1941), pp. 230 f. This jury proposal is an interesting attempt to get away from the conservatism of courts, in providing for constitutional interpretation. Yet is it not, in fact, a "verbal" solution? Functionally, any body interpreting a legal document is a kind of court. One might recall, also, the old adage that the Supreme Court follows the election returns.

9. This provides the explanation for Abraham Lincoln's supposed inconsistency when he enunciated the doctrine of the people's right to abolish the government and later denied that right to the seceding states.

10. Mims, *op. cit.*, p. 38, appropriately cites Webster's brief before the Supreme Court in *Luther v. Borden:* "The Constitution goes on the idea that, within and under the Constitution, no new form of government can be established without the authority of the existing government. Unless there be some authentic way of ascertaining the will of the people . . . all is anarchy . . . and all constitutions and legislative rights are prostrated and disregarded."

11. Cf. for a splendid exposition of this kind of democratic group pluralism, Eduard Heimann, *Communism, Fascism, or Democracy?* (1938), especially pp. 267 ff. "The popular notion that democracy consists in acting as the majority desires is obviously very wrong, if it is not confined to secondary decisions." How Kendall, in the light of this statement, can claim Heimann as an adherent of his view I do not understand.

12. Heimann, *op. cit.*, p. 279.

13. The movement known as agrarianism, largely supported by Southern writers and poets, has made much of this issue. See, e.g., *I'll Take My Stand; the South and the Agrarian Tradition; by Twelve Southerners* (1930). It has always been central in the Catholic Church's view of property.

14. Soil conservationists might take courage from the fact that Faust is planning a drainage program here.

Notes

CHAPTER V

1. Parts of the discussion which follows were presented in an article entitled "Democracy and Dissent," by the author, published in Vol. X (October–December 1939), of *The Political Quarterly* (London).

2. *Parliamentary Government in England*, pp. 4 ff.

3. See, e.g., G. D. H. Cole, *The Intelligent Man's Guide Through World Chaos* (1932), p. 603.

4. See Robert H. Jackson, *The Struggle for Judicial Supremacy* (1940). Also Erich Hula, *Social Research*, Vol. VI, p. 284, and compare pp. 269–272, as well as 301–302, and William Yandell Elliott, *The Review of Politics*, Vol. II, No. 1 (January, 1940), pp. 1–11.

5. Eduard Lindeman, *Leisure — A National Issue* (1939), p. 35.

6. Louis Adamic, *From Many Lands* (1940), p. 297.

7. See R. Bassett, *The Essentials of Parliamentary Democracy* (1935), p. 126.

8. See Chapter III, the discussion of "Education versus Propaganda."

9. See *My Battle* (1933), pp. 47 ff.

10. For Niemöller see *I Was in Prison* by Charles S. Macfarland (1939); for Bishop Count von Galen, see the *Pilot* for October 18 and 25, 1941, and January 24, 1942.

11. See Donald Strong, *Organized Anti-Semitism in America* (1940).

12. Archibald MacLeish, "American Letter," *New Found Land* (Houghton Mifflin Company, 1930).

13. H. L. Mencken, *American Language* (1923), p. 294 ff.

14. See, for an elaborate description of the crisis which arose, Josef Redlich, *The Procedure of the House of Commons* (1908), Vol. I, pp. 137–163.

15. In what follows I have benefited by a study made for me by Samuel Beer.

Notes

16. For this legislation see K. B. Smellie, *A Hundred Years of English Government* (1937), and E. L. Woodward, *The Age of Reform* (1938).

17. These and many other lines of development have been treated over and over again by textbook writers on English political, social, and economic history. See, e.g., K. B. Smellie, *op. cit.*, or R. C. K. Ensor, *England 1870–1914* (1936).

18. See William H. Chamberlin, *Russia's Iron Age* (1934), p. 152.

19. *Works*, Vol. III, p. 165 (Boston, 1839).

20. *Op. cit.*, p. 424.

21. See Walter Bagehot, *The English Constitution* (1867), pp. 49, 50. It will be noted that these views are close to those of Plato's *Republic*, with its guardian class.

22. For further discussion of the elite concept, see Chapter VIII.

23. See *Constitutional Government and Democracy* (1941).

24. This is what my highly esteemed friend Erich Hula did when he wrote: "There can be no doubt that such an agreement (upon consent rather than force) presupposes in itself common fundamental objectives." See *Social Research*, Vol. VI, p. 284. Common objectives, yes! But why "fundamental"?

25. Other quotations from McWilliams and documentation of his fascist connections will be found in a pamphlet, "The Case Against Joseph E. McWilliams," issued by Friends of Democracy, Inc., in 1940.

26. See *Freedom of Assembly and Anti-Democratic Groups*, Democracy in Action Series, No. 1, Council for Democracy.

27. I have good reason to believe that Mr. Maverick would recognize that it was his job as mayor to arrange matters so that such a riot should not occur. If the application for the permit had been brought to his attention in the first place, he would have handled the situation successfully. What happened was that Mrs. Brooks went to a clerk, and the clerk treated the permit as a routine matter. If you are realistic you can see

that a very important factor in the situation was that the meeting was held in a place which was felt by the community to be a memorial to patriotism. It was like hoisting the red flag on the Lincoln Memorial.

CHAPTER VI

1. James Beck, *Our Wonderland of Bureaucracy* (1932); Lord Hewart, *The New Despotism* (1932).

2. See the valuable, though somewhat meandering, comments by Joseph Dorfman in *Thorstein Veblen and his America* (1934), pp. 165 ff.

3. Thorstein Veblen, *The Instinct of Workmanship and the State of the Industrial Arts* (1914).

4. How this problem may be analyzed from the administrative standpoint, the author has shown in two related studies: *Responsible Bureaucracy* (1932 — with Taylor Cole), and "Responsible Government Service under the Constitution" in *Problems of the American Public Service* (1936), pp. 3–29.

5. As in mining, quarrying, electric light and power. See Leverett S. Lyon, Myron W. Watkins, Victor Abrahamson, *Government and Economic Life* (1939), Vol. I, p. 47, and p. 494.

6. See James Burnham, *The Managerial Revolution* (1940).

7. See Lewis Meriam, *Public Personnel Problems* (1938), and W. E. Mosher, *Public Personnel Administration* (1941).

8. Chester I. Barnard, *The Functions of the Executive* (1938), p. 71.

9. Childs and others have distinguished four. Cf. *Introduction to Public Opinion* (1940), p. 42.

10. *The Oxford English Dictionary* defines responsibility by describing a responsible person as one who is answerable for his acts to some other person or body. This person or body to whom responsibility is owed is called "the principal."

Notes

11. Chester I. Barnard, *op. cit.,* p. 283.

12. We deal here primarily with the second of these levels, where the common man-citizen operates. We have dealt with the common man-functionary in a separate study, "Public Policy and Administrative Responsibility," in *Public Policy,* Vol. I (1940).

13. See Chapter III, pp. 114–117.

14. See *Variety,* July 9, 1941, p. 26, where a review of the first time is found. The story of the Treasury's campaign is discussed at some length in Peter H. Odegard and Alan Barth, "Millions for Defense," *Public Opinion Quarterly,* Vol. V, No. 3 (Fall 1941), pp. 399–411.

15. See C. J. Friedrich, *Constitutional Government and Democracy* (1941), pp. 445 ff.

16. For the theoretically important "rule of anticipated reactions" in interpreting such contexts, see *op. cit.,* pp. 589 ff.

17. The limitations on majority decisions which this brings about have been previously discussed in Chapter IV.

CHAPTER VII

1. His most recent statement of the case is found in *On the Agenda of Democracy* (1941), pp. 72 ff. But see also *The New Democracy and the New Despotism* (1939), pp. 145 ff. and still earlier his *Role of Politics in Social Change* (1936). About that time the author also adumbrated this view in "Some Thoughts on the Politics of Government Control," *Journal of Social Philosophy,* Vol. I (1936), pp. 122 ff.

2. See *The Wisdom of Confucius* (ed. Lin Yutang), p. 163.

3. See René de Visme Williamson, *The Politics of Planning in the Oil Industry under the Code* (1936), p. 18. Williamson there defines an *end* as "the symbol of an ideal social order, conceived as intrinsically and ultimately valuable, which is a

Notes

standard of action and principle of ethical justification." His analysis is based upon a closely reasoned, if brief, survey of the issue as he sees it.

4. See Chester I. Barnard, *The Functions of the Executive* (1938), pp. 55 ff., especially. Barnard warns his readers that "efficiency" is often used in a purely technological sense in which it has no applicability to organization problems. See p. 92.

5. For example, the friendly treatment of the Plan by Sidney and Beatrice Webb in *Soviet Communism*, p. 642 and elsewhere.

6. Charles E. Merriam takes a very broad view of resources; see, e.g., his new *On the Agenda for Democracy* (1941), p. 76.

7. See William Henry Chamberlin, *Russia's Iron Age* (1934), ch. viii; Douglas Miller, *You Can't Do Business with Hitler* (1941); Gunther Reimann, *The Vampire Economy* (1939); and many others.

8. Fritz Morstein Marx deserves high praise for having made this point emphatically in his *Government of the Third Reich*, especially pp. 115 ff. (rev. ed.). Others, such as Frederick Schumann, also early called attention to this aspect of Nazi Germany.

9. For this point, compare the author's *Constitutional Government and Democracy*, ch. v.

10. See for confirmation the several works of Charles E. Merriam cited. To these might well be added Sir Henry Bunbury's *Governmental Planning Machinery* (1938).

11. From an interview with Professor Hilliard as reported by one of my students.

12. The original research on this matter was done under my direction by Mr. George Ingram, then Fellow at the Graduate School of Public Administration.

13. See John Gaus, *Public Administration and the United States Department of Agriculture* (1940), pp. 104–105, 149–152, 158, 393, 468–471. Also John D. Lewis, "Democratic Planning in Agriculture," the *American Political Science Re-*

Notes

view, Vol. XXXV, Nos. 2 and 3 (April and June 1941), pp. 232–249, 454–469.

14. Report of the Temporary National Economic Committee. Also F. Frankfurter, *The Public and Its Government* (1930), p. 162.

15. See *Constitutional Government and Democracy*, ch. xxiii, and the works of E. P. Herring referred to there.

16. See Lionel Robbins, *Economic Planning and International Order*, Part I (1937).

17. This viewpoint is also taken by Merriam, *On the Agenda of Democracy* (1941), pp. 53–70.

CHAPTER VIII

1. Horace M. Kallen in the *Encyclopedia of the Social Sciences*.

2. *The Mind and Society* (edited by Arthur Livingston, 1935), Vol. I, §§ 246 and 2027 ff. It is Pareto's particular method to obscure the triteness of his basic insights by two devices, (1) by a fantastic vocabulary, (2) by continuously inserting brilliant asides which, like the obiter dicta of a great judge, make no pretense of being supported by any evidence such as Pareto chooses to parade in support of his more obvious points.

3. *Op. cit.*, § 2244.

4. Gaetano Mosca, *The Ruling Class* (edited by Arthur Livingston, 1939), p. 50.

5. *The Mind and Society, op. cit.*, § 2239.

6. For a more extensive discussion, see *Constitutional Government and Democracy* (1941), ch. xxiv, and the bibliography cited there, where a less pretentious conception of "science" is developed.

7. In the light of these quotations, it is hardly too much to say that *Past and Present* is "in a real sense an essay on

Notes

fascism," as Benjamin Lippincott puts it in his admirable *Victorian Critics of Democracy* (1938), p. 26.

8. *Wille zur Macht*, Book IV, § 960.

9. See, for a more extended discussion, two recent books which well supplement each other: George Allen Morgan, Jr., *What Nietzsche Means* (1941), and Crane Brinton, *Nietzsche* (1940).

10. *Past and Present*, Book IV, ch. i.

11. We shall speak here of Marx, although we recognize that recent research has brought to light the independent contribution of Friedrich Engels, notably in this matter of the elite.

12. See the able discussion in Arthur Livingston's introduction to Mosca's *The Ruling Class*, pp. xxxvi ff. However, in line with his general enthusiasm for Pareto, Livingston somewhat misstates the situation when he claims: "There is no dialectical or historical connection between Pareto's theory of the elite and Mosca's theory of the ruling class." Pareto's "governing elite" seems largely identical with Mosca's "ruling class."

13. Instead of *residues*, we shall use the term *sentiments*, and instead of *derivations*, the term *ideas*. These substitutions are justified by Pareto's own use; he called his second volume "Analysis of Sentiment (Theory of Residues)," and his third "Sentiment in Thinking (Theory of Derivations)."

14. *The Mind and Society*, § 2051.

15. *The Mind and Society*, § 2032. Lewis, *op. cit.*, discusses the analogy between the choice of governors and the choice of "persons skilled in any other profession, art or handicraft. . . ." pp. 255 ff.

16. Compare *Constitutional Government and Democracy*, *op. cit.*, ch. xv, and the literature cited there.

17. "Revolutions come about through accumulations in the higher strata of society of decadent elements no longer possessing the residues (sentiments) suitable for keeping them in

Notes

power, and shrinking from the use of force; while meantime in the lower strata of society elements of superior quality are coming to the fore, possessing residues suitable of exercising the functions of government and willing enough to use force." The major purpose of constitutional democracy is to forestall this sort of thing.

18. "The Nazi Dictatorship in Action" in *Democracy Is Different* (edited by Carl Wittke, 1941).

19. George Gallup and Saul F. Rae, *The Pulse of Democracy* (1940), ch. xxi.

20. Gallup and Rae, *op. cit.*, p. 272.

21. See *Constitutional Government and Democracy, op. cit.*, ch. xviii.

CHAPTER IX

1. See Charles E. Merriam, *The Making of Citizens, A Comparative Study of Methods of Civic Training* (1931), and the following: Samuel N. Harper, *Civic Training in Soviet Russia;* John M. Gaus, *Great Britain;* Oscar Jaszi, *The Dissolution of the Habsburg Monarchy;* Herbert W. Schneider and Shepard B. Clough, *Making Fascists;* Paul Kosok, *Germany;* Robert C. Brooks, *Civic Training in Switzerland;* Carleton J. H. Hayes, *France;* Bessie L. Pierce, *Civic Attitudes in American School Textbooks;* Elizabeth Weber, *The Duk-Duks.*

2. Henry David Thoreau, *Walden* (1854), p. 98.

3. *Op. cit.*, pp. 56–57.

4. *The Education of Free Men in American Democracy.* This document is the result of five years of exploration by the Educational Policies Commission of the National Education Association.

5. See Herbert Spiegelberg, *Gesetz und Sittengesetz* (1934) and the author's review in *Isis* No. 73 (Vol. XXVII, 1), May, 1937; as well as Max Scheler, *Der Formalismus in der Ethik*

[371]

Notes

und die materiale Wertethik (1921). For Jaeger see *Paideia: The Ideals of Greek Culture,* translated by Gilbert Highet (1939).

6. See A. Lawrence Lowell, *Conflict of Principles* (1932).

7. *The Education of Free Men in American Democracy.*

8. John Tunis, *Democracy and Sports* (1941).

CHAPTER X

1. See, for example, Zechariah Chafee, Jr., *Freedom of Speech in the United States* (1941), and Walter Nelles, *A Liberal in Wartime, the Education of Albert DeSilver* (1940).

2. Carl Schurz, "True Americanism," *Speeches* (1865), p. 63.

3. Walter Lippmann, *Preface to Morals* (1929), p. 329.

4. John Stuart Mill, *Representative Government* (1861), p. 49.

5. Quoted from William Paton, *The Church and the New Order* (1941), p. 160, itself an important contribution to a broader outlook.

6. Chateaubriand, *Mémoires d'Outre-Tombe,* Book I.

EPILOGUE

[1] Hadley Cantril, "The World in 1952: Some Predictions." Clinical Supplement to the *Journal of Abnormal and Social Psychology,* Vol. 38 (April 1943). A cogent analysis of the problem of prediction and prophecy is given by Karl R. Popper in *The Open Society and Its Enemies,* Vol. II, entitled *The High Tide of Prophecy — Hegel, Marx and the Aftermath* (1945); this remarkable book, and the first volume dealing with Plato, constitute striking support for some of the key positions regarding the common man.

[2] This same lack of belief in the common man is at present troubling relations with the Soviet Union, both in certain quarters in the United States and in Europe.

Notes

[3] For further aspects of this basic fact see the vast literature on democracy published in the U.S. since 1940.

[4] For a magistral discourse elaborating this theme, see Quincy Wright, *A Study of War* (1942).

[5] Lenin, *State and Revolution*, chap. V. Stalin, "Leninism," in Report to the Eighteenth Party Congress; as well as his speech, Feb. 8, 1946, reported in *The New York Times*, Feb. 9, 1946.

[6] The essay is contained, in a new translation, in my *Inevitable Peace* (1948), in which what is said in the text above is fully developed, showing the background of past traditions and the way in which the idea of peace is linked to Kant's general philosophy. His essay on history and a number of other writings are included in my *The Philosophy of Kant* (1949).

[7] See *Inevitable Peace*, p. 160, for an analysis of this passage.

[8] I am hoping to offer a more thorough analysis of these ideas in a forthcoming continuation of *Inevitable Peace* entitled *The Haunting Spectre.*

[9] "We Build the Future" was the title of a short paper in the *Atlantic* in which I rejected the defeatist prophecies of Anne Morrow Lindbergh's *The Wave of the Future* (1940).

[10] Clyde Kluckhohn, *Mirror for Man* (1949), pp. 232 ff., especially pp. 257–59.

[11] See above, pp. 25 f.

[12] Granville Hicks, *Small Town*, p. 208.

[13] See *The Boston Contest of 1944: Prize Winning Programs.* See also *The Structure of the Metropolitan Community: A Study of Dominance and Subdominance*, by Don J. Bogue (Ann Arbor: The University of Michigan, 1949); and the very stimulating discussion by Guy Greer, *Your City Tomorrow* (New York: The Macmillan Company, 1947).

[14] See my article "The New Constitutions" in *The Review of Politics*, May, 1950, as well as the forthcoming new edition of *Constitutional Government and Democracy* (1950), chap. IX.

[15] Christopher Hollis in *Horizon*, Sept., 1949, p. 208.

INDEX

Index

Bureaucracy, 188, 216; in a democracy, 39, 192–193; in large organizations, 278

Burke, Edmund, 11, 135, 161, 266; his doctrine of fundamental agreement, 38, 153, 154, 155, 240; quoted, 175; defender of *status quo*, 255

CALHOUN, JOHN C., 47, 246

Carlyle, Thomas, 265; an elitist, 17, 239, 245, 247, 251, 263, 269; quoted, 210, 249–250; criticism of, 248–250, 252–253; a great moral challenger, 254

"Carol of Occupations" (Whitman), quoted, 16

Character, of common man, 6, 41; importance of, 33–35, 153; as an educational goal, 281, 295

Chateaubriand, François René, Viscount de, quoted, 315–316

Christianity and the state, 68, 72, 78, 79

Church versus state, 68–70; in medieval theory, 70–73; Renaissance view of, 73–75; in Lutheran and Anglican tradition, 75–78; and education, 100–101, 274, 275

Churchill, Winston, 91

Cicero, 275

Civics, 280, 308

Civil Disobedience (Thoreau), 19, 51; quoted, 19

Civil liberties, 126–127, 178–180, 297, 298. *See also* Freedoms

Civitas, 69–73

Clay, Henry, 224

Coker, Francis, quoted, 50

Cole, G. D. H., 154

Common man, history of belief in, 3–5, 6–15; mind of the, 5–6, 29–

30, 109; character of the, 6, 33–35, 153; in American literature, 15–25, 43–44, 61–62; Dewey's belief in, 25–26; antirationalist views of, 26–28; fallible, 30–31, 141; collective, 31–32, 35, 119, 174; judgments of, 32–37, 98, 113–114, 127, 132; sense of workmanship in, 39, 112, 188–193, 208, 265; versus elite, 39–40, 109–111, 133–134, 175–177, 186, 240–241, 245, 246, 258; political capacity of, 41–42; Laski's belief in, 51–52; and the state, 53–61, 62–65; as world citizen, 79–80, 118–119, 234–235, 270, 300, 302–305, 315–317; and mass communication, 81–84, 98, 106–109, 120; Lincoln as archetype of, 111–112, 269–270; and governmental policy, 114–118, 133, 194, 200–205, 208, 269; non-Utopian view of, 135, 149–150, 239–240; in Germany, 145–146; and property, 147–149, 166–171; and responsibility, 197–199, 209–211; and planning, 215–232, 235–237, in pressure groups, 232–234; sampling the opinions of, 266–268; education for, 271–295, 307–311; in democratic politics, 311–312; and freedom from fear, 299–300, 314–315

Common Sense (Paine), quoted, 8–9

Communication, 83–84, 86, 108, 195–197

Communism, 57–58, 78, 142, 144, 309

Communist Manifesto, 254

Communists, 27, 29, 38, 144, 183, 184, 254–255

Confucianism, 68, 307, 311

Index

Confucius, quoted, 214

Constituent power, 56, 129–134, 149

Constitutional Code (Bentham), 9, 31

Constitutional Government and Politics (Friedrich), 154

Constitutionalism, democratic, 39, 123–124, 134, 140, 149–150, 157, 159–160, 166, 167–168, 172, 179–181, 185–186; power under, 53–54; consent in, 56, 57, 62–63; medieval, 56, 70–71, 77–78; problem of modern, 73

Cooley, Thomas McIntyre, 133

Co-operation, elicited, 199–202, 204, 206–207, 216, 217–220, 225, 240

Coughlin, Charles E., 99

Council for Democracy, 151

Creel, George, 81, 84, 106

Culture, national, 163–166, 272–274, 308–309; educational concept of, 275

Culture of the Renaissance (Burckhardt), 244

DECLARATION OF INDEPENDENCE, 5

Democracy, rests on belief in common man, 3, 6–7, 11, 17, 28–30, 35, 41, 42, 52, 58, 62–63, 106, 146, 258–260, 265, 269–270; Dewey's view of, 25–26; its need for dissent, 38–39, 156, 157–159, 162, 163, 164–166, 167–174, 177–181, 185–186; and bureaucracy, 39, 188–189, 191–193, 199, 201, 205, 207–208, 210–211; education for, 40, 280–283, 286–295, 308–310; anarchic strain in, 51, 61–62; people in a, 54–55, 57, 64–65, 79–80, 146, 149–150, 194, 198, 266–268; crisis of, 57, 59–60; in Greek

thought, 67–68; religion under, 69, 159–162; propaganda and, 81, 82, 83–84, 89, 92–93, 94, 95–96, 98, 106, 108–109, 110, 119–120; foreign policy of a, 117–119; moderation in, 121–123; and majority rule, 125–128; and sportsmanship, 152–153; role of pressure groups in a, 232–234; and nationalism, 273–274; a never-finished task, 284–285, 293; politics in a, 311. *See also* Constitutionalism, Planning

Democracy and Sport (Tunis), 152

Department of Agriculture, United States, 114–117, 196–197, 199, 228–230

Department of Justice, United States, 204

Dewey, John, 31, 32, 83; quoted, 25–26

Diary of a Country Priest (Bernanos), 104

Discipline of free men, 286–294

Dissent, democracy's need for, 38–39; importance of, 157–159, 177, 185; tolerance of, 179–180, 185–186

Dostoevski, Feodor Mikhailovich, quoted, 103–104

Drums Along the Mohawk (Edmonds), 12

"Due process of law," 138–139

Duke of Stockbridge, The (Bellamy), 13

ECONOMIC DISAGREEMENTS, 166–171

Economic Interpretation of the Constitution of the United States (Beard), 224

Edmonds, Walter, 12

[376]

Index

Index

[378]

Index

Index

Index

Roosevelt, Theodore, 14, 224–225
Rousseau, Jean-Jacques, 37–38, 41; his view of sovereignty, 46, 51, 78; his view of majorities, 127–128; quoted, 127–128; his doctrine of "real constitution," 134–135, 158
Rule, majority, 38, 122–124, 150; minority, 123, 137–139
Ruling Class, The (Mosca), 256
Ruskin, John, 245

SAINT-SIMON, Claude Henri, Count, quoted, 194
San Antonio Case, 183–184
Sandburg, Carl, 22, 270
Schiller, Friedrich von, 270
Schurz, Carl, quoted, 304
Self-preference, principle of, 10, 11
Shaw, George Bernard, 245
Shays' Rebellion, 13
Sieyès, Abbé Emmanuel Joseph, 129
Silone, Ignazio, quoted, 104–105
Slavery in Massachusetts (Thoreau), quoted, 19–20
Smith, Alfred E., 160
Sovereignty, 45–46, 50, 52, 77–78, 79, 132, 305; popular, 46–47; state, 47–49; pluralist theory of, 50–52; of majority, 54–55
Spinoza, Benedict, 45
Stakes of Diplomacy (Lippmann), 82
Stalin, Joseph, 49, 60, 78, 172, 185
State, concept of, 37, 44–47; sovereignty of, 47–52; as sovereign association, 52–54; incompatible with belief in common man, 57–59, 61; deification of, 60, 62, 65–68, 76, 78; piratical view of, 63–65; church versus, 68–71; in

Aquinas, 71–73; in the Renaissance, 73–75; in Lutheran and Anglican tradition, 75–78; symbol of totalitarian government, 78–80
State in Theory and Practice, The (Laski), 52
Stein, Lorenz von, 255
Steinbeck, John, 25, 148
Stendhal (Marie Henri Beyle), 246
"Stereotypes," 82, 119, 201
Subordination, training in, 278–279
Supreme Court, 131, 138, 139
Switzerland, democracy in, 47, 53, 121, 128, 243; order in, 63; constitutional amendments in, 140; conflict situations in, 160, 164, 171; planning in, 231
Synthesis, new educational, 280–283

TAINE, HIPPOLYTE ADOLPHE, 246
Taste, 32–33
"This Progressive Education" (Friedrich), 277
Thoreau, Henry David, 16, 23, 43, 51, 62, 148, 169; quoted, 19–21, 121, 274, 276
Thus Spake Zarathustra (Nietzsche), quoted, 248
Tocqueville, Alexis de, 255, 260
Toynbee, Paget, quoted, 314
Trade unions, 52
Treasury, United States, 200–201
Treitschke, Heinrich von, 246
Tunis, John, 152

UNAMUNO, MIGUEL DE, 246
United States, common man in, 12–15, 21; democracy in, 47, 53–54, 121–122, 128, 194; order in, 63; religion in, 69, 160; a service state, 140–141; conflict situations in,

Index